SPOILING AND COPING WITH SPOILERS

INDIANA SERIES IN MIDDLE EAST STUDIES
Editor, Mark Tessler

SPOILING AND COPING WITH SPOILERS

Israeli-Arab Negotiations

Edited by Galia Golan and Gilead Sher

INDIANA UNIVERSITY PRESS

This book is a publication of

Indiana University Press
Office of Scholarly Publishing
Herman B Wells Library 350
1320 East 10th Street
Bloomington, Indiana 47405 USA

iupress.indiana.edu

© 2019 by Indiana University Press

All rights reserved

No part of this book may be reproduced or utilized in any form or by any means, electronic or mechanical, including photocopying and recording, or by any information storage and retrieval system, without permission in writing from the publisher. The paper used in this publication meets the minimum requirements of the American National Standard for Information Sciences—Permanence of Paper for Printed Library Materials, ANSI Z39.48-1992.

Manufactured in the United States of America

Library of Congress Cataloging-in-Publication Data

Names: Golan, Galia, editor. | Sher, Gilead, editor.
Title: Spoiling and coping with spoilers : Israeli-Arab negotiations / Galia Golan and Gilead Sher, editors.
Description: Bloomington, Indiana, USA : Indiana University Press, 2019. | Series: Indiana series in Middle East studies | Includes bibliographical references and index.
Identifiers: LCCN 2019011412 (print) | LCCN 2019016210 (ebook) | ISBN 9780253042408 (ebook) | ISBN 9780253042361 | ISBN 9780253042361 hardback : paper) | ISBN 9780253042378pbk. : paper)
Subjects: LCSH: Arab-Israeli conflict–1993—Peace.
Classification: LCC DS119.76 (ebook) | LCC DS119.76 .S796 2019 (print) | DDC 956.05/4—dc23
LC record available at https://lccn.loc.gov/2019011412

1 2 3 4 5   23 22 21 20 19

*To the memory of Naomi Kaplansky,
a beloved source of inspiration to so many,*

*and to the memory of Ron Pundak,
a sorely missed force for peace.*

CONTENTS

Acknowledgments ix

Introduction: Theoretical and Historical Contexts / Galia Golan 1

1. Spoiling International Peace Negotiations from within the Room / Gilead Sher and Deborah Shulman 9

2. The Leadership as a Spoiler / Roee Kibrik and Maya Kornberg 30

3. Israel's Domestic Legal Struggle against the Settlements: Spoiler-Advancing, Spoiler-Hindering, or Spoiler-Exposing? / Shlomy Zachary 58

4. The American Jewish Diaspora as a Spoiler / Ofira Seliktar 93

5. Visual Spoilers? Peace and Conflict in Israeli Political Cartoons / Tamir Shaefer, Ilan Danjoux, Shira Dabir-Gvirsman, and Shaul Shenhav 118

6. The Psychological Effects of Forced Evacuation: The Case of Jewish Settlers in the West Bank / Sivan Hirsch-Hoefler, Tamar Saguy, and Gilad Hirschberger 133

7. Coping with Spoilers: A Comparative Analysis / Galia Golan 153

Index 193

ACKNOWLEDGMENTS

We would like to thank Deborah Shulman for her devoted, efficient, and wise assistance in preparing this volume, from its inception. As a researcher in the Center for Applied Negotiations of the Institute for National Security Studies (INSS), Deborah was an invaluable resource, as well as a contributing coauthor, and we are most grateful to her. Our thanks also to Mor Ben-Kalifa, who masterfully and graciously completed the many tasks in the final preparation of the book for publication after Deborah moved on from INSS to other work.

We wish also to thank our contributors to this volume. We thank them for their patience and cooperation throughout our many communications, queries, and requests, taking the time from their busy schedules and important work to join us in the examination of this critical topic. We are grateful for the resources and support provided to us by the INSS.

We are hopeful that this international, interdisciplinary, and multifaceted study of spoilers and coping with spoilers will contribute to a normalization of relations between Israel and the Arab world. Within that context, we hope that it will contribute in the future to the successful realization of peace between Israel and the Palestinians.

SPOILING AND COPING WITH SPOILERS

INTRODUCTION

Theoretical and Historical Contexts

Galia Golan

Theoretical Background

There are many obstacles on the path of peacemaking, and many factors contribute to the failure of such efforts, particularly in the case of long-standing armed conflicts. Among the many factors, the acts of spoilers have often figured prominently, perhaps critically, as groups or individuals strive to influence, disrupt, or defeat negotiations or peace-building endeavors. The concept of spoilers in the resolution of conflicts has generally been treated in connection with violent actions taken during peace negotiations or following an agreement, in an effort by one side, or a faction or group on one side or the other, to "spoil"—disrupt or end—the peace effort. Past analyses have occasionally expanded the concept to nonviolent spoilers and potential spoilers, particularly during the period of negotiations or peace processes prior to an agreement. Violent spoiling may produce catastrophic results, but other forms of spoiling can also be critical to the process insofar as they may also disrupt negotiations or even bring them to a halt. The success or failure of nonviolent spoilers depends on a large number of factors, such as the identity and motivation of the spoilers, their influence or strength, the methods they employ, the context or circumstances of their efforts, and the measures adopted by the "custodians" of the peace process for coping with the spoiling efforts. We shall examine these factors, with attention also to the less-examined matter of coping with nonviolent—primarily political—spoilers, reviewing examples of past peace processes with a focus on spoiling by Israelis (or their supporters abroad) in connection with Israeli-Arab negotiations.

Israeli spoilers provide an interesting, and, in fact, relatively rare, case of nonviolent spoilers operating in a democratic society (in which there are varied nonviolent methods for expressing opposition) within a broader context of violence. In some cases, for example, the efforts to spoil the peace process with Egypt took place within the broader context of an ongoing conflict that sporadically exploded into armed conflict and war. In other cases, particularly those connected with Israeli-Palestinian negotiations, Israeli spoilers acted within a context of near-constant violent spoiling actions that came from within the ranks of the adversary, namely almost-daily terror attacks by Islamist elements from the Palestinian side. Although ultimately Israeli spoiling became violent with the assassination of Prime Minister Yitzhak Rabin, this fateful act of violence was in fact an isolated case in an increasingly volatile but nonetheless nonviolent process of domestic opposition. While the broader context during any period of the conflict must be borne in mind and may be assumed to have played at least some psychological role for spoilers, our interest is to examine the phenomenon of nonviolent spoiling, in quite varied forms, during different instances of Israeli peace efforts. Such an examination may throw light not only on the specific problem of nonviolent spoilers to Israeli peacemaking and possibly the means of coping with them, but also elucidate the more general topic of nonviolent spoilers and spoiling.

Originally the studies of spoilers focused on the motivation and identity of the spoilers, based on the premise that if one knew the reasons behind the spoilers' actions, primarily their goals, one would be better able to cope with them. Steven Stedman, who introduced this area of study, identified three types of spoilers, according to motivation/objectives: limited, greedy, and total (opposition).[1] Limited spoilers seek redress of grievances or certain assurances regarding their interests or fears; they may simply seek to be a part of the negotiations. Limited spoilers could be perceived as pragmatists. Greedy spoilers might be similar to limited spoilers regarding motivation, but they adjust their demands according to a cost/benefit analysis, seeking increased gains as risks are reduced. Some might consider them to be more cynical than merely pragmatic. Total spoilers are opposed to the process altogether, usually out of ideological convictions, but they may be simply those who believe their political interests have been or would be thwarted, or even those who profit from continuation of the conflict.[2] Moreover, the degree of commitment—to the process or to their own demands—may well determine if a limited or greedy spoiler will turn into a total spoiler.

The position of all these types of spoilers is of importance. They may be on the same side as one party to the process or they may be among the adversary's camp. In this sense, a two-level game may be needed, namely to persuade not only one's own camp but also spoilers, or potential spoilers, from the adversary's side.[3] Position is also a factor insofar as the spoilers may be inside or outside the process. If they are inside, their influence can vary even to the point of wielding veto power, depending on their role (part of the leadership or coalition, head of a large faction or party, etc.).[4] Even a total spoiler can be found inside a process—that is, a person or group with what Oliver Richmond calls "devious objectives" (a "devious actor") that enters negotiations with objectives other than reaching agreement.[5]

In such cases, the motive for joining (possibly even initiating) the process may, for example, be to counter domestic or international pressure, to gain time to recoup and strengthen positions, to gain political favor from a constituency, or to promote personal political fortunes within a power struggle. Spoilers outside the negotiating process may come from civil society as well as political groupings, including a ruling coalition, and from third parties altogether, such as other countries, diaspora, international organizations, or groups. Two subtypes of spoilers could be added to the list, whether inside or outside the process itself: skeptics and potential spoilers. Skeptics might be inadvertent or unintentional spoilers—namely, limited or greedy spoilers (to use the classic categories) who generally support the process (or, at least are not totally opposed) but who, out of mistrust or strong doubts, make demands that constitute deal breakers.[6] Such skeptics are actually prime suspects as potential spoilers, emerging as spoilers due to events during the process (for example, statements or actions, especially violence, by the adversary to the conflict; changes in public opinion; third-party, regional, or international involvement). Alternatively, they may turn into spoilers in response to the content (or their understanding of the content) of the emerging agreement. In either case, their mistrust or skepticism reaches the level of deal-breaking demands that constitute spoiling, even if their original motivation had not been total opposition. Other potential, even inadvertent, spoilers may be those who—for the purposes of bargaining, to reassure followers, or to further other domestic considerations—engage in harsh statements or actions that send the wrong signal to the other side and thus spoil the process.[7]

Some have argued that virtually any person or group could be viewed as a potential spoiler under changing circumstances, or that none are spoilers until or unless they actually spoil the process. Semantics and typology aside, those who make these claims argue that an additional element must be taken into consideration: capabilities, including resources.[8] Regardless of motivation, the potential or "latent" spoilers would be those who will act *only* if they have the means with which to conduct spoiling. Such resources might be sufficient numbers of supporters or political influence (outside as well as domestically), or financial backing, media access, organizational ability, and so on. One might link capacity with opportunity,[9] created perhaps by changed circumstances, such as those mentioned above (violence, harsh statements by the adversary, etc.), or domestic changes in leadership, party strength, public opinion, etc. Opportunity may be linked to timing; for example, when the process has just begun, it may be particularly vulnerable, while at a later stage, confidence in the process may have grown, the initial hurdles may have been overcome, or the commitment of the "custodians"—due to the time and effort invested—may be stronger.[10]

Thus, in addition to types of spoilers according to motivation, objectives, position, and role, one must look at opportunity, timing, capabilities, and resources, as well as degree of commitment. However, to further understand the phenomenon of spoiling, we must also take into account the strategy and tactics employed by the spoiler, and these are often connected with the coping efforts undertaken by the "custodians."

This Volume

The essays in this volume address spoiling of a nonviolent nature, whether by political or other types of domestic actors, whether successful or not. Indeed, much can be learned from failed as well as successful attempts to spoil a peace process and the methods employed by advocates or "custodians" of the process to cope with nonviolent spoilers or spoiling. Thus, we shall investigate, in a comparative framework, coping measures and the way in which they were attempted in past Israeli peace efforts. In some cases, a distinction is indeed made between spoilers and spoiling—that is, spoiling behavior—in part because some acts of spoiling may be unintentional, on the one hand, or on the other hand, disguised, as in the behavior of "devious actors."[11] Moreover, we shall examine spoiling on the part of new actors on the international scene, diaspora groups or personalities, and an often neglected but potentially influential spoiling by the media, namely political cartoons. Further, contributors to this volume will reveal spoiling in unexpected places, such as the negotiations room, the leadership itself, and even in the courts, presumably inadvertently. As our analyses are in the context of Israeli peacemaking, we offer a social psychological experiment testing the circumstances under which a major spoiler in the past, Israeli settlers, will respond to enforced evacuation in the future, determining the likelihood and nature of future spoiling and potentially effective coping measures.

Historical Context

Throughout the history of the Israeli-Arab conflict, there have been initiatives, negotiations, secret meetings, and even groundbreaking agreements. Arguably, resolution of the conflict could not reasonably have been expected prior to 1967, for the conflict between Israel and the Arab states appeared to be a zero-sum game, given the Arabs' total rejection of Israel's existence in the region. This view may be challenged; some may argue, and have argued, that Arab rejection was not total.[12] But it does seem to be the case that following the 1967 war and Israel's occupation of lands belonging to neighboring states, a bargaining situation was created: peace might be forthcoming in exchange for return of the newly acquired territories. Yet security demands, born primarily of Israeli mistrust regarding Arab intentions, prevented breakthroughs with the neighboring states—for example, in 1971 and 1973 with regard to Egypt.[13] In time, however, following more armed encounters and wars, and, among other factors, changes in leadership in both countries, Egypt and Israel eventually entered negotiations and made the exchange: the return of the Sinai Peninsula for the Israeli-Egyptian Peace Treaty of 1979. Regarding Jordan and the West Bank (including East Jerusalem), similar Israeli security concerns were often joined by ideological and religious aspirations for the biblical land of Israel (*Eretz Israel*), ultimately blocking a land-for-peace exchange with Jordan. The possibility of such a trade with Jordan came to a close—actually became irrelevant—when Jordan relinquished its claim to the West Bank in favor of the Palestinians in 1988.

With Jordan no longer negotiating over territory previously under its control, the way was open for the eventual peace treaty with Israel in 1994. However, Jordan's abandonment of the West Bank returned the conflict to the zero-sum, core issue of the conflict: the claims of both Israel and the Palestinians to pre-1948-mandated Palestine, of which the West Bank was just a part. Once again, however, increased violence intervened, but so did a number of other factors as well. In large part due to the outbreak of the

First Intifada in the occupied West Bank and Gaza Strip, but also due to the regional and international environment (such as the demise of the Soviet Union), Palestinian policy underwent a total change. In 1988, the Palestinian Liberation Organization (PLO) proclaimed its acceptance of Israel's right to exist and resolved to seek a state only in the territory of the West Bank and Gaza. Leadership change, specifically the 1992 election of Yitzhak Rabin in Israel, among other factors, led Israel and the PLO to enter negotiations that resulted in the 1993 Oslo Accords, including mutual recognition. Only an interim agreement, these accords did not culminate in a peace agreement but rather in several more temporary agreements (e.g., Oslo II, the Wye River Memorandum), further leadership changes (after the 1995 assassination of Rabin), failed negotiations (Camp David, 2000), and renewed violence, followed by outside mediation and failure once again (US secretary of state John Kerry's talks, 2013–14). Israel also held talks with Syria, beginning prior to Oslo under Rabin and conducted by his successors, Shimon Peres, Benjamin Netanyahu (indirectly), and Ehud Barak; all of these ended in failure.

Clearly, there are many facets to the Israeli-Arab conflict, and perhaps even more histories, interpretations, and analyses, all presumably engaged in trying to understand this long-standing conflict. Spoilers, that is, those who try to foil or who unintentionally spoil an effort to make peace are but one of the many factors contributing to past Israeli-Arab attempts at making peace. There were many other factors beyond the spoilers, such as mistrust, fed by periodic violence and terrorism; negative public opinion, weak leadership or absence of legitimacy; ideological or religious dogmatism; and, of course, problems from other parties, be they the adversary or regional or international protagonists. There were also many obstacles along the path, some of a structural nature, such as social or economic differences; others of a psychological nature; and still others of a more concrete political nature—local or otherwise.[14] Often spoilers and spoiling could have been defined as falling into both categories, constituting both a factor for failure and a serious obstacle to success.

Spoilers and spoiling were neither the only nor necessarily the most important factor in past failures, just as successful coping with spoilers was not necessarily the key to the few successes or breakthroughs achieved—for example, the peace with Egypt and the limited breakthrough of the Oslo Accords. Similarly, spoilers and spoiling did constitute an obstacle to one degree or another in almost all of Israel's peacemaking (with the exception of the 1994 peace agreement with Jordan), while methods to overcome these obstacles were not always the prime consideration of Israeli decision-makers. Perhaps it should have been, at least in some cases. Be that as it may, it is indeed quite likely that domestic spoilers of the types addressed in this volume will reappear in any future Israeli peacemaking effort.

Notes

1. Stephen John Stedman, "Spoiler Problems in Peace Processes," *International Security* 22, no. 2 (1997): 5–53.
2. Oliver Ramsbotham, Hugh Miall, and Tom Woodhouse, *Contemporary Conflict Resolution* (New York: Polity, 2011).
3. Robert D. Putnam, "Diplomacy and Domestic Politics: The Logic of Two-Level Games," *International Organization* 42, no. 3 (1988): 427–460. Putnam discusses situations in which leaders bargain with the other side but also have to deal with their own colleagues and public as well as the public on the other side.
4. Hendrik Spruyt, "Territorial Concessions, Domestic Politics, and the Israeli–Palestinian Conflict." *Democracy and Conflict Resolution: The Dilemmas of Israel's Peacemaking* (2014): 36.
5. Edward Newman and Oliver Richmond, eds., *Challenges to Peacebuilding: Managing Spoilers during Conflict Resolution* (Tokyo: United Nations University Press, 2006), 59–77; Wendy Pearlman, "Spoiling Inside and Out: Internal Political Contestation and the Middle East Peace Process," *International Security* 33, no. 3 (2009): 79–109.
6. Ramsbotham, Miall, and Woodhouse, *Contemporary Conflict Resolution*, 186.
7. Roger R. Mac Ginty, "Northern Ireland: A Peace Process Thwarted by Accidental Spoiling," in Newman and Richmond, *Challenges to Peacebuilding*, 154; Mac Ginty defines this as an activity that erodes support for a peace process as a "by-product" of its primary intention.
8. Kelly M. Greenhill and Solomon Major, "The Perils of Profiling: Civil War Spoilers and the Collapse of Intrastate Peace Accords." *International Security* 31, no. 3 (2007): 7–40.
9. Oded Haklai, "Linking Ideas and Opportunities in Contentious Politics: The Israeli Nonparliamentary Opposition to the Peace Process," *Canadian Journal of Political Science/ Revue canadienne de science politique* 36, no. 4 (2003): 791–812.
10. Mac Ginty, "Northern Ireland," 169.
11. Oliver Richmond, "The Linkage between Devious Objectives and Spoiling Behaviour in Peace Processes," in Newman and Richmond, *Challenges to Peacebuilding*, 59–77.
12. Elie Podeh, *Chances for Peace: Missed Opportunities in the Arab-Israeli Conflict* (Austin: University of Texas Press, 2015).
13. Galia Golan, *Israeli Peacemaking since 1967: Factors behind the Breakthroughs and Failures* (London: Routledge, 2014).
14. Gilead Sher and Anat Kurz, *Negotiating in Times of Conflict* (Tel Aviv: Institute for National Security Studies, 2015).

GALIA GOLAN is Professor Emerita of political science at the Hebrew University of Jerusalem. The most recent of her many publications is *Israeli Peacemaking since 1967: Factors behind the Breakthroughs and Failures*. Golan is the recipient of the 2016 Distinguished Scholar Award of the International Studies Association (ISA) for her work in peace research.

1

SPOILING INTERNATIONAL PEACE NEGOTIATIONS FROM WITHIN THE ROOM

Gilead Sher and Deborah Shulman

INTRACTABLE CONFLICTS ARE CHARACTERIZED BY REPEATING CYCLES OF violence, often interspersed with several rounds of failed negotiations and agreements that are never implemented. A peace process may be spoiled by excluded groups and disgruntled constituents who act forcefully to derail negotiations, or by leaders and groups included in the peace process that destroy it from within the negotiating room. Scholars and journalists, however, seldom focus on spoiling within the negotiating room itself, and accordingly, the undercurrents and dynamics in the room are less frequently examined and are rarely reported in mainstream media. This is in part because many negotiations are confidential, and relatively few individuals actually take part in the process. There is also a tendency to examine the success of peace processes by exclusively assessing whether agreements were reached. This chapter thus aims to address a topic that requires greater attention and analysis: how spoiling behavior in the room can cause and contribute to the failure of peaceful resolution.

As outlined in the introduction, Steven Stedman's concept of spoilers refers to actors who deliberately undermine negotiations.[1] His typology categorizes spoilers as limited, greedy, or total. Limited spoilers have specific goals that can be met by inducements, such as official recognition or power-sharing agreements. Greedy spoilers also have specific demands, but demands increase when the risk and cost are low and benefits are high. Total spoilers have demands for total power and are not prepared to make compromises. Whereas there may be ways to manage limited and greedy spoilers within the negotiating room, there is no place for total spoilers at the table. The intentions of potential spoilers in the room are extremely difficult to accurately identify. Whereas some negotiators attempt to appear accommodating but actually aim to subvert the negotiations, others may appear to be total spoilers, spouting rhetoric to appease followers, but in practice may have negotiation flexibility. Second, spoilers may move between categories depending on the existing opportunity structures. Greenhill and Major argue that, depending on the given context, "every real or potential spoiler will be as greedy as he thinks he can afford to be."[2] If a party believes that it can unilaterally achieve a better deal than the one on the table, it is likely to resort to spoiling, either within the room or outside of it.[3] On the other hand, if peace becomes more beneficial than the continuation of war, actors who previously spoiled talks may become genuinely interested in reaching a negotiated settlement. There are many examples of spoiler categorization changing over time. For instance, the Palestinian Liberation Organization (PLO) was once classified by many Israelis as a total spoiler, and until 1992 it was illegal for Israelis to talk to members of the PLO, but, subsequently it became a negotiating partner.[4] On the contrary, a party may start spoiling only during the process, despite promoting the continuation of talks during the prenegotiation phase.

Spoiling within the negotiating room is less predictable and identifiable, and perhaps occurs less frequently, than spoiling behavior of excluded political or extremist groups, but it can be just as detrimental. Stedman's typology may help us to be extra vigilant when negotiating with previous spoilers or rebel groups with a brutal past.[5] However, too much reliance on spoiler labels might lead one to overlook less obvious but equally troublesome spoilers, or alternatively, write off groups as "total" spoilers and thereby miss opportunities for constructive engagement. Therefore, we prefer to shift the emphasis from labeling groups as spoilers to looking at spoiling behavior. Actors may have an incentive to partake in a negotiation process other than reaching an agreement, such as to stall decisions, divert attention, avoid sanctions, gain leverage on another issue, involve a third party, or avoid sanctions and win international approval. Actors with these motivations are more likely to deliberately engage in spoiling behavior. However, in addition to these duplicitous actors, most negotiators use potentially spoiling behavior at some point during negotiations in a bid to further their interests and shape the outcome.[6] Even negotiators who want a peace process to succeed might use strategies that put the process in jeopardy as they try to increase bargaining power—for instance, by prolonging negotiations to gain concessions from the other side in the eleventh hour. By using an expansive definition of spoiling, we hope to better capture the complex reality of negotiations in which a multitude of behaviors can result in the collapse of talks.

The Negotiating Room in International Political Conflicts

The negotiating room is a place where "two or more parties interact in the search for an acceptable position with regard to their differences and concerning the same issue of conflict."[7] Within the room, heads of state may be present, but a more common setup involves representative delegations headed by chief negotiators, often with a third-party present to help facilitate or mediate the process or merely provide a venue without being involved in the talks. In order not to provoke external parties with an interest in spoiling talks, the parties may arrange for the goings-on within the room to be entirely confidential with no press interaction whatsoever. Alternatively, to create legitimacy for what is going on in the negotiating room, the parties may decide on a policy of a joint or an agreed-upon press outlet, or when a third-party broker is the host, it might brief the press. The latter was the case in the Camp David summit in 2000, where the single daily press release was provided by the US delegation. This was designed to minimize contact with the press to avoid spoiling.

The physical location and setup of the room, such as seating arrangements, impact the decision-making process and the outcome of the negotiations more than is often realized, and they can even lead to talks being spoiled. Reaching a consensus on the location of talks and aspects of the setup can represent the first hurdle in the process. A high-profile location increases ongoing awareness of the talks and may create more visible opposition, such as protests and media attention outside the venue, in turn affecting negotiators on a psychological level and changing the dynamics within the room. If the location is not neutral and or elements of the setup provide an advantage to one of the parties, relations within the room are likely to be tenser, increasing the likelihood of parties engaging in spoiling behavior. For example, the initial negotiations that took place in Paris in May 1968 on the future of South Vietnam consisted of many disagreements on a number of procedural issues that reflected the parties' concerns over representation in the room, such as the use of flags, the speaking order of participants, and most notably the shape of the table.[8] North Vietnam and the National Liberation Front (NLF) demanded a four-sided table to emphasize equality between the parties, whereas the United States and South Vietnam insisted on a two-sided arrangement, because they did not want the NLF to be represented on equal footing with the other parties. Only after eight months were all the players in the room finally able to reach a compromise: no flags or nameplates, speaking order arranged by the drawing of lots, and a round table with two smaller rectangular tables at opposite sides, as suggested by Soviet diplomats.[9]

Actions that jeopardize the confidentiality of the exchange, such as the host state or a third party recording the talks, are likely to increase the fear of leaks. This may result in negotiators censoring themselves in the room, for fear that their legitimacy and even their life could be in danger, making them less willing to discuss sensitive topics. These examples show that even matters that appear prosaic and unrelated to the substantive issues of negotiations can end up spoiling the process.

The Mandate

Absence of a clear mandate—that is, official instructions regarding negotiators' authority and limitations—may lead to spoiling during negotiations. If there is doubt about the limits of a party's authority at the table, negotiations are unlikely to be effective. This is a common scenario in negotiations, especially in an international political setup, that can lead to negotiators becoming frustrated in the room when they realize they have been effectively wasting their time partaking in a redundant process. In rare instances negotiators may partake in talks without any mandate, putting the peace process at risk. In an exposed Israeli-Palestinian secret negotiation channel between Yitzhak Molcho, the personal legal counsel and envoy of Israeli prime minister Benjamin Netanyahu, and a confidant of Palestinian president Mahmoud Abbas that ran alongside the official 2013–2014 negotiations, Abbas's presumed secret negotiator was operating without a real mandate.[10] According to Amir Tibon, the journalist who exposed the talks, the formula for final-status negotiations discussed in the secret channel included concessions that the Israeli and Palestinian leaders had repeatedly refused to make. When US secretary of state John Kerry, facilitator of the official talks, merged the secret and official channels, it became apparent that Abbas was either unaware of the progress in the secret channel or did not recognize it. Engaging in talks as a negotiator without a mandate is potentially spoiling behavior. More than just being irrelevant due to a questionable mandate, the secret track destabilized the official track as tensions rose between leaders, with Abbas rejecting the American framework and Netanyahu claiming that the framework had already been agreed upon.[11]

Negotiators can also spoil talks by entering them with a restrictive mandate, meaning that they do not have the authority to discuss or negotiate certain topics. It was reported, though not verified, that Palestinian chief negotiator, Saeb Erekat, refused to hear the Israeli position on the security issue, claiming that he did not have a mandate to discuss security without first receiving a detailed document from the Israeli team about borders and security.[12] In earlier rounds of talks, such as the official process in the fall of 1999, following the signing of the Sharm el-Sheikh Memorandum, it was asserted that neither the Israeli head of delegation, Oded Eran, nor his Palestinian interlocutor, Yasser Abed Rabbo, had substantive leeway for negotiating anything but procedural matters. Likewise, in the January 2001 Taba talks, after the presentation of US president Bill Clinton's parameters, it was clear that the Palestinian head of delegation, Abu Ala, was heavily constrained by a restricted, narrow mandate from PLO chairman Yasser Arafat. The reluctance to put forward clear negotiating positions, on the grounds of a limited mandate, generally exemplifies greedy spoiling, utilized by parties trying to work out how many concessions they can receive without putting their cards on the table. Refusing to discuss substantive issues could also be the work of parties who have reasons to remain part of the process but are not willing or able to make concessions.

Inside the Room: The Effect of External Spoilers

The principal challenge for a negotiator is producing an outcome that is acceptable to the other side, while also being acceptable to domestic constituents.[13] This challenge, named by Robert Putnam as the "two-level game," is essential if agreements are to be reached and then realized. Ignoring the public is likely to render agreements very difficult to implement. On the other hand, negotiators who are constrained by sectors in the public who oppose negotiations will struggle to make concessions, putting a significant strain on the relationship between the negotiating parties. This is one way that external spoilers can affect what goes on inside the room.

There are many instances of negotiators engaging in spoiling behavior themselves, because they appear more concerned about how the public will perceive the agreement than about reaching an agreement. Following the Camp David Summit in 2000, intensive talks resumed in Jerusalem. Akram Haniyeh, a close political advisor of Arafat and the editor-in-chief of the Palestinian daily *Al-Ayyam*, joined one of the first sessions. During this session, Mohammad Dahlan of the Palestinian negotiating team bluntly and loudly renounced all the understandings reached on security issues in Camp David. This sudden apparent backtracking on the Palestinian side immediately created a crisis in the room between the Israelis and Palestinians, and the negotiators had to ask the American team to check their accounts from Camp David. US Middle East envoy Dennis Ross, a key member of the American mediation team, happened to be in Jerusalem for personal reasons at the time and rushed to the negotiating room. Ross informed the teams that the US team had no reports documenting the summit negotiations. One cannot rule out that the presence of an influential media actor in the room provided an opportunity for Dahlan to amplify a rigid and uncompromising standpoint in security matters, thus gaining a stronger position within the Palestinian constituency.

There are also cases in which those inside the room may actually benefit from the spoiling behavior of excluded parties and thus fail to prevent or actually encourage it. To take an example used by Wendy Perlman, in the Oslo peace talks between Israel and the PLO, the PLO initially did not crack down on terrorism carried out by the excluded groups, Hamas and the Palestinian Islamic Jihad, who opposed the negotiations. The PLO's failure to prevent terrorism likely reflected concern over losing public support and legitimacy. But a further explanation may lie in the fact that the terror attacks that were perpetrated during the peace process initially provided a potential advantage to the Palestinians. Hamas and the Palestinian Islamic Jihad terrorism arguably increased the PLO's bargaining power at the table, as Israel became more desperate to put an end to the violence. The prevention of terrorism was effectively a bargaining chip for the PLO—the May 1994 agreement granted limited Palestinian self-rule in exchange for a commitment from the PLO to take all measures necessary to prevent terrorist attacks against Israelis. The PLO managed to avoid direct responsibility for the attacks, while their position at the table was possibly strengthened due to the spoiling behavior of external players.

If parties inside the room are genuinely interested in peace and are willing to make the necessary compromises but are concerned about excluded extremists spoiling an agreement or certain sectors opposing one, they may benefit from taking time in the room to try to resolve these issues together. James K. Sebenius suggests ways that negotiators should help each other construct a strategy for increasing the legitimacy of an agreement among both domestic constituencies together.[14] They could decide, for instance, on one side agreeing not to make a speech detailing how many concessions it received from the other side, in order not to provoke the public on the other side. Alternatively, negotiating parties could agree that one side will make a victory speech to appease their public.

Inclusion

Whether to include the most hardline parties within the room or exclude them in an attempt to marginalize and weaken them is a recurrent dilemma. At times, spoilers have been purposefully excluded from the negotiation process, such as in Guatemala (1997) and El Salvador (1994). In Rwanda (1994), however, the exclusion of extremists may have contributed to the escalation of violence after the peace agreement was reached.[15]

A growing body of literature suggests that a more inclusive negotiation process has a higher chance of producing a lasting stable peace than a military victory.[16] An inclusive approach may involve trying to integrate such groups as rebels, terrorists, prisoners, and other extreme factions. Simply by partaking in the process, extremists may form personal ties with others in the room, diminishing the chance that they will escalate the conflict outside the room, especially if they feel that they would benefit more by participating than by walking away. Although governments are instinctively resistant to engage with such groups, they do often end up talking with them, and groups that at one time were written off as spoilers do sometimes moderate and turn away from violence toward a more political approach.[17] This was the case in the peace process in Northern Ireland in the 1990s that led up to the signing of the Good Friday Agreement. The series of negotiations that ended apartheid in South Africa provides another example of when inclusiveness was crucial to the success of a lengthy and difficult process. To limit the spoiling potential of certain groups in the room, the concept of "sufficient consensus" was employed.[18] This decision-making mechanism meant that if no agreement was reached after prolonged debate, a judge would decide whether there was enough agreement to reach a decision. George Mitchell also adopted a modified version of the principle of sufficient consensus during the Northern Ireland negotiations. Any proposal had to gain majority support from parties representing the majority of the voting population, parties representing both Catholics and Protestants, and from both governments. In both South Africa and Northern Ireland, this concept ensured that the largest parties, the African National Congress and the National Party, and the Ulster Unionist Party and the Social Democratic and Labour Party, respectively, effectively had veto power over decisions in the talks.[19] Inclusion thus became less risky for the major parties, as they still maintained significant control over the process.[20]

Attempting to engage with extremists means inviting groups into the room that may be more likely to engage in spoiling behavior. Parties are not always moderated after they are brought on board, and they may instead try to spoil the peace process while being situated within it. Nevertheless, trying to marginalize extremist groups rarely works. Inclusive negotiation processes have repeatedly been shown to bring about more durable peace agreements. The challenge is to find strategies, such as sufficient consensus, that allow one to reap the benefits of inclusion, while keeping the risks associated with it at bay.

The Divided Team

In an ideal world, all negotiators on the same team should be in agreement about their position on issues under discussion before they enter the room. However, in reality, negotiating teams are often not homogenous, and according to Ira William Zartman, "the dynamics within the sides and parties are usually as dramatic as those between parties."[21] Members of the team may reflect fundamental splits within the government or society, and they may end up negotiating between themselves at the table or in caucuses.[22] During the 2013–2014 Israeli-Palestinian direct negotiations, Israeli chief negotiator and justice minister Tzipi Livni was joined at the table by Yitzhak Molcho. According to commentators, whereas Livni entered negotiations set on reaching a deal with the Palestinians, Molcho was arguably present to keep an eye on negotiations so that no concessions would be made that would upset Netanyahu. It was reported that while Livni wanted to discuss details, Molcho was preoccupied with procedural issues and insistent that Israel would not put a map on the table until the negotiators had agreed on the security conditions that would govern a Palestinian state.[23] As such it was almost impossible for any progress to be made inside the room.

A split in the Israeli team also developed during negotiations at Bolling Air Force Base near Washington, DC, in December 2000, following the Camp David Summit and preceding the laying out of the Clinton Parameters. During talks, it became clear that negotiator Shlomo Ben-Ami was taking a far more flexible stance toward making concessions on core issues, namely the Temple Mount, than Ehud Barak's mandate would allow. Ben-Ami appeared determined to reach an agreement, perhaps partly due to the political consideration that Shimon Peres would replace him as foreign minister if he was not able to reach an agreement. Israeli delegation member Israel Hasson, critical of Ben-Ami's conduct, temporarily resigned from the team; other Israeli delegates informed the Americans and Palestinians that Ben-Ami's offers should not be considered as representative of Barak's position, and there were private discussions with Ben-Ami about the confusion he had created in the room by diverging from the official Israeli standpoint. This incident lasted for a good number of hours and temporarily disassembled the Israeli team. It brought about confusion and uncertainty both for the American facilitators and the Palestinian negotiators and required urgent consultations to bring the team together and make sure all parties were on the same page. From then on, although the situation was stabilized, positions expressed by individuals in the Israeli negotiating team were challenged by Palestinian interlocutors, who had become less trusting. Even when good intentions are involved without any intention to spoil, which evidently was the case with Ben-Ami, actions that create confusion and cause the other side to question the integrity and legitimacy of the team with whom they are negotiating put the process in jeopardy.

In complex negotiation processes with multi-issue, multiparty, multilevel setups—such as the intensive rounds of talks on the 1995 Interim Agreement and the permanent-status negotiations in Camp David (2000), Taba (2001), and Annapolis (2007–2008)—it is common to see a wide array of participants, each with a different professional and social circle, on each side of the negotiation table. This fact in itself provides fertile ground for internal tension within the team, often greatly diminishing the chance of an agreement being reached. However, the advantages of a diversified or even divided team might mean that the interests of various political groups and parties are better represented at the table. Therefore, if an agreement is reached with an internally divided team, it may be better received by the domestic constituents on that side as a whole. But the potential for the same diversity actually spoiling the negotiations may sometimes outweigh this advantage.

Potentially Spoiling Tactics and Behavior

In his book *Negotiating Peace*, former CIA agent Paul Pillar maintains that negotiations may be utilized as a means for parties to extend combat, but through diplomacy rather than violence.[24] Strategies of war can be brought into the negotiating room, such as eroding the enemy's strength and sapping its morale, in an attempt to achieve victory rather than to achieve a mutually acceptable agreement. In intractable conflicts, when parties are never quite sure of the intentions of the other side, there is inherent mistrust between sides. Unless a negotiating team is therefore convinced that their interlocutors are negotiating in good faith, they will be reluctant to make concessions, and negotiations are likely to become deadlocked.

Behavior that signifies a lack of integrity or sincerity has a long-lasting effect through the negotiation process and can potentially spoil talks. Besides outright deception and falsification of facts, common tactics used at the table include walking out as a means to get the other party to make concessions; pretending to have an opposed interest on an issue very important to the other party in order to gain an advantage on other issues;[25] and "tag teams" in which one "nice" decision-maker makes a show of persuading the other "tough" decision-maker to offer or agree to more, so that the team appears to be making a big concession.[26] These types of tactics may work—that is, produce favorable outcomes for a one-off negotiation. However, in ongoing negotiations, reputation is important, and such tactics are likely to weaken trust between parties and potentially backfire. A bad reputation prevents even skilled negotiators from maximizing gains at the negotiating table and can put a whole negotiation process in jeopardy.[27]

Actions that signify disrespect to the other party or a lack of commitment to the negotiation process can become central issues in the room, overshadowing the tangible issues.[28] In the 2000 Camp David Summit, during a round of particularly tense negotiations, US president Bill Clinton suggested a secret negotiation exercise comprising just a small circle of Israeli and Palestinian negotiators selected by both leaders: Yasser Arafat appointed Saeb Erekat and Mohammed Dahlan, and Ehud Barak appointed

Shlomo Ben-Ami and Gilead Sher. The exercise aimed to provide negotiators with the flexibility to negotiate on core issues and be conducive to breaking impasses that had emerged. It was decided that negotiators would meet for a continuous twenty-four hours—Clinton's security guards were positioned at the door, preventing anyone from entering or leaving the cabin. After a few hours, Erekat decided to take a nap on a sofa in the cabin where the secret negotiations were being held; by doing so, he was bluntly breaking the conditions of the negotiations. Ben-Ami was furious and ran over to Erekat shouting, "Are you crazy? This is the last chance we have, and you are getting tired? This is how you work? Don't you want a state?"[29] Erekat's spoiling behavior, whether intentional or not, caused the Israeli team to question his commitment. Even once an actor stops spoiling, as Erekat did when he got up from the couch and continued negotiating in the back channel, the effects can be long-lasting.

Unintentional spoiling can involve not taking time to acknowledge and understand the other side's needs, concerns, and interests. This is perhaps the most detrimental behavior in a negotiation room. At worst, it can lead parties to unwittingly diminish the value of the other party, causing significant offense. At best, it stops parties from making headway in the room as they remain fixated on their own positions and arguments, rather than gaining familiarity with those of the interlocutor, with whom they need to strike a deal.[30] The core needs and interests of the other side, as well as their positions, need to be explored. Because this approach uncovers the underlying needs of the parties, more creative options for resolution are likely to emerge.[31]

Back-Channel Negotiations

One way that parties in conflict attempt to circumvent spoiling is by holding official sanctioned talks in secret, known as back-channel negotiations. Back-channel talks may be conducted in parallel to front-channel negotiations, sometimes even with the same negotiators, or as an alternative to the front channel. Back-channel talks are often used in between rounds of official negotiations in order to explore possible avenues for compromise and degrees of flexibility in confidence, and to convey pragmatic messages from one party to the other, often representing mutual deposits made by the respective leaders, without the interference of the media, the public, and opponents of a negotiated settlement. Because of the secret and exploratory nature of the talks, parties may be more willing to consider a wider range of options in the room and commit to a tentative agreement.[32] Back-channel negotiations are credited with effectively facilitating early breakthrough agreements—for example, the Oslo Accords.[33] In contrast, the high-profile multinational 1991 Madrid Conference and follow-up Washington, DC, talks, which took place simultaneously with the Oslo secret talks, failed to achieve results and became redundant.

Implementing agreements that emerge from back-channel negotiations may, however, be more challenging. If talks are discovered, external spoilers may work hard to derail the process.[34] Moreover, if the back channel involves only a few individuals, which it often does, it will not address the internal divisions within each side, and the agreement will not be easy to implement. Take, for example, the negotiations that led to the signing of the Evian Accords by France and the Provisional Government of the Algerian Republic. Spoiling was impressively averted during the negotiations that took place in the secluded Chalet du Yeti in the Jura Mountains in Switzerland, but as Alistair Horne writes, "almost every one of the provisions was to remain a dead letter" as events on the ground superseded the official agreement.[35]

One can nonetheless gain valuable insight into how spoiling was averted in the room from Horne's analysis of the French-Algerian Yeti talks. First, the location of the talks, Switzerland, was neutral territory. Second, the specific location allowed for absolute secrecy: the chalet was inconspicuous, basic, and small, and unlike the Evian hotel in which the previous round of negotiations was held, it did not resemble a place for high-status delegates to meet. According to Horne, this was an unintended bonus that actually helped negotiators form ties, as they had more human contact with each other. The negotiators also went to huge efforts to keep the press in the dark: French negotiator Louis Joxe disguised himself as a winter-sports enthusiast on his way to the chalet, and in one instance, an Algerian negotiation team's car skidded and blocked the road when it was being followed by the press, giving the delegates time to flee. The secrecy of the talks by itself may have built trust and mutual understanding and improved personal ties, as disputants took part in an ongoing shared task that only they and very few others knew about.[36] Third, Joxe had the backing of the elected leader, de Gaulle, giving him room to maneuver. When talks began to reach an impasse in the room, due to the Algerian team becoming hardened in its position as violence escalated on the ground in Algeria, Joxe phoned de

Gaulle for advice on how to proceed. De Gaulle instructed him to reach an agreement comprising a ceasefire and self-determination that day and not to get stuck on details. Joxe returned to the table with the authority and freedom to negotiate, and after an all-night session, some agreement was reached. Negotiators managed to avoid spoiling behavior inside the room because their teams were each cohesive, consisting of only a few individuals, and because the French had a broad mandate from the decision-makers. A final round of negotiations to iron out the details took place in Evian, where an agreement was officially reached on March 18, 1962. However, following the agreement there was an upsurge of violence by far-right French groups determined to preserve French rule in Algeria, which was met with an increase in terrorism toward the French residents, driving almost a million out of Algeria, and many of the remaining settlers were killed.

This case highlights both the most beneficial and the most detrimental effects of secret negotiations. The secrecy of negotiations eased tensions between parties in the room and sparked the process that facilitated the end of 132 years of French occupation and ultimately the end of the crisis. But with the far-right French parties absent, the agreement met great resistance when presented to the public, resulting in a violent backlash and most of the terms of the agreements being breached. The secrecy of the negotiations ensured that violence did not erupt while negotiations were taking place to spoil the talks, but spoiling did happen at the implementation stage. As Anthony Wanis-St. John explains, reaching a peace agreement at the table is not equivalent to peacebuilding, and excluding key parties is likely to exacerbate splits within each side and provoke spoilers, rather than resolve them. This does not mean that the back channel should be abandoned, but rather that it should be used with caution, specifically at the earliest stages of a negotiation process or to help break an impasse.[37] Back-channel negotiations must be used in conjunction with the front channel, and increasing and continual efforts should be made to expand support for talks on each side in an inclusive fashion.

Third Parties

A third party often enters or initiates negotiations in an attempt to control spoiling behavior inside the room. Third parties can be more or less official, can be states or international organizations, and can be involved to a greater or lesser extent: they can act as advisors, they can facilitate communication, they can suggest alternatives for resolution, and they can use tactics aimed at coercing parties to shift their positions.[38] Parties in conflict are likely to want a third party to mediate if they believe it is actually able, and not just not willing, to help.[39] In conflicts where a power discrepancy exists between sides, a more powerful third party can work toward redressing the balance through incentives (e.g., increased legitimacy, financial gain) or deprivations (e.g., sanctions, withdrawal of aid), to propel the parties toward resolution.[40] Stronger parties can also offer security guarantees, although these are neither necessary nor always sufficient for securing resolution: in Cambodia, Angola, Liberia, and Somalia, even with security guarantees from third parties, the agreements reached were not implemented.[41] In addition to material leverage, a third party's credibility, based on a strong rapport with negotiators and key players, plus a high degree of knowledge about the core issues of the conflict, can be utilized to help parties reach an agreement.[42] A third party can supply missing information, highlight common interests, keep the parties focused on the issues, and help facilitate a different pattern of communication between disputants caught in a cycle of actions and reactions.[43] If a third party is more involved and proposes a solution, it can take personal responsibility for the concessions made so that leaders can "blame" someone else aside from their side's negotiators.[44] As such, negotiators may be more willing to accept a solution put forward by an impartial third party than to put forward the same solution themselves. Intervention methods must be adapted to the specific negotiations, in order to effectively curb, and not exacerbate, spoiling behavior.

Daniel Curran, James K. Sebenius, and Michael Watkins compare Richard Holbrook's aggressive and coercive approach to ending the war in Bosnia and Herzegovina with George Mitchell's patient and facilitative approach to negotiating peace in Northern Ireland, illustrating the importance of the type of third-party involvement.[45] In the summer of 1995, backed by NATO air strikes and economic sanctions, Holbrook engaged in three months of intensive shuttle diplomacy with the minimum necessary number of parties, leading to a series of agreements and a cease-fire that was followed by the Dayton Accords. Holbrook warned of the dire consequences of not reaching an agreement and followed up this threat with the NATO bombing of Serbian targets. He employed coercive tactics, telling Serbian President Milosevic that he did not have the authority to ease sanctions, although he did, saving it to use as an incentive for an eventual peace agreement. He was determined to reach a deal and wielded his power and authority to coerce Milosevic to reach an agreement, while Milosevic was acting as a greedy spoiler, responding to the West's sticks and carrots.[46] In contrast to Holbrook's hard approach, Mitchell acted as a neutral facilitator, seeking to build trust between party leaders and create institutional and constitutional frameworks in Northern Ireland. Mitchell took a facilitative role in negotiations from 1995 until 1998, with no clear mandate or powers to reward and punish. He acted with patience, determined to keep the process going, and sought wide participation in the negotiations. Unlike Holbrook, Mitchell claimed to be impressed by the parties he was mediating between and believed he could be most effective by gaining their trust and confidence. Through this approach he was able to bring previous and potential spoilers on board with the process.

Although third parties often have the power to control spoiling behavior in the room, the threats and incentives offered can sometimes bring parties to the table who are actually not interested in peace. For instance, Israeli prime minister Yitzhak Shamir agreed to participate in the 1991 Madrid peace conference, then later admitted that he did so mainly in order to avoid US pressure. In speeches made during the conference, he showed no willingness to make concessions. Then in 1992, after losing the Israeli general elections, he revealed his prior hopes to expand settlements and prevent the establishment of a Palestinian state.[47] Shamir uncovered his true agenda and his tactics, stating, "In my political activity, I know how to display the tactics of moderation, but without conceding anything on the goal—the integrity of the Land of Israel" in an interview for an Israeli newspaper.[48] After this speech it was clear that Shamir had no intention to compromise and was using the negotiation process to buy time. In hindsight, from a negotiation perspective, Shamir can be categorized as a total spoiler, and thus it is doubtful whether any third party would have been able to facilitate or mediate an agreement with him in the room.

Finally, having a "middle man" in the negotiation process can bring with it an added danger of misunderstanding, which may inadvertently spoil talks. In the 2013–2014 Israeli-Palestinian negotiations, Kerry was accused of communicating inaccurate messages to the Palestinians around the thorny issue of Israel's release of Palestinian prisoners.[49] Israel had agreed to release a number of Palestinian prisoners, but not Israeli-Arab prisoners, as Abbas had requested. According to Israeli negotiator Michael Herzog, Kerry had guaranteed the release of the Israeli-Arab prisoners to Abbas, later claiming a misunderstanding. Moreover, there was confusion over the terms of release—Kerry had apparently promised Abbas that the released prisoners would be sent "to their homes"; however, the Israeli side claimed it had never agreed to this term and insisted that a number of the most high-risk prisoners be sent to Gaza, Jordan, or abroad, and not to the West Bank.[50] Ultimately, and based on this "confusion," Israel refused to release the fourth batch of high-risk prisoners that it had promised. What may be seen as third-party unintentional spoiling entered the picture. Israel's refusal to meet its commitment on the fourth prisoner release led the Palestinians to take unilateral "spoiling" steps. They dispatched requests to join various international bodies, violating their commitment not to take unilateral steps toward gaining Palestinian recognition and effectively waging diplomatic warfare against Israel. In turn, Israel reacted by accelerating construction in East Jerusalem. Thus, as seen in this series of events, third parties can intentionally or unintentionally breed misunderstanding as they shuffle between the sides delivering key messages. Nonetheless, the benefits of a third party in curbing spoiling behavior do, generally, outweigh this risk.

Structure and Timing

There is a saying that 90 percent of the negotiation takes place during the final 10 percent of the allocated time.[51] When no realistic deadlines for the negotiations are set by the respective leaders or a third party, the negotiators within the room tend to be indifferent to time issues, unless they serve their interests. It has been argued that the realistic deadline in the Northern Ireland peace process was an essential part of its success.[52] The deadline created an intense negotiating environment in which parties were more motivated to make concessions. However, in the 2013–2014 Israeli-Palestinian negotiations, setting deadlines for the completion of the talks proved redundant and perhaps destructive. The US State Department aimed to reach a permanent peace agreement within nine months, which was unfeasible. If a deadline is unrealistic, it will not provide the motivation that it was intended to create, and the parties may be less likely to take the process seriously.

When a third party facilitates the talks by hosting the negotiators or shuttling between the parties, it has a duty to provide an orderly setup and to manage the process with the utmost sensitivity to timing. The Clinton parameters for an Israeli-Palestinian peace accord of December 2000 were practically ready as early as mid-September 2000. They followed up on as many as forty extensive secret daily direct negotiations, recapping the convergences reached between the parties during the detailed negotiations at the Camp David Summit. Had President Clinton presented them opposed to, capitalizing on the momentum remaining from the summit, the outcome might have been different. The events that followed, however, consisted in an upsurge of violence, and the potentially historic opportunity for all parties concerned was lost. Sadly, there was no realistic US contingency plan in place, and no fallback or exit strategies were prepared in anticipation of failure.

Conclusion

Spoiling from within the negotiating room can be as hazardous to peace efforts as the spoiling actions of those outside the process. This chapter has detailed several decisions and behaviors that can lead to negotiations being spoiled from within. If negotiators have not been granted a comprehensive mandate from the decision-maker, their hands are tied at the table—they have no room to discuss substantive issues, let alone conclude an agreement. Negotiators might also engage in spoiling behavior in the room if they, or the decision-maker, begin to fear the public's response to the negotiations or to an upcoming agreement, specifically when the public opposes the peace process. Negotiators often fail to consider that the other side also faces the challenge of "selling" the agreement to the public. Additionally, splits within the same negotiating team, which are a frequent occurrence, can create tension and confusion in the room. Furthermore, a negotiation process that is inclusive of the most hardline parties may be more vulnerable to being spoiled in the room. However, despite this, an inclusive process is often necessary for an agreement to be implemented, and thus efforts need to be taken to minimize potential spoiling behavior of more extreme parties once they are in the room. When negotiators employ tactics at the table—for example, storming out of the room in an attempt to achieve a better deal—it can often backfire, as trust is lost between the sides.

To overcome the threats of spoiling behavior in the room, a heavier emphasis should be placed on mechanisms to cope with different types of spoiling as they emerge in talks throughout the process. Such mechanisms may include a back channel or third-party facilitation, but even these need to be used carefully—the back channel cannot be utilized as a substitute for garnering support for an agreement among the public, and third-party pressure can sometimes bring parties to the table who are not interested in negotiations and are thus liable to spoil them. Internal spoiling potential has seldom been highlighted to date, even though it can determine whether peace is reached or conflict is refueled.

Notes

1. Stephen John Stedman, "Spoiler Problems in Peace Processes," *International Security* 22, no. 2 (1997): 5–53.

2. Kelly M. Greenhill and Solomon Major, "The Perils of Profiling: Civil War Spoilers and the Collapse of Intrastate Peace Accords," *International Security* 31, no. 3 (2007): 7–40, quotation from p. 11.

3. Julius Mutwol, *Peace Agreements and Civil Wars in Africa: Insurgent Motivations, State Responses, and Third Party Peacemaking in Liberia, Rwanda, and Sierra Leone* (Amherst, NY: Cambria Press, 2009).

4. Marie-Joëlle Zahar, "Reframing the Spoiler Debate in Peace Processes," in *Contemporary Peacemaking: Conflict, Violence and Peace Processes*, ed. John Darby and Roger Mac Ginty (London: Palgrave Macmillan, 2003)

5. Stephen John Stedman, Donald S. Rothchild, and Elizabeth M. Cousens, eds. *Ending Civil Wars: The Implementation of Peace Agreements* (Boulder, CO: Lynne Rienner, 2002).

6. Ben Shepherd, *"The 'Spoiler' Concept, Conflict and Politics: Who 'Spoils' What, for Whom?"* Foreign and Commonwealth Office/London School of Economics and Political Science (2010): 11–16.

7. Frank R. Pfetsch, "Hypotheses about the Nature, Environment, Rules of Conflict, Third Parties, and Outcomes/Solutions," in *Negotiating Political Conflicts* (London: Palgrave Macmillan, 2007), 189–195.

8. Paul R. Pillar, "The Long Road of Negotiations," *National Interest*, April 15, 2012, http://nationalinterest.org/blog/paul-pillar/the-long-road-negotiations-6785.

9. "Summary: 1964–1968, Volume VII, Vietnam, September 1968–January 1969," US Department of State Archive, Foreign Relations, information released online from January 20, 2001 to January 20, 2009, accessed August 30, 2016, http://2001–2009.state.gov/r/pa/ho/frus/johnsonlb/vii/22443.htm.

10. Amir Tibon, "The Secret Back Channel That Doomed the Israel-Palestine Negotiations," *New Republic*, November 26, 2014, accessed August 30, 2016, http://www.newrepublic.com/article/120413/secret-negotiations-between-yitzhak-molho-abbas-representative.

11. Ibid.

12. Tzvi Ben-Gedalyahu, "Kerry Jumps on Okay for Freeing Terrorists, Announces Peace Talks," *Jewish Press*, July 29, 2013, accessed August 30, 2010, http://www.jewishpress.com/tag/molcho/.

13. Peter B. Evans, Harold K. Jacobson, and Robert D. Putnam, eds. *Double-Edged Diplomacy: International Bargaining and Domestic Politics* (Berkeley: University of California Press, 1993).

14. James K. Sebenius, "'Level II' Negotiation Strategies: Advance Your Interests by Helping to Solve Their Internal Problems," in *Negotiating in Times of Conflict*, ed. Gilead Sher and Anat Kurz (Tel Aviv: Institute of National Security Studies, 2015), 107–124.

15. Wendy Pearlman, "Spoiling Inside and Out: Internal Political Contestation and the Middle East Peace Process," *International Security* 33, no. 3 (2009): 79–109.

16. For example, see Fen Osler Hampson, *Nurturing Peace: Why Peace Settlements Succeed or Fail* (Washington, DC: United States Institute of Peace, 1996); and Roy Licklinder, "Obstacles to Peace Settlements," in *Turbulent Peace: The Challenges of Managing International Conflict*, ed. Chester A Crocker, Fen Olser Hamspon, and Pamela Aall (Washington, DC: United States Institute of Peace, 2001), 697–718; and Daniel Scher, "Managing Spoilers at the Bargaining Table: Inkatha and the Talks to End Apartheid, 1990–1994," Innovations for Successful Societies, Princeton University, 2010, http://successfulsocieties.princeton.edu/sites/successfulsocieties/files/Policy_Note_ID137.pdf.

17. Erik Solheim, "Always Try Engagement," in *Negotiating in Times of Conflict*, ed. Gilead Sher and Anat Kurz (Tel Aviv: Institute of National Security Studies, 2015), 17–28.

18. Robert H. Mnookin, 2003. "Strategic Barriers to Dispute Resolution: A Comparison of Bilateral and Multilateral Negotiations," *Journal of Institutional and Theoretical Economics*, 159, no. 1: 199–220.

19. Daniel Curran, James K. Sebenius, and Michael Watkins, "Two Paths to Peace: Contrasting George Mitchell in Northern Ireland with Richard Holbrooke in Bosnia-Herzegovina," *Negotiation Journal* 20, no. 4 (2004): 513–537.

20. Ibid.

21. Ira William Zartman, *Engaging Extremists: Trade-offs, Timing, and Diplomacy* (Washington, DC: US Institute of Peace, 2011), 284.

22. Brigid Starkey, Mark A. Boyer, and Jonathan Wilkenfeld, *Negotiating a Complex World: An Introduction to International Negotiation* (Lanham, MD: Rowman & Littlefield, 2005).

23. Ben Birnbaum and Amir Tibon, "The Explosive, Inside Story of How John Kerry Built an Israel-Palestine Peace Plan—and Watched It Crumble," *New Republic*, July 20, 2014, accessed August 30, 2016, http://www.newrepublic.com/article/118751/how-israel-palestine-peace-deal-died.

24. Paul R. Pillar, *Negotiating Peace: War Termination as a Bargaining Process* (Princeton, NJ, Princeton University Press, 1983).

25. Kathleen M. O'Connor and Peter J. Carnevale, "A Nasty but Effective Negotiation Strategy: Misrepresentation of a Common-Value Issue," *Personality and Social Psychology Bulletin* 23 no. 5 (1997): 504–515.

26. David Wachtel, "How to Succeed When Working with Tactical Negotiators," Negotiation Experts, accessed August 30, 2016, http://www.negotiations.com/articles/negotiation-tactics/.

27. Catherine H. Tinsley, Kathleen M. O'Connor, and Brandon A. Sullivan, "Tough Guys Finish Last: The Perils of a Distributive Reputation." *Organizational Behavior and Human Decision Processes* 88, no. 2 (2002): 621–642.

28. Bert Brown, "Face Saving and Face Restoration in Negotiation" in *Negotiations: Social-Psychological Perspectives*, ed. D. Druckman (Beverly Hills, CA: Sage, 1977), 275–300.

29. Gilead Sher, *Israeli-Palestinian Peace Negotiations, 1999–2001: Within Reach* (Oxfordshire, UK: Routledge, 2013), 73.

30. Aldo Matteucci, "Language and Diplomacy—A Practitioner's View," in *Language and Diplomacy*, ed. Jovan Kurbalija and Hannah Slavik (Malta, Diplo Foundation, 2001), 55–66.

31. Marwan Sinaceur et al., "Good Things Come to Those Who Wait: Late First Offers Facilitate Creative Agreements in Negotiation," *Personality and Social Psychology Bulletin* 39, no. 6 (2013): 814–825.

32. Anthony Wanis-St. John, "Back-Channel Negotiation: International Bargaining in the Shadows." *Negotiation Journal* 22, no. 2 (2006): 119–144.

33. Ibid.

34. Ibid.

35. Alistair Horne, *A Savage War of Peace: Algeria 1954–1962* (New York: New York Review of Books, 2006, first published in 1997), 521.

36. Niall Ó Dochartaigh, "Together in the Middle: Back Channel Negotiation in the Irish Peace Process," *Journal of Peace Research* 48, no. 6 (2011): 767–780.

37. Wanis-St. John, "Back-Channel Negotiation."

38. Ira William Zartman and Saadia Touval, "International Mediation: Conflict Resolution and Power Politics," *Journal of Social Issues* 41, no. 2 (1985): 27–45.

39. Mutwol, "Peace Agreements and Civil Wars in Africa."

40. Barbara Walter, *Committing to Peace: The Successful Settlement of Civil Wars* (Princeton, NJ: Princeton University Press, 2002).

41. Michal Glenn Findlay, *Spoiling the Peace or Seeking the Spoils?: Civil War Outcomes and the Role of Spoilers* (PhD diss., University of Illinois at Urbana-Champaign, 2007).

42. Lindsay Reid, "Examining Leverage in Civil War Mediation: A Dynamic Theory of Mediator Leverage," Department of Political Science University of North Carolina at Chapel Hill, Paper prepared for a presentation at the Duke-UNC IR Research Workshop, April 30, 2014, accessed August 30, 2016, http://polisci.duke.edu/uploads/media_items/reid.original.pdf.

43. Oliver Ramsbotham, Hugh Miall and Tom Woodhouse, *Contemporary Conflict Resolution* (Cambridge: Polity, 2011).

44. Starkey, Boyer, and Wilkenfeld, "Negotiating a Complex World."

45. Daniel Curran, James K. Sebenius, and Michael Watkins, "Two Paths to Peace: Contrasting George Mitchell in Northern Ireland with Richard Holbrooke in Bosnia-Herzegovina." *Negotiation Journal* 20, no. 4 (2004): 513–537.

46. Roger D. Petersen, *Western Intervention in the Balkans: The Strategic Use of Emotion in Conflict* (Cambridge: Cambridge University Press, 2011).

47. Karin Aggestam, "Internal and External Dynamics of Spoiling: A Negotiation Approach" in *Challenges to Peacebuilding: Managing Spoilers during Conflict Resolution*, ed. Edward Newman and Oliver Richmond (Tokyo: United Nations University Press, 2006), 23–39.

48. Andrew S. Buchanan, *Peace with Justice: A History of the Israeli-Palestinian Declaration of Principles on Interim Self-Government Arrangements*, (London: Macmillan Press, 2000).

49. Michael Herzog, "The Kerry Legacy: Inside the Black Box of Israeli-Palestinian Talks," *The American Interest*, February 27, 2017, accessed June 15, 2017. https://www.the-american-interest.com/2017/02/27/inside-the-black-box-of-israeli-palestinian-talks/

50. Ibid.

51. Thomas R. Colosi, "The Iceberg Principle: Secrecy in Negotiation," in *Perspectives on Negotiation: Four Case Studies and Interpretations*, ed. Diane B. Bendahmane and John W. McDonald, Jr. (Washington, DC: Center for the Study of Foreign Affairs, 1986), 243–262.

52. Timothy J. White, "Lessons from the Northern Ireland Peace Process: An Introduction" in *Lessons from the Northern Ireland Peace Process*, ed. Timothy J. White (Madison: University of Wisconsin Press, 2013), 3–33.

GILEAD SHER was Senior Negotiator at the 2000 Camp David summit and the 2001 Taba talks and served as Prime Minister Barak's chief of staff. Sher leads the Center for Applied Negotiations (CAN) at the Tel Aviv Institute for National Security Studies (INSS). His books include *The Israeli-Palestinian Peace Negotiations, 1999–2001: Within Reach* and *The Battle for Home*.

DEBORAH SHULMAN is a PhD student in social psychology at Friedrich Schiller University Jena and a member of the Psychology of Intergroup Conflict and Reconciliation Lab at Interdisciplinary Center (IDC) Herzliya.

2

THE LEADERSHIP AS A SPOILER

Roee Kibrik and Maya Kornberg

To date, most of the literature regarding spoilers has looked at actors outside of the government, taking it as a given that if the leadership chooses to participate in negotiations for peace, it will not, in itself, undermine it. This chapter, however, looks at the political leadership itself as a spoiler in the peace negotiations in which it takes part, and we shall focus on spoiling activity during the negotiation phase before an agreement is signed. The assumption that there is a dividing line between the leadership in negotiations and spoilers outside of it is too narrow. We argue that the political leadership can indeed be a powerful spoiler during the negotiation phase of a peace process, and sometimes it is necessary for supporters of a peace process to cope with the leadership itself as spoiler.

There have been a number of different applications of spoiling in analyses of leadership involvement in peace processes, though few if any have focused on spoiling during the negotiations. George Katete Onyango, for example, has dealt with the Sudanese government's spoiling activity, focusing on the implementation phase of peace agreements.[1] Others—for example, Carlo Nasi—examine the way leadership has coped with spoilers, looking at the peace process in Colombia, and the spoiling actions of rebel groups, the Colombian Congress, the US government, drug traffickers, the armed forces, and other prominent actors.[2]

The concept of spoiling has also been applied to the Israeli context, as seen in earlier chapters. Oded Haklai applies "spoiling" to the Israeli domestic institutional structures, looking at organized settler movements as spoilers to the peace process.[3] He argues that these spoilers have most capacity to spoil in situations with low state cohesion (the extent to which polity is unified and integrated) and state expansiveness (the social and physical space occupied by an institutional framework). Magnus Ranstrop also applies a spoiling framework to the Israeli-Palestinian Oslo negotiations, looking at perceptions of the others' narrative as a key cause of "devious objectives" in the peace process.[4]

Recognizing a need to broaden the investigation of spoiling and spoilers, Edward Newman and Oliver Richmond advocate a more comprehensive definition of spoilers that accounts for more actors, beyond the protagonists, such as parties in the international arena. Moreover, they argue against normative judgments about spoiling as entirely negative behavior, pointing out that defining someone as a spoiler can be a political statement in itself.[5]

Our definition of spoiling is largely based on Stedman's basic definition. To avoid the normative judgment in defining a spoiler as one who acts against the liberal-democratic-Western-valued peace process, following Newman and Richmond's warning,[6] we define a spoiler as one who acts to spoil the negotiations. The act of spoiling is what defines the spoiler, and not an independent definition of someone as a spoiler per se. In addition, our approach espouses Roger MacGinty's and others' inclusive definition of spoilers as either violent or nonviolent.[7]

It is difficult to differentiate between spoiling and simply failing to bring negotiations to a successful conclusion. Indeed, in many cases the political leadership fails in its attempts to reach an agreement. Sometimes its attempts at supporting, strengthening, and promoting the negotiations for peace actually harm their efforts. Spoiling, however, is not a behavior that achieves unintended results; rather it is an intentional action designed to hurt the negotiations and the peace process as a whole.

We deal with these challenges by developing an original set of criteria, based on the existing literature on spoilers. To differentiate between failing and spoiling, we propose a list of behaviors that can be defined as spoiling behavior, such as the leadership betraying trust, introducing new demands, or delegitimizing the negotiations. We then test our assertion by applying our criteria to two test cases. We show that the Israeli leadership acted as a spoiler during the 1999–2000 Israeli-Syrian negotiations as well as during the 2013–2014 Kerry Initiative.[8]

There is a distinction between a peace process and the negotiations themselves. Negotiations constitute just one component of a peace process between enemies—a process that must include fulfillment of the agreement, changes of attitudes toward the other, changes in one's own practices and identity, and more. Moreover, there are phases of negotiations. Spoilers to negotiations may aim to tackle the negotiation activity itself, and they could focus on any or all of the three main phases of negotiations. First, they can spoil what may be seen as a prenegotiation phase, though actually this may be a first stage of the negotiation process in which there are negotiations over the terms or conditions and the agenda for the talks. Secondly, spoilers may hurt the management and continuation of the negotiations. This second phase—what we shall call the phase of negotiation—consists of talks about the issues arising from the conflict, their resolution, and the conditions for implementation. Thirdly, spoilers can try to prevent the conclusion of an agreement in the last phase of the negotiation process. In this last phase, negotiators return to their constituents and the public (or others) to gain support or approval (and possibly formal ratification) of the negotiated agreement. This may be needed to proceed to the actual signing or to implementation. This division into phases is far from perfect; in reality the three phases might be mixed and the differences between them blurred, but they will be useful for our analysis.

The leadership has tremendous power to spoil peace negotiations. Its centrality in negotiation activity; its economic, political, rhetorical, cultural, and coercive resources; and its access and perhaps even control of relevant information all make the leadership a powerful spoiler, if it chooses to act as one. We define leadership as the person or group of people who act as the key decision-makers in a given society. In some cases the leadership may be composed of a single leader determining the course of a policy issue or the whole process. In other cases, the leadership comprises a heterogeneous group of people who together lead their society, though they may not agree among themselves. The nature and character of leadership is different depending on the country and can even change within the same society during different periods of time and contexts.

In this context it is important to distinguish between the leadership as a spoiler and the leadership as a "devious actor." It may very well be the case, as we will show in our first example, that political leadership enters negotiations with noble intentions but *changes* as the negotiations progress. It is also possible for the leadership to enter negotiations with intentions other than promoting peace, and still not spoil them because the negotiations themselves, and their success, serve to further its objectives.

There are various reasons why the leadership may decide to enter the negotiations with the intention of spoiling. Most of them have already been mentioned by Richmond in his discussion about the connection between devious objectives and spoiling.[9] First, it may have had no other alternative but to negotiate due to outside pressure and/or the risk of a heavy political (or other) price had it not entered negotiations. External pressure can be direct or indirect—for example, in the form of encouraging domestic pressure on the leadership (i.e., a public demand for negotiations). Second, the leadership may view entering the negotiations as a way to spoil the overall peace process. Third, internal debates and struggles can lead the political leadership to decide upon negotiations solely to balance the contradictory views within its coalition, or to buy time, with the intention of spoiling at some point when necessary. A fourth explanation is that a leader may choose to enter negotiations without the intention of reaching a compromise, but rather to use the negotiation to promote his/her interests. One can use the negotiation as a discursive arena for delegitimizing and undermining the other side's positions and claims. In this case, to paraphrase Clausewitz, the negotiation is merely the continuation of conflict (war) by other means. A fifth explanation, which has not been discussed by Richmond, pertains to ontological security, a concept that refers to preserving one's own identity as one perceives it. In order to preserve identity and avoid tension, a leadership that defines itself as peace loving may not have a choice but to enter negotiations.[10] Sixth, practical political calculations (beyond the above) may sway the political leadership to enter negotiation but spoil it from within, not only to preserve a certain desired identity as a peaceful entity, but perhaps in order to strengthen alliances, or as a way to gain other political dividends without committing to further steps. If the other side tries to do the same, there may be a struggle over who comes out of the failed negotiations as the peacemaker and who is labeled the spoiler. Further, once engaged in negotiations, the political leadership may seek to improve its own position, gain greater public support, or cooperation, against domestic opponents. This may also include an attempt to gain legitimacy for coercive acts (e.g., in fighting terror or even violent spoilers) or for security cooperation (e.g., with former adversaries), as well as legitimacy externally, to combat outside sanctions or other pressure, or internally for placating propeace factions in its society.

Ten Ways for the Leadership to Spoil Negotiations

The behavior of the leadership is manifested in its rhetorical practices, decisions, legislative behavior, and regulatory activities. Therefore, the materials used to assess the two test cases included government decisions, formal and informal deliberations, statements, testimonies from the negotiations, and interviews with practitioners. Our focus, as noted above, is on actions or behaviors that spoil rather than the characterization of an actor as a spoiler. The list of spoiling actions is as follows:

1. *Intentionally delegitimize the negotiations and/or the negotiators themselves (from either side).*
   It is a difficult task for the leadership to damage the legitimacy of the negotiations and emerge unscathed when it is involved in them itself. Nonetheless, it is possible. For example, a leader can kill two birds with one stone in sending a domestic competitor to head the negotiations and then delegitimizing the negotiator and the negotiations themselves. It can also undermine the adversary's legitimacy by trying to divide the adversary and create or exploit its internal divisions. This is most strategic in the prenegotiation phase, when hurting the other side's legitimacy will not harm one's own standing. For example, one can portray the adversary's leadership as not having complete control over its people and/or not being able to deliver any agreement. These are just small examples, and the list is long.
2. *Hurt the internal political base and/or resources of the propeace forces at home and on the other side.*
   Acting to weaken the propeace forces, either at home or on the other side, is an act of spoiling. The leadership may describe these factions as traitors, pass legislation to cut their budgets or discredit their political legitimacy, censor or deny access to the media, or arrest them, among other actions. One might also strengthen the adversary's opposition forces by releasing prisoners who belong to the adversary's opposition rather than its leadership group.
3. *Intentionally engage in actions that will exacerbate tensions to improve position (limited spoiling), but also as an act to prevent the possibility of finding future solutions (total spoiling).*
   The leadership can try to improve its bargaining power by changing the facts on the ground. This can be done through legal measures, coercive steps, or by other means. These are acts of limited spoiling. In addition, the leadership can change the situation on the ground in a way that would hinder a future agreement, and in this way act as a total spoiler. This can be done best when the actions of the leadership are designed to touch the very core issues or the "casus belli" issues as expressed by the partners for negotiations.
4. *Intentionally betray the trust of the adversaries.*
   Damaging mutual trust is particularly destructive because trust is an essential part of negotiation, or at least one of the basic objectives of the peace

negotiations. If, for example, one party engages in uncoordinated leaks from the talks, goes back on prior commitments, or lies, trust may be jeopardized or completely lost. Therefore, such behavior can be seen as spoiling behavior.

5. *Introduce new demands or issues not previously raised or retreat on earlier understandings.*

    The move from the first phase of negotiations to the second obligates the sides to agree on a framework of how to conduct the negotiations and on the issues to be discussed. When one side introduces new demands regarding the framework (e.g., another mediator, a different timetable, or a change in the structure of the proceedings), or new issues that have not previously been mentioned, this can be interpreted as spoiling behavior. It is especially true if the new demands come at the second phase of negotiations or late in the process.

6. *Avoid compromises and/or shifts in demands.*

    As Richmond emphasizes, from the perspective of the liberal peace, the decision to enter negotiations is tantamount to the willingness to compromise.[11] When there is no shift at all in demands or stance over time, this signifies spoiling. One of the tactics that has been used to avoid a compromise is demanding symmetry at all levels, in cases where the economic strength, military might, and other powers are asymmetric. Insisting on symbolic or physical symmetry in concessions when the two sides are not on equal footing can be seen as an attempt of the more powerful side to thwart the success of negotiations as a whole or improve its relative position. Other tactics to avoid compromise include insisting on fine print, demand for personal changes . . . or stalling in any other possible way.

7. *Emphasize the points/issues in the domestic narrative that contradict central components from the adversary's narrative.*

    For negotiations to be successful, both sides need to change parts of their identity, or at least avoid those components of their identity relating to the conflict. The mission is twofold. The sides must both change their own narrative in a way that casts the peace process in a positive light, and simultaneously support the other side's efforts to do the same. If the leadership acts to reinforce certain elements of the domestic narrative, such as the portrayal of the other side as the implacable enemy or the conflict itself as a central element of identity, this is an act of spoiling.

8. *Support or strengthen the opponents on the other side directly or indirectly.*

    When one side takes steps to bolster the domestic opposition to the peace process of the other side, this is a spoiling action. This can be done through (covert) financing, releasing prisoners, acknowledging the opposition's stance in the internal debate, providing that opposition a platform for publicity or access to media, or undermining the standing of the adversary's leadership, or by other means.

9. *Delegitimize the mediators.*
   The mediator, if there is one, becomes an important part of the constellation of negotiation. Delegitimizing the mediator by emphasizing its own interests, stressing its biases, or even hurting its credibility altogether, may hinder the talks themselves. Though sometimes the mediator is indeed biased or may have devious objectives that are difficult to identify, acting to delegitimize it may be treated as spoiling action.
10. *Support other spoiling forces on the home front.*
    Sometimes the leadership does not want to be blamed for the failure of the negotiations or, even worse, to be blamed for intentionally spoiling them. Thus, the leadership may subcontract activity, using the home opposition groups for this task, for example. Using one's own domestic opposition during negotiations may be part of the negotiation tactics (to highlight the red lines, to stress the political price at stake, to introduce the limitations of possible solutions, and more) in order to improve the negotiation's outcomes, rather than to spoil them altogether. In this case, not all of the activities of the opposition groups are spoiling actions; it depends on the content, target, and aim of the activity. However, when the leadership supports the actions of domestic groups in one of the behaviors enumerated above, it can be seen as an act of spoiling. Sometimes it may be even outside groups that gain the support of the leadership in order to promote spoiling actions (e.g., diaspora groups, international organizations, etc.).

Barak Gets "Cold Feet" and Spoils: Israel-Syria Negotiations on 1999–2000

In 1999, the Barak administration in Israel entered into a series of negotiations with Hafez al-Assad in Syria. The negotiation ended in a crushing failure. There had been several previous attempts at peace with Syria. Under Prime Minister Shamir, Yossi Ben-Aharon led the Israeli negotiation team in the 1992 post–Madrid Conference "Washington Talks." Itamar Rabinovitch headed the 1993–1995 negotiations under Prime Minister Rabin. Uri Savir negotiated in 1996 under Prime Minister Peres. In addition to the public negotiations, there were secret talks under Netanyahu in the late 1990s, led by his friend, US citizen Ron Lauder. Ehud Barak was elected prime minister in May 1999 and immediately started secret lower-level talks with the Syrians. One reason that Barak may have been eager to negotiate with Syria was his pledge to get Israeli troops out of Lebanon within a year, a step that he believed hinged on an agreement with Syria. High-level official talks between Syrian Foreign Minister Farouk Shara and Ehud Barak then took place in Washington, DC, on December 15–16, 1999, and in January 2000 in

Shepherdstown, and a final meeting took place between President Clinton and President Assad in Geneva in March 2000. The United States played a powerful role as mediator during the negotiations in the 1990s as well as in the Barak negotiations. In a speech before the National Defense College, Barak said that "our links with the United States have been and are the central anchor of not only the strengthening of Israel, but also in advancing the peace process with our neighbors."[12]

A central issue in the negotiations with Syria was the area from which Israel would withdraw—that is, to the international border of 1923 or the June 4 line of 1967 (at which point Syrian troops had advanced over the years through a demilitarized zone westward from the 1923 line and were on the banks of the Sea of Galilee).[13] The roughly two hundred meters between the two lines were the subject of controversy, with the Syrians claiming that Rabin had agreed to "full withdrawal," namely withdrawal to the June 4, 1967, line. Such agreement was referred to as the "Rabin pocket" offered to the American mediator during the 1993–1995 negotiations, and it became crucial in the 1999–2000 Israel-Syria talks.

Throughout the negotiation process, Barak, as well as different actors within the government, acted to undermine its success. Even early in the negotiations, various coalition factions signaled their displeasure. Uri Sagie, the head of Barak's negotiation team, writes that in an early government meeting, various members of the coalition, especially from Shas and Yisrael B'Aliyah, spoke out publicly against the negotiations.[14] Before the December 1999 Washington negotiations, the National Religious Party and Yisrael B'Aliyah threatened to leave the coalition if a land-for-peace deal was reached. This signaled an unwillingness to relent—clear spoiling behavior. American negotiator Dennis Ross writes that Barak was "isolated in his own cabinet on Syria."[15] This isolation and these threats may very well have deterred Barak from moving forward at Shepherdstown in January. While the Sheperdstown talks were going on, Eli Yishai, leader of the Shas party, publicly called for Barak to suspend talks and return home.[16] This type of public call also strengthened domestic spoiling forces, such as the large protest movement of the settlers,[17] delegitimizing both the negotiations and the negotiators. In mid-January, immediately after the failed Shepherdstown talks, Natan Sharansky of Yisrael B'Aliyah and Yitzhak Levy of the National Religious Party spoke out against pulling out of the Golan Heights at a huge rally, thereby strengthening domestic spoiling forces.[18] Though the coalition did engage in spoiling, the primary focus of this analysis will be on Barak, rather than his coalition, as he held the most power and was the main cause for the collapse of negotiations.

Spoiling Activity in the Prenegotiation Phase

In the prenegotiation phase, Ehud Barak did not engage in any spoiling activity. On the contrary, he acted to promote the continuation of negotiations. It seems clear that even before he took office, he was resolved to move forward with the Syria negotiations. In 1998, as chairman of the Labor Party, Barak wrote that "pursuing the strategy of peace, we must move purposely down a long, complex corridor of negotiations with patience and resolve."[19] In January 1999, months before his election, he expressed his interest in negotiations with Syria to Uri Sagie (who became his chief negotiator with the Syrians). After taking office, in his September 1999 Rosh Hashanah interview with a leading Israeli newspaper, *Yediot Ahronot*, Barak reaffirmed his public promise to make peace with Syria.[20] In an address in Sharm el-Sheikh, Egypt, the same month, Barak said, "From here I call on President Assad to put aside all past disagreement and together find the appropriate way to resume peace negotiations between Israel and Syria."[21] On October 4, 1999, Barak asked Assad in a speech to "engage in negotiations toward a peace agreement of 'courage and honor.'"[22] In addition, Barak privately told President Clinton in the summer of 1999 that he was eager to negotiate with Syria.[23] Both Uri Sagie and Dennis Ross describe Barak's great enthusiasm for and commitment to reaching an agreement during the prenegotiation phase. According to Ross, in the fall of 1999, Barak asked that substantive talks be organized as soon as possible, and in September, two sets of secret meetings took place between Uri Sagie and Assad's personal emissary, Riyad Daudi, in Switzerland and Washington, laying the groundwork for the official negotiations.[24] The United States also took part in these meetings as a mediator.

Theoretically, peace was within reach. Because negotiations had been going on since the mid-1990s, the outline was already in place. It soon turned out, though, that the issues from the previous talks continued to haunt negotiations. One major problem that the Barak team encountered in the prenegotiation phase was the loose ends from the Lauder talks and conflicting evidence regarding certain issues that arose in the talks. Lauder's team initially told Barak's team that Assad had agreed to the 1923 lines rather than the June 4, 1967, lines. Barak later found a Lauder document containing agreement on the June 4, 1967, line, leading Barak to believe that he could restart negotiations from this comfortable place presumably agreed to by Netanyahu (or at least his emissary).[25] The Syrians insisted the negotiations resume from what they claimed was agreement on the June 4, 1967, line (the "Rabin pocket"). In a meeting with Clinton in July 1999, Barak told him he would not confirm the Rabin pocket, but he was vague about his final position. He did agree, however, to the Americans using the June 4 line as a "guide" in the talks. When pressed by the Syrians, who claimed previous Israeli agreement to the "Rabin pocket," Barak ambiguously answered, "While my government has made no commitment in advance, we do not erase previous history."[26] This statement was neither a commitment nor a refusal of the 1967 lines. According to Rabinovich, Barak's phrasing gave him room to negotiate further as they moved forward and shaped the specifics, although Clinton believed that Barak had in fact agreed to the June 4 line.[27] In hindsight, we see that the issue of the "Rabin pocket" continued to haunt the negotiations and ultimately led to their demise. Still, Barak's behavior at this point cannot be interpreted as an act of spoiling. By all accounts, he enthusiastically pushed for the negotiations to move forward to the official negotiations phase, and though his statement was vague, it did not impede the progress of the talks. He may have appeared hesitant and noncommittal, but he did not intentionally engage in any spoiling activity during this phase.

Spoiling Activities during the Negotiations Phase

Barak exhibited several characteristics of spoiling behavior during the official talks. First, he went back on commitments several times throughout the negotiation process. After several months of prenegotiation-phase meetings, official talks were organized at Blair House in December 1999. Although he had pressed the United States to set up official talks, Barak called two days before the meeting to say the Blair House talks should be about process and not substance.[28] Once the official negotiations started in December at Blair House, Barak also added new demands. After his hefty statement "While my government has made no commitment, we don't erase history," Barak showed signs of backing down. In the lead up to the January Shepherdstown talks, he introduced a whole series of completely new demands: Syrian agreement to simultaneous discussions between Israel and Lebanon, improvement of relations between Israel and Tunisia, announcement of a free-trade zone for the Golan, requests for additional US military aid to compensate for leaving, and more.[29]

Barak also quibbled over minor details, stalling the negotiations. Uri Sagie compares him to a "surgeon in the surgery room, arguing pedantically about the order of using the surgical tools, while in front of him the patient is turning white and losing blood."[30] According to Martin Indyk, the moment Barak got off the plane in Shepherdstown for the January talks, he told Indyk that he "can't do it."[31] Sagie describes how the first few days at Shepherdstown were consumed with Barak arguing over minor details and the agenda and insisting that certain teams meet at specific times.

Even after the procedural issues were sorted out, Barak also showed no willingness to relent. Ross writes, "I drew the conclusion that Barak intended to leave after a week with the objective of being able to show his public he had made no concessions."[32] After Syrian foreign minister Shara showed an interest in negotiating and flexibility about Israeli sovereignty over the Sea of Galilee, Barak demanded the resumption of the Lebanon talks before he agreed to anything. These actions signaled little willingness to make concessions.

An even more serious blow to the negotiations came when an American version of an agreement showing Syrian but not Israeli concessions was leaked, possibly by Barak himself. Deeply embarrassed, the Syrians called an indefinite recess, virtually ending the talks. Sagie writes, "I have no legal evidence and want to be cautious, but in my opinion there is a good chance that the initial leak came from our side, as a test balloon, to feel and prepare public opinion in Israel."[33] Akiva Eldar, the reporter who received the leaked draft, later also disclosed that the leak came from a source inside (at the very least) the prime minister's office, implying that Barak himself could be the source.[34] We cannot conclusively define this as an act of spoiling, as it may be argued that it was done to prepare the Israeli public for a possible deal and build legitimacy. Indeed, it is impossible to know for certain who leaked the documents or what their intentions were. Still, it is possible that it was done to hurt the trust with Syrian negotiators, and thus it may have been an act of spoiling.

Perhaps Barak's greatest act of spoiling was going back on his promises and betraying the trust of the other side. At the closing dinner of Shepherdstown, Shara complained, "I don't understand. What is Barak telling me here? That he is not true to his word? I thought he was a man of his word, of honor, and now I feel I've been cheated."[35] The Shepherdstown negotiations ended without an agreement. Ross writes that because of the perception that Barak had misled Syria by coming to Shepherdstown without truly wanting to negotiate, Ross left feeling that "Shepherdstown was a disaster. Syria had been flexible and exposed concessions and gotten nothing in return. Barak was not serious."[36] Clinton was angry with Barak, telling him, "I went to Shepherdstown and was told nothing by you for four days."[37]

After the failure of the Shepherdstown negotiations, Clinton met Assad in March in Geneva in one final attempt to reach an agreement. According to various sources, Barak was the one who pushed for the Clinton-Assad meeting to take place. Possible evidence in confirmation of Barak's push for a meeting was that one month earlier, Danny Yatom, head of Barak's staff, confirmed the existence of the "Rabin pocket" to the Americans. However, the Geneva talks failed, once again, apparently because of Barak's unwillingness to relent and what Assad construed as a betrayal of trust. A briefing put together by Barak's staff in the lead-up to the Geneva meeting told Barak, "The Syrians are arriving to Geneva without trust in the Israelis. From their point of view, Israel tried, under your leadership, to mislead Assad and stall, despite the promises given."[38] Tainted by the mistrust created in Shepherdstown, the talks in Geneva did not take long to unravel. To be precise, they took exactly six minutes. Reportedly what transpired was that between January and March, Barak had agreed to retreat to what Clinton said would be "commonly agreed upon borders."[39] This was conveyed by Clinton to Assad at Geneva, and, according to Sagie, Assad replied that this (apparently the vague wording) was a problem. Clinton then continued that Israel wanted sovereignty over the Sea of Galilee and the sources of the Jordan River, some distance to the east of the June 4 line. Assad replied, "Then they do not want peace," and he was not ready for any further discussion. While it is impossible to know the precise reasons behind Assad's refusal, Sagie writes that Barak's failure to be true to his word and his wavering made it difficult for Assad to trust him. Assad's quick refusal in Geneva signaled that he did not believe Barak was committed. Others reinforce this point. Clinton's interpretation was that the Syrians "had been burned once by being flexible and forthcoming, and they weren't about to make the same mistake again."[40] Ross remarked that "for a brief period of time [in January], Assad was ready to conclude an agreement. Barak made a decision that he wasn't able to implement politically. Assad lost confidence in the peace process."[41] Barak's betrayal of trust succeeded in thwarting a possible agreement in Geneva.

In conclusion, the behavior of Barak and his government during the Syria negotiations in 1999–2000 clearly fits the criteria for spoiling behavior. Though Barak did not engage in spoiling during the prenegotiation phase, he showed clear signs of spoiling in the negotiation phase. This change is notable because it is unlike many other cases in which leaders consistently spoil throughout the negotiation process. Barak suddenly introduced new demands, stalled, showed no willingness to relent, and betrayed the Syrians' trust. All in all, his actions severely damaged the peace negotiations with Syria. Ultimately, the negotiations ended in March 2000. Hafez al-Assad passed away in June 2000.

A Devious Objective Ideal Type: Netanyahu's Government and the Kerry Initiative

On February 1, 2013, John Kerry was sworn in as secretary of state of the United States. Among his first calls as secretary of state were those to Prime Minister Netanyahu, President Mahmud Abbas, and President Shimon Peres, in which he underscored his concern regarding the conflict in Israel/Palestine and his commitment to solving it.[42] He immediately launched a campaign to bring the two sides to the negotiating table; thus the prenegotiation phase began.

At that time Netanyahu was busy with his recent reelection and the construction of the third Netanyahu government. A temporary partnership between the right-wing Zionist-religious party "HaBayit HaYehudi" and the secular center party "Yesh Atid" led Netanyahu to cast aside his former alliances with the ultra-Orthodox Jewish parties and to form a coalition with these two parties as well as with Tzipi Livni's center party, "Hatnua." As a result, part of Netanyahu's political base found itself in the government (Halikud-Israel Beiteinu and HaBayit HaYehudi), while others were in the opposition (mainly some representatives of the religious party Shas). The new government was sworn in on March 18, 2013. Although on several issues, particularly civil affairs and state-religion relations, the coalition members saw eye to eye, the new government was internally divided regarding the negotiations with the Palestinians. At one side stood Yesh Atid and Hatnua, supporting the negotiations (to varying degrees), and on the other side stood Netanyahu's party, Halikud-Israel Beiteinu, and HaBayit HaYehudi, which were, to put it mildly, far more recalcitrant.

Meanwhile, Palestinian Authority president Mahmud Abbas's internal politics distracted him as well. His longstanding conflict with his prime minister, Salam Fayad, reached a climax with Fayad's resignation on April 13, 2013, after almost six years in office. Abbas needed to appoint a new prime minister and also manage relations with the Hamas movement that had taken control of the Gaza Strip in 2007 and did not recognize the government appointed by Abbas.

Against this domestic political backdrop, during the following months, Kerry conducted numerous talks with leaders and ministers in the Middle East to promote the idea of reviving direct negotiations between the Israelis and the Palestinians. In the six months after entering office, Kerry visited the region six times for this purpose. He even succeeded in bringing President Obama to the region on March 20–22, 2013, to support these efforts. Finally, on July 19, 2013, Kerry was ready to announce the renewal of direct talks between the sides.[43] The talks were designed to be semiconfidential—that is, the public would know there were talks, but the content was to be confidential.

The second phase of negotiations, direct talks between the sides regarding the core issues, started on July 29, 2013. A nine-month period of direct negotiations began with a meeting between Tzipi Livni, minister of justice and the minister responsible for the negotiations, along with the prime minister's advisor, Yitzhak Molcho, on the Israeli side, and on the Palestinian side, chief negotiator Saeb Erekat and Muhammad Shtayyeh, a senior advisor to Abbas. Although theoretically both sides had agreed to move to the second phase of negotiations, they continued for some time to dwell on prenegotiation-phase issues such as the conditions for the talks and the agenda, with each threatening to withdraw and end the negotiations. At the end of April, after nine months of negotiations, the Kerry Initiative stood at a total standstill, each side blaming the other for the halt in the talks.

To be sure, many factors contributed to the failure of the negotiations: unsuccessful mediation, internal politics, lack of preparation, absence of effective brokers, and more. Thus, one cannot in fact place the blame solely on Netanyahu's government. Nevertheless, Netanyahu's government spoiled the negotiations in several ways.

Spoiling Activity in the Prenegotiation Phase

At the end of the prenegotiation phase, Netanyahu's government decided to proceed to the next phase and entered official talks with the Palestinians. Technically, the prenegotiation phase had taken place for six months, starting when Kerry took office and ending with the announcement of negotiations, but as mentioned above, it persisted into the negotiation phase as well.

The prenegotiation phase dealt with two central issues. It was first necessary to agree on the terms and preconditions for beginning talks, and second to agree on the agenda. Kerry succeeded in reaching an agreement with both Netanyahu and Abbas regarding the preconditions for starting talks. The Palestinians withdrew their demand to freeze settlement construction, and they committed to halt their appeals to join several international institutions, receiving in exchange an Israeli agreement to the release 104 prisoners from the pre-Oslo period (though Israel was to divide the release into four stages over the duration of the negotiations). The Israelis withdrew their demand for the Palestinians to recognize the Jewish character of the state of Israel *as a precondition*. Thus, each side withdrew its most important demand, and the United States placated them by accepting their basic demands: the Palestinians received a letter from Kerry that confirmed the position set forth by President Obama in his May 2011 speeches, which was that Palestine's borders with Israel should be based on the 1967 lines—a major Palestinian demand regarding the future borders—with mutually agreed swaps (understood to accommodate Israeli annexation of two settlement blocks). The Israelis received a letter that emphasized the American commitment to Israel as a Jewish state, as well as silent US approval for limited constructions in the settlements.[44]

While the sides entered the second phase of negotiations—discussion of the core issues—they continued to express disagreements about the agenda. The Israelis strove to put all the issues on the table simultaneously, while the Palestinians wanted to start with borders and later move on to security.

Although at the end of the prenegotiation phase Netanyahu's government agreed to proceed to the negotiation phase, its behavior in the prenegotiation phase fit several of the criteria for spoiling. One major spoiling action was the government's activities regarding construction in the settlements. Construction was only temporarily halted, until after Obama's visit to Israel in March. It was resumed shortly after, including building in the unauthorized outposts as well. This decision to resume construction was partly the result of pressure from the settler community, who feared that a building freeze might actually have been a precondition agreed to by Israel for the commencement of negotiations.[45] For the Palestinians, the settlements not only symbolize the Israeli occupation but also demonstrate that Israel has no intention of evacuating the West Bank. Thus, from the Palestinian perspective, the decision to continue construction in the settlements seemed tantamount to a decision to continue the occupation. Indeed, as already noted, halting settlement construction had been the first Palestinian precondition for opening negotiations.[46] Although this demand had been dropped, Israel had avoided building temporarily; the resumption of building was a problem that in effect constituted spoiling.

In addition, Netanyahu emphasized the demand that the Palestinians recognize the state of Israel as a Jewish state. Though this demand had come up in discussions between negotiators in the Annapolis talks as well, it was never declared a precondition to negotiations. Furthermore, whereas in Annapolis the issue remained in the negotiation room, in the Kerry Initiative negotiations the government utilized it to fuel a public debate and as a political tool to weaken the propeace forces inside Israeli society. This new demand continued to play a part in the negotiation phase as well. To further strengthen the spoiling potential of this action, a new law entitled "Israel as a Jewish State" was submitted to the Knesset by several MKs from the coalition. In the explanation attached to the proposal, supporters explicitly pointed to the connection between this proposal and the negotiations with the Palestinians, explaining that this was a step that would limit, from the outset, discussions regarding the right of return of the Palestinian refugees.[47]

Moreover, the government strengthened other domestic spoilers, at least indirectly, by its weak response to Jewish hate crimes, commonly known as "Tag Mehir" ("Price Tag"), against Palestinians. In fact, 2013 saw an increase of about 32 percent in Tag Mehir activities.[48] Netanyahu and his government publicly opposed these acts, but when Justice Minister Tzipi Livni and the General Security Services pushed to define these activities as "acts of terror," the government explicitly refused to do so. In this way, it actually bolstered domestic spoiling forces, thereby also hurting the negotiations and the peace process.[49]

Eventually, Kerry succeeded in bringing the sides to sit together and move onto the second phase: actual negotiations. However, Netanyahu capitalized on the announcement to make a statement emphasizing problematic elements of the Israeli narrative that strengthened the image of the Palestinians as the enemy. In a message to citizens, he stressed that the goals of the negotiations were "the prevention of a creation of a bi-national state . . . which will endanger the future of the Jewish state . . . and the prevention of the establishment of a terror state . . . on the borders of Israel."[50] The latter implied a nefarious enemy while avoiding the word "peace" altogether.

Spoiling Activities during the Negotiations Phase

During this phase, the government engaged in spoiling activity mainly by delegitimizing the negotiations. On July 28, 2013, one day before entering the second phase, the government of Israel approved the opening of the negotiations with the Palestinians. At the very same meeting, the government also approved the draft for "Basic Law: Referendum,"[51] which states that any concession of territory belonging to the state must be approved by a referendum. Although this step can be interpreted as an attempt to strengthen democratic processes, or as a step to cope with other spoilers, the explanation attached to the law, as well as the public perception of it, indicated that it also symbolized delegitimization of the negotiators or, at the very least, limited the legitimacy of the negotiations and those working to reach a final agreement.[52] This step also strengthened other spoilers, not just in a symbolic way but also in a practical way, while paving the way for future spoiling attempts on the societal level during the referendum process.

Netanyahu's government's efforts to delegitimize negotiations are present elsewhere as well.[53] Netanyahu appointed attorney Yitzhak Molcho as his personal delegate in what many read as a strategy to monitor and in fact limit Livni, the official leader of the negotiations. Indeed, various members of the coalition bluntly and repeatedly disrespected Livni. In addition, American secretary of state Kerry, the mediator, also received his fair share of delegitimization. Minister of Defense Ya'alon, for example, bluntly described him as "messianic" and "obsessive," "with a personal aspiration to gain the Nobel Prize."[54]

Netanyahu's government also continued to support other domestic spoiling forces as well. To supplement the lenient treatment of spoiling activities such as Tag Mehir, it also weakened the propeace and pronegotiations groups inside Israeli society. This spoiling behavior was clearly evident in government activities to hurt the funding of propeace associations, to limit their activities, and to delegitimize them once and for all. These activities of the government did not start with the Kerry negotiations,[55] but they gained momentum in this period. Legislative proposals, accompanied by discursive actions, were submitted by members of the coalition during the prenegotiation phase and into the negotiation phase—for example, calling for a 45 percent tax on external funding to (basically peace and human rights) NGOs. In addition, during the negotiation phase, the government introduced a bill to prevent these groups from even registering as legal associations, but rather as agents of foreign governments.[56]

Another tool the government used to hinder the negotiations was the legislative process. The legislative process has two dimensions: that of the formal law, and that of shaping the public attitudes (even without proceeding to formal legislation). Members from the coalition submitted numerous legislative proposals to the Ministerial Committee for Legislation[57] aimed at delegitimizing the negotiations and hindering their progress. Examples include proposals to annex the Jordan Valley, to apply Israeli law to the occupied territories, or to obligate the government to obtain consent from the Knesset in order to negotiate the issues of Jerusalem or the refugees. After accepting the draft regarding "Basic Law: Referendum" at exactly the same time as announcing the launch of the negotiations, the government continued to promote the bill, even in the face of tremendous opposition. The coalition passed the law in second and third readings on March 12, 2014, while the entire opposition boycotted the discussion and abstained from voting. Furthermore, the Ministerial Committee rejected proposals from the opposition designed to promote reconciliation and support the peace process.[58] All of these steps strengthened Palestinian mistrust of Israel's intentions, strengthened domestic spoiler narratives, and undermined the propeace forces.

Netanyahu's government also exacerbated tensions and changed the status quo in a way that prevented, or at least challenged, the possibility of future solutions by continued building in the settlements. In the prenegotiation phase, release of Palestinian prisoners apparently outweighed the building in the settlements insofar as the Palestinians were concerned, and so the negotiations had continued. Nevertheless, building in the settlements was still a spoiling activity. Initially the Ministry of Construction did not release any new tenders for housing in the occupied territories, but a few days into the negotiations themselves, on August 11, 2013, it released tenders for more than one hundred units beyond the green line.[59] The minister himself put the new marketing in the context of the negotiations, stating that "no state in the world accepts dictations from other states where it is allowed for her to construct and where not." This statement contradicted an earlier Government Housing Cabinet policy that had prioritized construction in areas in great demand—in the center of the country[60]—suggesting that the intention was to (negatively) influence the negotiations with the Palestinians. Announcements of new tenders for construction in the settlements surfaced again and again as the negotiations continued.[61]

On August 12, 2013, the government of Israel publicized the list of prisoners to be released according to the understandings between the two sides. The Palestinians were disappointed by the identity of the prisoners selected for release as none of them were very well-known figures. This made it more difficult for the Palestinian leadership to gain support; indeed, the prisoner release was criticized in the Palestinian streets rather than celebrated. It is not clear, though, that the list of prisoners was indeed a spoiling activity. There is evidence that the committee in charge of compiling the list had tried to strengthen Abbas, not weaken him, but it was limited by the internal Israeli discourse and what was perceived as legitimate. Even so, the Israeli leadership was not united on this issue. A few days before the release of the second group of prisoners, one of the coalition parties HaBayit HaYehudi submitted yet another legislative proposal aimed at preventing the release of "terrorists" (implying that all the prisoners involved had been imprisoned for acts of terrorism).

The party took advantage of the occasion to once again delegitimize both Livni personally and the negotiations as a whole, stating that "release of terrorists in return for Livni's dubious right to meet with Erekat [chief Palestinian negotiator] is very serious. With all due respect, stopping the release of murderers is even more important than Livni's raison d'être for being a part of the Government."[62]

As time passed and the two sides approached the April 29, 2014, deadline for the end of negotiations, they retreated to issues of the prenegotiation phase, such as the conditions under which talks could continue after the deadline. It became quite clear that the sides would not reach a final agreement, or even a framework agreement, by the deadline. Therefore, at this point both sides spoiled the negotiations and went back on former commitments: the government of Israel went back on its commitment to release the fourth group of prisoners, and the Palestinians sent an application to join fifteen international institutions.[63]

Discussion and Conclusions

Using the examples of the Israel-Syria negotiations in 1999–2000 and the Kerry Initiative in 2013–14, we showed how the political leadership can act as a spoiler in peace negotiations. There are similarities, yet in many ways each case is unique. The leadership is a different spoiler type. Barak is a "cold feet" case, while Netanyahu's government can be seen as a "devious actor" case.

From the analysis of the prenegotiation phase in the Israeli-Syrian negotiations, it is clear that Barak wanted to negotiate and reach a peace agreement. Uri Sagie further emphasizes this point, writing, "We really wanted to succeed in the negotiations; so did he (Barak), I am sure of it to this day."[64] Accounts of the negotiations themselves stress that spoiling activity was less the result of intentional foiling and more of a manifestation of fears. The reasons for Barak's "cold feet" are less clear. Many argue that Barak got cold feet because of poll phobia. In a December 24, 1999, poll, Stanley Greenberg, an American pollster working for Barak, found that 59 percent of Israelis felt that Barak was moving too fast in the negotiations, and his image as a tough negotiator fell from 45 percent to 35 percent. Greenberg wrote to Barak, "We clearly find ourselves at a dangerous point if you intend to bring the country to a new Eden. The public wants to see tough, cautious negotiations in connection with such critical issues."[65] Clinton also inferred that Barak "decided, apparently on the basis of polling data, that he needed to slow-walk the process for a few days in order to convince the Israeli public that he was being a tough negotiator."[66] Though we will never know what went on in Barak's mind, many, including President Clinton, seem convinced that he was afraid of public opinion. Clinton believed that because Barak was new to politics, he attached too much importance to public opinion, which was highly variable and inconsistent.[67] One could also argue that Barak's spoiling activity in the 1999–2000 negotiations was meant to show Israelis and Syrians that he was a tough negotiator so that he could succeed in future negotiations. Still others contend that the reason for Barak's cold feet was innate, a part of his hot-and-cold personality. Though the reasons for Barak's change of heart remain unclear, it is clear that the actions themselves were spoiling behavior: he added new demands, stalled, showed no willingness to compromise, at least appeared to retreat on commitments, and betrayed the trust of his adversaries.

In the Kerry Initiative, Netanyahu's government fit the description of a devious actor. It is evident that the Israeli government was reluctant to enter the negotiations and to press for a successful conclusion. In accordance with Richmond's arguments, sometimes parties choose to enter negotiations with objectives other than making peace.[68] These "devious objectives" include providing time to regroup and reorganize, wanting to internationalize the conflict, searching for an ally, legitimizing negotiation positions and current status, mitigating internal pressure, face saving and ontological security aspects, avoiding costly concessions by prolonging the process itself, and avoiding or mitigating external pressure.

The Netanyahu government exhibited several of these devious objectives. The first was the desire to strengthen relations with an ally. It entered the negotiations as a result of external pressure from the United States and other international players. The government's second "devious objective" was the desire to mitigate internal political pressures from settlers and their political supporter in the coalition, while other coalition partners, Livni and Lapid, had promised their voters that they would promote the peace process.[69] It is also possible that the Netanyahu government entered the negotiations because of ontological reasons in an attempt to reinforce its own perception of itself by emphasizing the propeace character of the Israeli state.

The Netanyahu government entered the negotiations because of these devious objectives rather than the desire to achieve a peace agreement, and this is evidenced by the government's spoiling actions during the negotiations. Netanyahu, the government as a whole, and individual coalition MKs spoiled the negotiations from the outset, through legislative proposals, public remarks, and other actions. It worked to change reality on the ground, mainly by renewed construction in the settlements and legislation to spoil negotiations in a total or limited way. Furthermore, they emphasized certain parts of the Israeli narrative that starkly contradicted the Palestinian narrative, such as the government's insistence on Palestinian recognition of Israel as the nation-state of the Jewish people. They acted to delegitimize the negotiations, the chief negotiator Livni, and the mediator Kerry, especially after the move to the second phase of the negotiations—the negotiations themselves. The government also strengthened domestic spoiler groups, or at least did not fight them, while hurting and delegitimizing the internal propeace forces. Lastly, the government betrayed the Palestinians' trust by going back on past promises regarding the release of prisoners, in addition to continuing construction in the settlements, and various legislative initiatives. It would appear that the Netanyahu government did not miss any spoiling activity from the list.

The internal power balance of the Netanyahu government and that of Barak were very different. Barak started negotiations with the intention of achieving peace, coping with domestic spoilers and opposition to negotiations even inside his own coalition. Netanyahu, on the other hand, was very much in agreement with the spoiling forces inside his government from the outset. This difference can be seen in the different spoiling tools used by the two leaders. Barak had initiated and fought hard to legitimize the talks with the Syrians, so he refrained from spoiling them through delegitimization when he later became a spoiler. Instead he used intranegotiation actions to spoil them. Netanyahu used a whole slew of different tactics from the start of negotiations, spoiling through his ministers and through the legislative processes as well as public statements.

With the understanding that leaders themselves can act as spoilers in the peace process, they must also be included in the discussion on coping mechanisms. Coping with insider spoilers must be analyzed in greater depth. When analyzing a peace process and negotiations, one must distinguish between propeace forces and spoilers, and not just between groups inside the negotiations and those outside. It is important for propeace forces to be cognizant of the ability of leadership to spoil in order to cope effectively. Determining the right response can bring even a devious actor on board.

Coping with a leader that is a spoiler, whether from the outset or becoming one in the course of the negotiations, is a complicated matter. One might, for example, combat delegitimization by linking the legitimacy of the leader himself to the talks. It would, therefore, be more difficult for the leader to delegitimize the negotiations, the adversary, or the mediator without delegitimizing himself. This might be achieved by insisting the leader actually take part in the negotiations directly and from the start.

The example of the Netanyahu government also highlights the importance of dealing with the leadership's political base[70] in order to minimize spoiling. This strategy may be especially effective when the leadership is weak and in situations where the leadership is heavily influenced by grassroots organizations and certain groups of people. The ways to bring these players on board and convince them to support peace are many and varied. They include economic incentives, ideological and identity arguments, and the use of influential public figures. In our example, this bottom-up strategy might include working to sway settlers and the secular right in the case of the Netanyahu government.

The Barak example suggests that efforts to strengthen vocal propeace elements and public support might be the major tool. Yet another strategy could be external pressure to restrain opponents to peace within the leadership. Such measures could be taken by individual countries as well international organizations and might include confiscating personal assets of leaders and supporters, "naming and shaming,"[71] diplomatic and economic boycotts, sanctions, and conditioning economic and military cooperation and membership in international organizations on the progress of peace talks. In cases where there is a high likelihood of creating the opposite "rallying around the flag" reaction to external sanctions or other measures, external pressure might not be strategic. Nevertheless, in certain circumstances external pressure can be a powerful coping mechanism.

* * *

Understanding the forces that ruin peace agreements before they are signed is key to the discussion of peace building. This understanding must include the egregious effects of leaders themselves. The present study shows how the leadership can act as a spoiler in peace talks, using the Kerry Initiative and the Israeli-Syrian negotiations as examples. We developed a set of criteria, based on previous literature, to classify behavior as spoiling and applied this set of criteria to the two cases. In both, the leadership clearly exhibited spoiling behavior. We also shed light on the ways in which Ehud Barak and Benjamin Netanyahu were similar in their spoiling styles and the ways in which they were different. While it appears that Barak began as a peace seeker and only later became a devious actor, Netanyahu had "devious objectives" and entered the negotiations with intentions other than achieving an agreement.

Our chapter looks at the different types of spoiling behaviors leaders engage in during negotiations, an important foundation. Future studies on coping mechanisms should examine how to cope with the efforts of leaders themselves to spoil the peace process. It is important to identify the coping mechanisms appropriate for each spoiling behavior. Perhaps in this way we can move toward a more holistic understanding of spoiling in peace processes and ultimately improve the processes themselves.

Notes

1. George Katete Onyango, "The Place of Spoilers in Peace Processes in Sudan," *African Journal of Political Science and International Relations* 6, no. 8 (2012): 167–180.

2. Carlo Nasi, "Spoilers in Colombia: Actors and Strategies," in *Challenges to Peacebuilding: Managing Spoilers during Conflict Resolution*, ed. Edward Newman and Oliver Richmond (New York: United Nations University, 2006), 219–242.

3. Oded Haklai, "Spoiling the Peace: State Structures and the Capacity of Hardliners to Foil Peacemaking Efforts," in *Democracy and Conflict Resolution*, ed. Miriam Elman, Oded Haklai, and Henrik Spruyt (Syracuse, NY: Syracuse University Press, 2014), 67–97.

4. Magnus Ranstrop, "The Israeli-Palestinian Peace Process: The Strategic Art of Deception," in Newman and Richmond, *Challenges to Peacebuilding*, 242–262.

5. Edward Newman and Oliver Richmond, "Obstacles to Peace Processes: Understanding Spoiling," in Newman and Richmond, *Challenges to Peacebuilding*, 1–21.

6. Newman and Richmond, "Obstacles to Peace Processes," 5.

7. Roger Mac Ginty, "Northern Ireland: A Peace Process Thwarted by Accidental Spoiling," in Newman and Richmond, *Challenges to Peacebuilding*, 153–173.

8. We acknowledge that there are many alternative explanations for the breakdown of any peace negotiation and of these two peace negotiations in particular. The literature speaks of many possible explanations for the breakdown of talks, including failures in mediation, structural failures, identity and historical narratives, and the content of the core issues. We argue that these alternative explanations are not mutually exclusive from ours. Our chapter focuses on the spoiling activities of the leadership as one part of the highly complex field of peace negotiations.

9. For detailed discussion regarding the connections between devious objectives and the plausibility of spoiling behavior, see Oliver Richmond, "The Linkage between Devious Objectives and Spoiling Behaviour in Peace Processes," in Newman and Richmond, *Challenges to Peacebuilding*, 59–77.

10. For a detailed account regarding ontological security and how it shapes the political behavior, see Jennifer Mitzen, "Ontological Security in World Politics: State Identity and the Security Dilemma," *European Journal of International Relations* 12, no. 3 (2006): 341–370.

11. Richmond, "Linkage between Devious Objectives," 59–60.

12. Prime Minister and Defense Minister Ehud Barak's speech to the National Defense College, August 13, 1999.

13. Other issues were also important, of course, such as the "nature of the peace" and the security arrangements, but the border—i.e., the extent of Israeli withdrawal—was the critical one.

14. Uri Sagie, *The Hand That Froze* (Tel Aviv: Yediot Ahronot and Hemed Books, 2011).

15. Dennis Ross, *The Missing Peace: The Inside Story of the Fight for Middle East Peace* (New York: Farrar, Straus and Giroux, 2004), 571.

16. Norman Kempster, "Clinton Tries to Speed Up Peace Talks," *Los Angeles Times*, January 7, 2000, accessed August 30, 2016, http://articles.latimes.com/2000/jan/07/news/mn-51640.

17. Joined by the political grouping known as "The Third Way."

18. David Landau, "How Will Israeli Premier Handle Opposition to Syrian Peace Deal," *J Weekly*, January 14, 2000, accessed September 01, 2016, http://www.jweekly.com/article/full/12389/how-will-israeli-premier-handle-opposition-to-syrian-peace-deal/.

19. Ehud Barak, "A Vision for the Future: Realizing the Promise of the Promised Land," *Harvard International Review* 20, no. 2 (1998): 60–63.

20. Jeremy Pressman, "Mediation, Domestic Politics, and the Israeli Syrian Negotiations," *Security Studies* 16, no. 3 (2007): 350–381.

21. Address by Prime Minister Ehud Barak, Sharem A-Sheikh Memorandum, Egypt, September 4, 1999, accessed August 30, 2016, https://www.jewishvirtuallibrary.org/jsource/Peace/ses_speeches.html.

22. Gilead Sher, *Within Reach: The Israeli-Palestinian Peace Negotiations, 1999–2001* (London: Routledge, 2006), 58.

23. Ross, *Missing Peace*, 571.

24. Ibid.

25. Itamar Rabinovich, *The Lingering Conflict: Israel, the Arabs, and the Middle East, 1948–2011* (Washington, DC: Brookings Institution, 2011), 90; as cited by Galia Golan, *Israeli Peacemaking Since 1967: Factors behind Breakthroughs and Failures* (New York: Routledge, 2015), 77, 79.

26. Ross, *Missing Peace*, 2004; Bill Clinton, *My Life* (London: Random House, 2005); as cited by Golan, *Israeli Peacemaking*, 80, citing a similar Barak comment to the Knesset.

27. Itamar Rabinovich, *Waging Peace: Israel and the Arabs, 1948–2003* (New Jersey: Princeton University Press, 2009), 128; Golan, *Israeli Peacemaking*, 80.

28. Ross, *Missing Peace*, 539.

29. Ross, *Missing Peace*, 544; as cited by Golan, *Israeli Peacemaking*, 53.

30. Sagie, *Hand That Froze*, 15.

31. Martin Indyk, *Innocent Abroad: An Intimate Account of American Peace Diplomacy in the Middle East* (New York: Simon and Schuster, 2009), 245.

32. Ross, *Missing Peace*, 555.

33. Sagie, *Hand That Froze*, 16.

34. As cited by Golan, *Israeli Peacemaking*, 56.

35. Sagie, *Hand That Froze*, 13.

36. Ross, *Missing Peace*, 563.

37. Jeremy Pressman, "Mediation, Domestic Politics, and the Israeli Syrian Negotiations," *Security Studies* 16, no. 3 (2007): 350–381, quotation on 370

38. Sagie, *Hand That Froze*, 165.

39. Pressman, "Mediation, Domestic Politics," 374.

40. Clinton, *My Life*, 887.

41. Pressman, "Mediation, Domestic Politics," 374.

42. John Kerry, "Remarks with Jordanian Foreign Minister Nasser Judeh after Their Meeting," Washington, DC, February 13, 2013, accessed August 30, 2016, http://www.state.gov/secretary/remarks/2013/02/204560.htm.

43. John Kerry, "Press Availability in Aman," Aman, Jordan, July 19, 2013, accessed August 30, 2016, http://www.state.gov/secretary/remarks/2013/07/212213.htm.

44. For a more detailed account of the road to negotiations and of the misunderstandings and mistakes along the way, see Ben Birnbaum and Amir Tibon, "The Explosive, Inside Story of How John Kerry Built an Israel-Palestine Peace Plan, and Watched It Crumble," *New Republic*, July 20, 2014, accessed August 30, 2016, http://www.newrepublic.com/article/118751/how-israel-palestine-peace-deal-died.

45. For examples, see publications on the news that linked negotiations and the government announcements on construction: Atilla Shmolfavi, "Livni, Kerry Meet as Ya'alon Advances Beit-El Construction Plan," Ynet, May 9, 2013, accessed August 30, 2016, http://www.ynetnews.com/articles/0,7340,L-4378030,00.html; Itamar Fleischman, "State to Supreme Court: Will Examine Legalization of 4 Outposts," Ynet, May 16, 2013, accessed

August 30, 2016, http://www.ynetnews.com/articles/0,7340,L-4380381,00.html; Itamar Fleischman, "More than 1,000 Housing Units in Territories Nearing Approval," Ynet, July 16, 2013, accessed August 30, 2016, http://www.ynet.co.il/articles/0,7340,L-4405719,00.html.

46. See, for example, Abbas statement to Kerry on 30.06.2013, in Arabic: http://tinyurl.com/nfgnxg4.

47. Proposal of Basic Law: Israel as the Nation-State of the Jewish People, July 22, 2013, The Ninetieth Knesset, No. 485717, in Hebrew, accessed August 30, 2016, http://index.justice.gov.il/StateIdentity/ProprsedBasicLaws/Pages/NationalState.aspx.

48. Yehushua Raizner, "32% Rise in Tag Mechir Incidents in 2013," *Walla News*, October 28, 2013, accessed August 30, 2016, http://news.walla.co.il/item/2689501.

49. See, for example, Barak Ravid, "Netanyahu: Price Tag Attacks Cannot Be Compared to Hamas Terror," *Ha'aratz*, June 17, 2013, accessed August 30, 2016, http://www.haaretz.com/news/diplomacy-defense/.premium-1.530205.

50. See the prime minister's announcement, and his letter to the citizens, right after Kerry's announcement on the resuming of the negotiations: http://www.pmo.gov.il/MediaCenter/Spokesman/Pages/spokemedini200713.aspx; http://www.pmo.gov.il/MediaCenter/Spokesman/Documents/OpenLetter270713.pdf.

51. Israel has no constitution. As a result of disagreement between Israel's political parties about drafting a constitution, they compromised on the idea of basic laws. A basic law is a more fundamental law and deals with issues usually dealt with in constitutions. It is normally more difficult to amend basic laws than other laws.

52. See, for example, the opposition reservation to the bill proposal. The first suggests changing the name of the law to "The Law for Eliminating the Representative Democracy in Israel," http://fs.knesset.gov.il//19/law/19_ls2_271757.pdf.

53. For a detailed account of the different ways the Netanyahu government delegitimized the negotiations, see Roee Kibrik and Gilead Sher, "Public Legitimacy as a Necessary Condition for a Peace Process: A Test of the Third Netanyahu Government," *Strategic Assessment* 17, no. 2 (2014): 17–32.

54. Shimeon Shiffer, "Ya'alon: Kerry is Messianic and Obsessive, Let Him Take the Nobel and Go Away," Ynet, January 14, 2014, accessed August 30, 2016, http://www.ynet.co.il/articles/0,7340,L-4476494,00.html.

55. For a detailed report on the government activities in former years against those associations, see Naomi Chazan, "Israel and the World: the Democratic Aspect," *Politika* 23 (2014): 105–134, in Hebrew, http://davis.huji.ac.il/.upload/%2023%20BOOKMARKS.pdf.

56. See, for example, the Shaked legislative proposal on July 31, 2013: https://oknesset.org/bill/7685/; the government decision on December 15, 2013; and the Regev proposal on March 13, 2013: https://oknesset.org/bill/5614/.

57. The Ministerial Committee for Legislation is a committee in the prime minister's office. The minister of justice is the head of the committee. The committee is primarily responsible for handling and approving legislative proposals before passing them to the Knesset, and for deciding the government's position regarding private law proposals. It is a very efficient and influential tool that the government uses to shape its policy and promote its ideology. It is very rare to witness a committee decision accepted without the agreement of the prime minister.

58. Examples of this include the proposals for conditioning any construction in the settlements on an eighty MK majority, for implementing coexistence programs in schools,

for the use of Arabic language in formal government publications, or for defining the activities of "Tag Mechir" (Price Tag) as terror acts.

59. See the ministry spokesman announcement on August 11, 2013, http://www.moch.gov.il/Spokesman/Pages/DoverListItem.aspx?ListID=5b390c93-15b2-4841-87e3-abf31c1af63d&WebId=fe384cf7-21cd-49eb-8bbb-71ed64f47de0&ItemID=513.

60. See how it is manifested clearly in the news at that time. For example, Ori Chudy, "Lapid Slams 1,200 Homes Tenders over Green Line," *Globes*, August 11, 2013, http://www.globes.co.il/en/article-1000870477; or see Einat Paz-Frankel, "Minister of Housing Defined Anew the Demanded Areas," *Calcalist*, August 11, 2013, in Hebrew, http://www.calcalist.co.il/real_estate/articles/0,7340,L-3609805,00.html.

61. In addition to the decision on August 11, 2013, more announcements have been made: in November 3, 2013 (1,560 units), November 12, 2013 (more than 20,000 units, from them more than 1,400 at the conflicted area of E1), January 10, 2014 (1,825 units), February 5, 2014 (558 units), February 19, 2014 (2,269 units), March 20, 2014 (184 units).

62. Jonathan Lis, "HaBayit HaYehudi against Livni: It is Better to Have a Coalition without Livni than a Danger to Israel," *Ha'aretz*, October 27, 2013, accessed August 30, 2016, http://www.haaretz.co.il/news/politi/1.2149862.

63. It is worthwhile to note that the Israeli government wished to continue the talks. It even offered the Palestinians other concessions regarding prisoners to continue the talks for six more months. As a devious actor, the government of Israel did achieve what it had hoped for in keeping the negotiations themselves alive. The Palestinians decided they had had enough, and that they could gain more without playing the negotiation game.

64. Sagie, *Hand That Froze*, 120.

65. Pressman, "Mediation, Domestic Politics," 374.

66. Clinton, *My Life*, 886.

67. Ibid.

68. Oliver Richmond, "Devious Objectives and the Disputants' View of International Mediation: A Theoretical Framework," *Journal of Peace Research* 35, no. 6 (1998): 707–722.

69. See, for example, Lapid's commitment to only join a government that enters peace negotiations with the Palestinians: Pinhas Wolf, "Lapid: We Will Sit Only in a Government That Will Conduct Negotiations," *Walla*, October 30, 2012, accessed August 30, 2016, http://news.walla.co.il/item/2580851; or Livni's commitment: Yinon Magal, "Livni to Walla News: I Will Promote the Peace Process or Sit in the Opposition," *Walla*, January 15, 2013, accessed August 30, 2016, http://news.walla.co.il/item/2607154.

70. We define the "political base" as the people and organizations, both inside the political party system and outside of it, who support the leadership and enable its governance. Their support can be manifested electorally, politically, ideologically-rhetorically, and financially, among other types of support.

71. Naming and shaming is a popular strategy to enforce international human rights norms and laws, but it is also a powerful tool in other fields of politics. For more on this, see Emilie M. Hafner-Burton, "Sticks and Stones: Naming and Shaming the Human Rights Enforcement Problem," *International Organization* 62, no. 4 (2008): 689–716; Claudia Hofmann and Ulrich Schneckener, "Engaging Non-State Armed Actors in State-and Peace-building: Options and Strategies," *International Review of the Red Cross* 93, no. 883 (2011): 603–621.

ROEE KIBRIK is an adjunct lecturer in the International Department at the Hebrew University in Jerusalem, and the director of research of Mitvim: The Israeli Institute for Regional Foreign Policies.

MAYA KORNBERG is a doctoral candidate in the Department of Politics and International Relations, Oxford University.

3

ISRAEL'S DOMESTIC LEGAL STRUGGLE AGAINST THE SETTLEMENTS

Spoiler-Advancing, Spoiler-Hindering, or Spoiler-Exposing?

Shlomy Zachary

Introduction

On July 29, 2015, while the bulldozers began implementing the final ruling ordering the demolition of residential units in the Beth El settlement in the West Bank,[1] an ordinance was issued by the Israeli prime minister's office, approving the construction of three hundred additional residential units in that same settlement.[2] Back in 2012, those same three hundred units had been promised by the Israeli government to the settlers' leaders, in the wake of another case wherein the government was compelled—against its will—to abide by another ruling ordering it to evacuate thirty residential units that were illegally built on private Palestinian lands.[3] However, the link between law enforcement on the one hand and the need to "compensate" the settlers' sector on the other hand was further solidified by the construction of new housing units. Several hours after the announcement of the approval of these three hundred units, various members of the international community voiced widespread criticism.[4] The expansion of Israeli construction in the West Bank, especially in settlements located outside the central recognized settlement block, had been viewed as an action undermining the peace process and the possibility of two states existing side by side. It now remained to be seen which path would be chosen by the State of Israel: whether it would allow the advancement of the beliefs of the national religious sector of Israeli society (the settlers), which had obtained a foothold within the Israeli government, or the continuation of a dialogue between Israel and the Palestinian National Authority (as well as between Israel and the international community) with the goal of achieving a two-state solution to the conflict.

Thus, the Beth El case of raises a number of questions: could the legal struggles against the building of settlements and outposts themselves be, unwittingly, spoilers of the peace process? Does the outcome of such legal proceedings—some of which led to the approval of illegal outposts or the expansion of settlements, and others which led to the establishment of new settlements in lieu of the evacuated outposts—consistently spoil the peace process? Are these outcomes merely reflections of the positions held by the State of Israel pertaining to the settlements, to the rights of the Palestinians (both as communities and individuals) as a party to negotiations, and to the peace process? Do the struggles against the expansion of settlements constitute an excessive part of the Israeli-Palestinian conflict or significant parts thereof, leading the parties to rely on a legal paradigm (either domestic or international), while gradually forsaking the classic path of dispute resolution in the form of bilateral or multilateral negotiations? And, finally, can such legal struggles hinder or prevent progress in the peace process?

This chapter will show that the settlement project (including the outposts) is a key element in how the Israeli-Palestinian conflict, and particularly its resolution, is viewed by the parties. Though there are many reasons for settlers to live in the West Bank (religious, national, economic, environmental, etc.), the settlements in the West Bank were intended, geographically, to prevent any possibility of Palestinian territorial contiguity, as can be seen by their expansion, their vast areas of jurisdiction, and their surrounding outposts.[5] As such, they may be deemed to be spoilers. This is the premise of the Palestinians, of the international community, and of significant parts of the Israeli population.[6] Even right-wing governments have acknowledged that the expansion of settlements and the establishment of new settlements do not contribute to the peace process.[7] Even if there is a dispute regarding the dominance of the settlement issue within the framework of Israeli-Palestinian negotiations (alongside other crucial issues such as security, Palestinian refugees, and the status of Jerusalem and the holy sites), no one disputes the centrality of the settlement issue in the peace process. This is because the expansions of settlements and the consistent increase in the number of Israeli settlers in the West Bank challenge the practical feasibility of the two-state solution. As such, the settlement project is a potential spoiler, and the Israeli Supreme Court treatment of this spoiler is therefore of great interest. Yet, as we shall argue, an additional spoiler, or spoilers, may be the legal struggle against the settlement project—and the court itself through its decisions, since these may have had an indirect effect on the peace process, as they have required authorities to make decisions that actually enhanced the settlement project.

In this chapter we shall commence with an examination of the Israeli Supreme Court decisions regarding the West Bank settlements and the outcomes of the early legal struggles against the settlements. Thereafter, we shall examine the effects of the legal struggles in more recent times pertaining to illegal construction in outposts and settlements and the increasing involvement of Israeli courts to see if the legal proceedings have effectively acted as an antispoiler—that is, prevented or slowed the spoiling. We shall examine the central question: whether, and if so, to what extent the legal proceedings and the Supreme Court itself were spoilers to the peace process. The issue of legal proceedings before international institutions and tribunals will also be examined, as well as the extent to which such proceedings may also have contributed to the spoil of the peace process.

The Israeli Supreme Court and the Settlement Question— One Step Forward, Two Steps Backward

Despite the perceived image of the Israeli Supreme Court by a vast part of the Israeli public as antisettlement, in actuality the court has not only abstained from preventing the establishment and expansion of the settlements in the past, but also, it has in many cases provided a quasi-legal umbrella for Israeli settlement building in the occupied territories. The court's rulings established the internal Israeli legitimization of such activities, even if such legitimization was occasionally provided only indirectly. It may be said that in terms of outcomes and from a historical perspective, the settlement project could not have flourished and developed to its current dimensions and level of expansion without the assistance, either direct or indirect, of the Supreme Court over decades.

The first settlements in the territories occupied by Israel following the Six Day War (1967) were erected on private Palestinian lands, which were expropriated for security reasons. The concept (then prevalent) led Israeli governments to perceive security and political interests as intertwined; the settlements themselves were perceived as reflecting a security need and as having security significance. Nonetheless, the establishment of the settlements on private lands raised real legal challenges even in the early days of the settlement project. For example, the seizure of many thousands of acres of Bedouin lands in the vicinity of the town of Rafah in the Sinai peninsula and denial of access for landowners were justified by the Supreme Court as based on security grounds, albeit combined with political purposes: "As for the removal of the Petitioners, there is no doubt that it is within the powers of the Respondents, provided that the latter acted on security grounds. Clearly, the fact that these lands, in whole or in part, are designated for Jewish settlement, does not detract from the security nature of this action as a whole."[8] The security considerations, thus concluded Supreme Court judges, were neither disproved nor discovered to be fictitious and a guise for other considerations; in addition, Jewish settlement was considered a security measure. As recent research exposed, that real and major goal for the evacuation of the Bedouin communities was for the establishment of an Israeli settlement.[9]

The Supreme Court also approved additional cases, based on similar claims, whereby private Palestinian lands were seized in the West Bank for the purpose of establishing Israeli settlements.[10] The most prominent of these was the Supreme Court approval of the establishment of Beth El in 1978.[11] In an extended chamber of judges, the court upheld the state's position whereby the seizure of the lands was indeed for military purposes; it was deemed that security needs were fulfilled by the establishment of a Jewish settlement on the seized Palestinian lands. The court further ruled that the settlement could remain intact for as long as military-political circumstances allowed, and thus hinted that the need itself was more political than it was military, and that the fate of the settlement would only be determined within the framework of future peace agreements with the Palestinian National Authority.[12]

One of the key rulings within the Beth El judgment pertinent to our discussion was a determination made by Justice Witkon. He clarified that in all matters pertaining to the political question of the actual existence of the settlements, as in all matters of foreign policy, the court would be disinclined to intervene, as that was a subject of negotiations between Israel and its neighbors, in light of the peace agreement between Israel and Egypt. However, the court would not concede the claim whereby the court should not intervene and rule on the issue of violation of individual rights in cases where this stemmed from political aspirations: "It is difficult to conceive that the Court shall deny recourse to such a person, merely because his right may be the subject of a disagreement in political negotiations."[13] Justice Landau was even clearer in his opinion in the Beth El case, stating that

> I was more willing to reach the conclusion that this Court should refrain from discussing this problem of civilian settlement in an occupied territory in terms of international law, knowing that this problem is subject to dispute between the Israeli Government and other governments, and that it may be subject to fateful international negotiations in which the Israeli Government is taking part. Any expression of opinion on such a delicate matter by this Court, which can only be an incidental utterance, shall neither add nor detract, and it is best that matters which by their nature belong to the sphere of international policy are discussed within that sphere alone.[14]

Legal struggles against Israeli settlements and outposts on privately owned Palestinian land have ended, in quite a few cases, successfully for the Palestinian landowner and contributed to restoring faith in the Israeli judicial system. Further, the court has made it clear that in all matters pertaining to human rights, it would not refrain from intervening and examining claims of violation. Nonetheless, even in these judgments, the court has hinted that its willingness to intervene in all matters pertaining to the political issue would be limited—in fact, nonexistent. In some cases, the court would even uphold the state's position whereby it is permissible to place civilians in an area seized for military needs, despite the inherent contradiction and the obligation prescribed in international law regarding the laws of occupation, which prohibit mixing between military and civilian targets.[15]

Shortly after the Beit El case, a similar case was brought in 1979 before the Supreme Court, regarding the establishment of the Elon Moreh settlement on the lands belonging to the Palestinian village of Rujeib.[16] In this case, the representatives of the Jewish settlement barefacedly argued before the court that the entire purpose of holding on to the land derived from religious-national motives, and that there was no military value to the seizure itself. Whether there ever existed a real military need for seizing the land was also questioned. Hence, in a monumental judgment, the court rescinded the military seizure. Following the Elon Moreh judgment, the practice of seizing private lands for the purpose of establishing Jewish settlements almost entirely ceased, at least as a matter of official policy.[17] Hence, the Elon Moreh case may be considered a legal turning point: not only did it assist the residents of the Palestinian village Rujeib in retaking their lands, but it also aided in exposing a widespread policy of the Israeli government to assist the settlers in taking over Palestinian lands under the guise of (nonexistent) security needs.

The change of policy by the government did not cause the establishment of settlements or the expansion of existing ones to be suspended; in fact, the exact opposite occurred. The restrictions set by the Supreme Court regarding establishing settlements on private lands became a justification for taking over public lands and allocating them exclusively for the purposes of the settlement project.[18] This led to new challenges regarding the settlement policy, as settlements were now established on public lands, and vast areas across the West Bank were declared as "state lands." The court approved the practices initiated by various Israeli governments, and their representatives in the military administration, with regard to the methods of declaring lands within the occupied territory as public lands, and never saw fit to involve themselves in the issue—that is, the allocation of lands for the establishment of settlements.[19] Based on a vague interpretation of the provisions of international humanitarian law with respect to the laws of occupation, the declarations of state land themselves have been viewed by the court as a duty obliging the military commander to save public property from invasions and other types of illegal use by others, while the court chose not to intervene on the issue of the allocation of such declared state lands for purposes of establishing settlements.[20]

Thus, while the Elon Moreh case can be considered a success as it led to almost complete cessation of the seizure of private lands for the purpose of establishing new settlements, the judgment, nonetheless, led to the expansion of the settlement project as a whole through Israel's declaration of state land on Palestinian public lands (lands originally intended for public use). As it turned out years later, land in areas under Israeli occupation[21] was allocated almost exclusively to the settlements and their ancillary support infrastructures.[22] Hence, the concrete victory in the Elon Moreh case led, in actuality, to the gradual expansion of settlements in the West Bank in the course of the 1980s, without there being any serious attempt or ability to challenge the legality of establishing settlements.[23] One should not blame the petitioners for the actual activities of the settlers or the government ("spoilers"), but one cannot disregard the fact that attempts to thwart such spoilers via the court eventually led to increased sophistication on the part of the spoilers and significant expansion of the settlement project.

The question of the legality of Israeli settlement in the occupied territories was finally brought before the Supreme Court in the early 1990s. The Bargil case, a petition that was filed by the Israeli NGO Peace Now,[24] raised the issue for the first time in a clear and unequivocal manner, seeking a declaration that the establishment of Israeli settlements in the occupied West Bank is an illegal action, primarily according to provisions of international law. Chief Justice Meir Shamgar dismissed the petition and ruled that the issue is one in which the dominant component is political rather than legal: "The prevalent nature of the issue raised in this petition is clearly political. The unsuitability of the subject-matter of this Petition for a judicial ruling in the High Court of Justice derives, in this case, from the combination of three characteristics which negate the justiciability of this matter: intervention in matters of policy within the purview of another authority, the absence of a concrete dispute, and the dominant political nature of the issue."[25] The court unequivocally ruled that this question is "injusticiable," as it belongs to the political sphere, and it denied the petition on the grounds of lack of justiciability.[26]

This approach also characterized the court's position in other instances, for example, that pertained to more concrete cases of expansion of the settlements' boundaries of jurisdiction, a practice that prevailed as a substitute for the establishment of new settlements once the peace process between Israel and the Palestinians began in the 1990s. The court's decision was to abstain from intervening in the issue of settlements due to the centrality of its political aspect, now in light of the existence of a political process between Israel and its neighbors, as elucidated by the Supreme Court judges in the case of Ma'ale Adumim, in 1998: "The matter raised in the Petition for our ruling shall undoubtedly be on the agenda of these neighborly negotiations. The entity responsible for this process as a whole is the government, and it would be inappropriate for the court to instruct it—within the framework of a public petition—to act one way or another. In such neighborly negotiations, it would be proper for the State to speak in one voice; in one voice and not in a voice and an echo which contradict one another."[27]

Thus, the court avoided, in its own terms, stepping on the legal landmine placed before it. In fact, following the Bargil case, it became impossible to examine through purely legal eyes and conduct internal Israeli judicial review of the settlement issue. However, in this context, it would be worthwhile to focus on one important point: prior to the Bargil ruling, for a period of about fifteen years, the Supreme Court had approved various practices that led, either directly or indirectly, to the establishment of new settlements, without discussing the central question of the legality of the settlements, based on various justifications as noted above. From this author's perspective, it seems that the Supreme Court believed there is basis under international law for the establishment of settlements, and that the issue would have been approved on a clear majority of cases (with the exception of the Elon Moreh case) regarding settlement building.

In the absence of any positive ruling declaring the settlements' legality, the court elected to bypass the issue, as it examined (and approved) only the manner of establishment of these settlements, providing a de facto legal umbrella for them. As previously put by one of the most senior jurists dealing with the issue of the settlements before the Supreme Court, David Kretzmer explained, the court has always served as "a trusty babysitter of the settlements."[28] Kretzmer observed, "It is hard to expect from a domestic court to make such a decision [ruling the settlements to be illegal], a decision which surely would have caused a head-on confrontation with the executive branch and a deep alienation between a large part of the Jewish public in Israel and the Court. This restraint does indeed exist, but its existence blatantly reveals the limitations of judicial review over the actions of the authorities in the Territories."[29]

Despite countless decisions made by various international institutions concerning the illegality of the settlements, and the comprehensive position of the international community,[30] the issue of the settlements' legality was never put to any practical test by any legal or judicial international institute until 2004. In 2004, the International Court of Justice (ICJ) was required to provide an advisory opinion regarding the legal implications of the construction of the separation barrier in the occupied Palestinian territories,[31] with the question of the settlements becoming involved therein, albeit through the back door. This occurred because a significant portion of the delineation of the barrier was designed to enclose major settlements and include them in the "Israeli" side of the separation barrier, with the possible eventuality of annexing them to the State of Israel. The ICJ ruled unanimously that the settlements themselves are illegal under international law, and that the Israeli wall constructed on the ground was intended to defend the settlements.[32] An advisory opinion of this type lacks any binding force according to international law,[33] yet one cannot disregard its legal gravitas, or the legal analysis presented therein. It may well serve as an inspiration in the future, since the Israeli Supreme Court has recognized the ICJ as the most senior institution in the practice of interpreting public international law.[34]

Has the fear of the potential legal internationalization of the settlement issue led the Israeli Supreme Court to reconsider the legality of the settlements or of the practices allowing them? Apparently not. In the course of one of the petitions pertaining to the delineation of the separation barrier in the vicinity of the Alfei Menashe settlement, a petition heard by the court after the advisory opinion of the ICJ was issued (thus compelling the court to confront the ICJ decision[35]), the court exempted itself from a profound and material discussion of the issue. It ruled that the wall could be constructed to safeguard the lives and security of Israeli residents in the West Bank, and for this purpose "it is irrelevant to examine whether such settlement in accordance with international law or in contravention thereto, as determined in the advisory opinion of the International Court in The Hague. For that reason, we shall not express any opinion on this matter."[36] This position of the Supreme Court was subject to much criticism. As Professor David Kretzmer stated, "I very much doubt whether the seizure of lands for the purpose of safeguarding a settlement whose mere existence on the ground is illegal, following a violation of international law by the military commanders who allocated the land for the establishment of the settlement and granted a permit for its construction, can be considered a seizure for military purposes."[37]

When putting the question of the court's involvement in the issue of settlements to the outcome test, it appears that with the exception of an extreme case at the margins of the settlement project, the court's involvement has not only failed to prevent the establishment of the settlements, in many cases it even led to its expansion, as it granted internal Israeli public legitimization to their establishment and expansion, deriving from the court's nonintervention. The court's conscious decision not to make a ruling regarding the legality of the settlements has stemmed, it appears, from its desire not to address the issue and thereby place itself during international negotiations between Israel and its neighbors—first Egypt (in 1978), later the Palestinians (in 1993) and the Hashemite Kingdom of Jordan (in 1994). Justice Cheshin clarified in the Iyad case[38] that the court did not want its rulings to somehow affect the negotiations and actually strengthen Palestinian demands for evacuation of the settlements. Similarly, as expressed in the ruling on the Bargil case, the Supreme Court ruled the matter suffers from "lack of justiciability" and belongs in the political sphere.

However, the Supreme Court actually has backed government policy regarding issues linked to important political processes, as can be seen in its approval of the law for implementation of the Gaza Disengagement in 2005. In 2004, the Israeli government under Prime Minister Ariel Sharon presented a plan for the withdrawal of IDF forces and evacuation of Israeli settlements from the Gaza Strip, as well as the evacuation of four other settlements in the northern West Bank.[39] Numerous petitions were filed against this policy and against the constitutionality of the legal framework on which it was based, as legislated and approved by the Knesset (Israeli parliament).[40] The Supreme Court, in a majority of ten to one, denied all the petitions that challenged the decision to execute the disengagement. The court upheld the state's position, in light of the temporary nature of occupation per se, that Israeli control and Israeli settlements within the occupied territories are in fact temporary. As a result, the disengagement, from a legal point of view, could go forward.[41]

In sum, the Supreme Court has approved the government's two major acts regarding the occupied territories over the years: both the actual establishment of the settlements and the expansion thereof, and the possibility of evacuating them, all as part of the government's general policy. The willingness of the court to intervene is limited, in most cases, to issues of violation of the rights of a concrete individual whose private land is being seized; however, such intervention often indirectly has led to the expansion of the settlement project as a whole. That said, the policy of the Supreme Court to restrict its intervention remained intact only so long as the settlements were institutionally sanctioned, based on the procedures, rules, and laws prescribed by the government.

The Renewed Struggle: The Rise of the Unauthorized Outposts and the Question of the Rule of Law

The Outposts

The emergence of unauthorized outposts in the mid-1990s undermined government decisions and procedures; it also brought the Supreme Court into the heart of the issue of Israeli settlement in the West Bank. Once the peace process between Israel and the Palestinians began in 1993 and until 2012, no new settlements were officially established by Israel, as a confidence-building measure on the part of the government. The settlers, often with the direct or indirect support of the political and military echelons, found two means by which to bypass this "moratorium." The first was expanding the areas of jurisdiction of the Israeli municipal authorities in the West Bank. In this manner, the areas controlled by the settlements were massively expanded from the mid-1990s, with no public notice issued prior to their expansion. The other approach was the establishment of various outposts throughout the West Bank, often with logistical or financial aid provided either directly or indirectly by official institutions of the State of Israel. A report commissioned by the Israeli government in 2005 regarding the outposts defined those minisettlements as illegal, if they failed to meet the following conditions: (1) they are the subject of a government resolution; (2) the nature of proprietary rights regarding the land allows their establishment, and the lands are not privately owned by Palestinians; (3) they are established according to a detailed city building plan, which allows the granting of building permits; and (4) they have a jurisdiction area determined by the commander of the IDF forces in the area.[42]

Thus, the outposts were deemed unauthorized and therefore illegal under domestic law and procedures prescribed by the Israeli governments, regardless of the question of their illegality under international law. The outposts were constructed in contravention of the declared policy of Israeli governments and without the issuance of the required permits, in an attempt to reshape the landscape of the West Bank by determining facts on the ground. In fact, the outposts were intended to spoil the political processes or their resumption once they had come to a standstill. Further, the outposts—like the settlements—were meant to thwart the existence of a viable Palestinian state with minimal territorial continuity in the West Bank.

The Legal Struggle against the Outposts and Illegal Construction in the Settlements and Its Outcomes

The initial attempts carried out by various Israeli peace groups to fight the outpost phenomenon were a failure. In 1998, a petition was filed seeking the immediate dismantling of the outposts that were built after 1996, under the first Netanyahu government.[43] This petition was denied shortly after, in 1999, in light of what was later entitled "the outpost agreement" between Prime Minister Ehud Barak (who replaced Benjamin Netanyahu following the 1999 elections) and the leaders of the settlers. In the agreement it was decided that the construction in most outposts would be suspended and some outposts would be consensually evacuated.[44] In fact, this agreement did not lead to a decrease in the number of outposts; it may even have led to the exact opposite. Until 1993, about one hundred settlements had been formally established by the various Israeli governments, but from the mid-1990s and until the publishing of the comprehensive report regarding the illegality of these outposts by attorney Talya Sasson in 2005 (the "Sasson Report"), over 105 new outposts had been built.[45] This was in addition to the expansion of both the area and the population of the existing settlements. Moreover, the outposts that were intended to be evacuated according to the agreement either remained in place or were relocated to nearby locations. That way the outpost phenomenon not only was not halted by the government, but was even assisted through financing, provision of infrastructure, IDF protection, and most importantly by the *deliberate* absence of law enforcement. The Israeli government may have found this duplicitous situation convenient. On the one hand, the establishment of the outposts throughout the West Bank was performed without any formal government resolution, allowing the government to claim it had nothing to do with it. On the other hand, practically speaking, by either direct support (through the financing and support of infrastructure) or indirect support (turning a blind eye and failing to enforce the law), the government encouraged and assisted these activities. The purpose of this practice was to thwart a two-state solution and to implement, albeit indirectly, the ideology of Israeli settlement building, contrary to proclaimed official government policy.[46] A second petition was filed in 2000, seeking the evacuation of all known outposts.[47] It too was denied shortly after filing, on grounds that it was excessively general and comprehensive, and did not contain the full factual infrastructure required with references to each and every one of the outposts.[48] However, the legal struggle did not end, but rather intensified and accelerated. Numerous specific petitions were filed against illegal construction in both outposts and settlements, relying on the fact that such activities, at least in the outposts, were—even according to the state's institutions—illegal construction. Additionally, in many cases, such construction took place on private Palestinian lands, an issue that involved also the violation of proprietary rights. The evacuation of nine permanent buildings in the outpost of Amona represented a milestone in the struggle against the outposts. In August 2005, extensive construction activities commenced throughout the West Bank, as a response to the disengagement evacuations. Right-wing organizations, disheartened by the relatively peaceful evacuation of the Gaza Strip settlements, considered the intended evacuation in Amona as a watershed, after which it would be impossible to evacuate any further buildings in the West Bank.[49] The Israeli NGO Peace Now filed a petition regarding

Amona in July 2005—days before executing the disengagement plan—as the Amona buildings were nearing habitation.[50] In its response to the petition, the state announced that it intended to execute demolition orders, but only after the disengagement. In January 2006, after the state's commitment was anchored by a court ruling, and after the court denied opposing petitions filed by outpost settlers, and local municipal councils seeking to prevent demolition of the buildings had been denied,[51] security forces were deployed to execute the demolition orders. Following a violent and tenacious struggle with settlers and outpost resisters, the buildings were evacuated and demolished.

The messages conveyed by vast sections of the Israeli right wing following the evacuations was abundantly clear: (1) no more submissive acceptance of the decisions of the political echelon or the rulings of the court, but rather a strong and possibly violent struggle against any future evacuation, and (2) every evacuation decided on would entail a clear price, in the form of a persistent struggle leading to the establishment of additional outposts and the expansion of existing settlements. Indeed, the decade following the Amona evacuation was characterized by numerous petitions against illegal construction on the one hand, and a persistent struggle, both at the political level and on the ground, against any intent to enforce the law on such illegal construction on the other hand. The state itself was forced, for the first time, to choose between favoring the rule of law in issues regarding the outposts and the settlement construction work in the West Bank, or allowing the number of settlements and housing units in the settlements to increase in a manner that would change the West Bank beyond recognition. A review of the state's responses in cases of illegal construction in the occupied territories and its position on rulings regarding the matter shed light on the question of whether the legal struggle against the outposts prevented (or at least delayed) these spoilers or served as a catalyst for such spoilers and thus also undermined political efforts for peace.

As noted, in the early days of the legal history of the settlements, as can be seen in the Beth El and Elon Moreh cases, the state asked the court to allow it to implement its policies regarding the settlements and not to intervene in these policies through legal proceedings. The court refused to accept such a position where the property rights of the individual might be in jeopardy but accepted it in all other cases. This position of the state reappeared within the framework of the renewed wave of petitions emerging after 2005. As it turned out, the court's ruling regarding the outposts became a bargaining tool in diplomatic negotiations. According to the state, the intervention by the court in an issue such as law enforcement might influence the international discourse conducted between the State of Israel and its neighbors, as well as between Israel and the international community.

At the same time that the Amona buildings case ended in 2005, a petition was filed by Peace Now in 2005 regarding the construction of twenty permanent buildings in the outposts named HaYovel and Haresha.[52] The fate of this petition was entirely different from that of Amona. During the many years the case was pending before the court, the state's position underwent numerous changes. While initially the state maintained that illegal construction in the outpost should be subject to enforcement according to the priorities of the enforcement institutions in the area, as years passed this position gradually eroded. When the court eventually faced the state and attempted to compel a schedule for enforcement under its direct supervision,[53] the state decided on a new enforcement policy: enforcement should focus on illegal construction located on private land; regarding illegal construction located on other lands, the enforcement would not be advanced, and the possibility of retroactive sanctioning of the outposts would be considered.[54] Outposts subject to this petition would eventually become part of existing, long-established settlements, and thus, their existence would be sanctioned. Had the petition not been filed, these outposts could have remained in place, and the Israeli government could have presented them as mere cases of illegal actions, contrary to actions representing the governmental policy. The belief was that once the government chose to uphold the raison d'être of the outposts, particularly in their specific strategic locations, the public perception of the state's intentions would also change in political terms. The expansion of existing settlements and the sanctioning of outposts belied the government's claims that the outposts did not reflect official policy and that it was not authorizing new settlements.

This became clear with additional petitions against the nonevacuation of illegal outposts, which led to a formal government resolution authorizing the establishment of new settlements in 2012. This was the case with the outposts Rechelim,[55] Bruchin,[56] and Sansana.[57] In petitions filed by organizations seeking the evacuation of the outposts' buildings due to their illegality, the state was required to present its position. For the first time since the 1990s, the state favored authorizing them as new settlements, for all intents and purposes, rather than evacuating them, and this became the first time since the 1990s that new settlements were approved.[58]

Alongside these procedures of retroactive authorization of illegal outposts on "public lands," the state made every effort to reverse or delay the implementation of the court order and to enforce the law on illegal construction in outposts built on privately owned lands. When this path was blocked by the court, the government quickly "compensated" the settlers' leadership by approving the establishment of new settlements and the addition of new neighborhoods in existing settlements. For example, in the case of the illegal construction in the Ulpanah outpost near Beth El, the state had committed before the court to evacuate the buildings. When the time of evacuation arrived, the state tried to retract from its commitment and requested the court reconsider its ruling, but the Supreme Court denied the request and noted that it was outrageous and extremely unreasonable.[59] In what could clearly be seen as a response, the government then passed a resolution authorizing the establishment of three new settlements—a hint to the petitioners that they should stop filing such petitions, since they would lose more than they would gain.[60]

The case of the Migron outpost reflects clearly how a struggle ending with a victory to the petitioners led to the expansion of the settlement project. Migron was the largest outpost in the West Bank, constructed almost entirely on private Palestinian lands. In 2006 a petition was filed by the landowners demanding evacuation of the outpost.[61] The state, in its response to the petition, said that the outpost was indeed illegal, and the only remaining question was when and how it would be evacuated.[62] Part of the compensation package given to the settler leadership included an expansion of the near settlement of Geva Binyamin, allegedly for the purpose of relocate the evacuees from Migron.[63] The expansion of Geva Binyamin was designed to include 1,400 residential units, despite the fact that the Migron outpost included only 50 units at the time. As this was a case of expansion of an existing settlement, the Supreme Court, adhering to its previous rulings, approved the proposed plan.[64] However, it turned out that the residents of Migron were unwilling to relocate to the new neighborhood prepared for them. Hence the idea was raised to establish a new settlement for them, "New Migron," which required modification of legislation.[65] Then the court faced a petition challenging the hasty establishment of this new settlement, but the court did not intervene, due to the fact that this was a matter of national policy.[66] The original Migron outpost was eventually evacuated, after countless legal proceedings aiming to delay its evacuation.[67]

The judgment rendered in this case—that the law must be enforced on those who violate it—was, legally speaking, a mere case of stating the obvious.⁶⁸ But what was the price paid for it? An outpost of fifty residential units was evacuated; instead another settlement was expanded, and another settlement was established. To this political price, one should add the public-legal price manifested in the continuing undermining of the statutes of the Supreme Court and the principle of the rule of law.⁶⁹ The evacuation of Migron did not lead to a decrease in the number of settlements or settlers, and possibly even led to the contrary. Nonetheless, from the perspective of the landowners, this was a significant victory. It was an official declaration of their right of the land, and the authorities were compelled to take active measures to protect these rights. Furthermore, in terms of public perception, it was also proved that contrary to the aftermath of the Amona case, the evacuation of illegal outposts in the West Bank is possible. However, in the government's willingness to make all efforts for the sake of an outpost that even according to its residents was illegal, the Israeli government revealed that it preferred prosettler policies over the evacuation of settlements in the West Bank.⁷⁰

During the deliberations regarding the Migron petition, the state claimed that the question of the evacuation of the outpost was a matter of political significance from an international perspective, and therefore, the court should adopt a restrained approach before deciding whether to intervene. In other petitions dealing with the outposts issue, the state repeatedly claimed that the issue of construction in the West Bank, including the matter of outposts' evacuation, is "a core issue in the political discourse between Israel and the Palestinian National Authority, as well as in political negotiations with the United States and other countries. Hence, the government's policy should be examined while taking such interests in to consideration."⁷¹ This implied that for the Israeli government, law enforcement regarding illegal outposts—or, in fact, the rule of law and the protection of the proprietary rights of Palestinians—had become a bargaining chip in political negotiations with the Palestinians and in diplomatic relations with other countries.⁷² In fact, from the government's perspective, the court intervention regarding the settlements would violate the executive branch's ability to conduct international relations and negotiations with the Palestinians.

The state explicitly expressed its position within the framework of a petition filed against illegal construction works carried out on private

Palestinian lands in the outskirts of the long-established settlement of Ofra.[73] In its response to the petition, the state argued that because the status of the buildings mentioned in the petition was not different from that of hundreds of other buildings in Ofra, this issue should be left for resolution within the framework of a future final agreement between Israel and the Palestinians, despite it being a case of illegal construction on privately owned lands.[74] The court ruled against the state's position: "If it has been decided to deny the Petition, this would have been tantamount to granting a permit to violate the rights of the area residents which is unacceptable."[75] In this ruling, the court returned to the classic approach that characterized its original rulings in the Elon Moreh case, whereby political reasons pertaining to the issue of settlements cannot serve as justification for building on the private property of Palestinians. However, the fact that the court restricted its determination solely to the nine buildings discussed in the petition, and did not address the other illegal buildings in that settlement, demonstrated once again the court's preference for examining settlement matters through a particularly narrow lens, disregarding the entirety of the illegality presented before it.[76] It has been argued that when the court makes the rare decision to evacuate a specific building (or a few specific buildings) in an outpost or settlement, it is actually stating that the other buildings are legitimate in its view—although such a determination was never positively made. Such tacit or hidden approval of the settlement project grants the Israeli government a sense of legitimization for its actions, especially in terms of internal Israeli discourse and the perceptions of the Israeli public.[77]

The most recent example of the results of the legal battle against illegal outposts can be demonstrated in the case of Amona. Though in 2006 nine houses were demolished as presented above, the entire outpost was subject to a separate legal proceeding, which started in 2008.[78] After several years of deliberations before the Supreme Court, the court ruled that the entire outpost that was built entirely on private land owned by Palestinians should be removed. Though the court provided the state with a long duration of time (two years) to execute its judgment, when the deadline approached, the state asked for a nine-month extension. The state decided to establish a new settlement next to Shilo (which would be considered allegedly only a neighborhood of Shilo), while at the same time the state tried to take over nearby property next to the current location of the illegal outpost.[79] That was the first time since the mid-1970s that the state was willing to use "abandoned" private property of Palestinians for the benefit of settlers, though several legal opinions had recommended against it in the past.[80] Shortly after, the court rejected this attempt to create a new settlement on private "abandoned" lands.[81] That led the government to declare the establishment of a new settlement: Amicay, the first governmental settlement created in almost twenty-five years.[82] The evacuation of Amona led to the creation of two new settlements, each one of them planned to be bigger than the outposts evacuated. Moreover, the failed attempts of the government to prevent the evacuation paved the way to legalizing the "regularization law" that will prevent future law enforcement regarding illegal outposts and buildings on Palestinian lands.[83] The law has led to widespread condemnations of Israel by the international community, not only because the declared purpose of the law that aimed to leave outposts as they are, but also because it was the first time that the Israeli Parliament legislated specifically about lands in the West Bank, an act that was viewed as annexation.[84] The legality of this controversial law is currently being subjected to a judicial review by the Supreme Court, both from constitutional aspects and due to its alleged contradiction of international law.[85]

In the majority of cases, the outcome of the court's decision was a government decision to take various steps in order to authorize illegal construction in settlements retroactively, to expand construction and the area of jurisdiction in existing settlements, and to establish additional settlements.[86] The court never saw fit to intervene in decisions of the government, or in the authorities' plans to approve establishment of settlements,[87] especially in cases where such decisions were made as "compensation" for evacuations of outposts, even when such compensation was disproportionate.

The Legal Struggle against Illegal Construction: Has It Done More Harm Than Good?

The study cases this article reviewed demonstrate how the legal proceedings not only failed in delaying the spoilers (the settlements), but eventually led to their intensification. The outcomes of the many legal struggles revealed the Israeli government policy—that is, to authorize outposts instead of evacuating them and to establish new settlements when the government was compelled to enforce the court's judgments. Such outcomes contradict the purpose of legal proceedings. In the eyes of the public, the purpose of the legal proceedings is to reach a just solution.[88] Considering the abovementioned cases, we can see that the legal proceedings regarding the settlements did reinforce the principle of justice in its direct sense—that is, they did provide assistance to individuals on whose lands settlements or outposts were established. These proceedings concluded with explicit orders of the court to the authorities: enforce the law, despite the government's reluctance to confront the political forces seeking nonenforcement of the law and of Supreme Court judgments.[89] From the perspective of the individual Palestinian, for example, whose lands might be restored instead of being used for the establishment of settlements, there were cases in which direct justice was achieved through legal proceedings. The court's confirmation of petitioners' claims and the granting of the welfare asked by them was the opposite of a spoiler to the peace process; such decisions have strengthened the Palestinians' (and others') faith in Israeli institutions and in the use of nonviolent measures such as legal actions or negotiations. The recognition of the injustice in the constructing of settlements on private lands helped to build trust between the people of the two nations.

Since the beginning of the legal struggle against the outposts and settlements, the number of cases regarding illegal construction on privately owned lands has increased significantly. The court has repeatedly clarified that it has no intention of allowing construction on privately owned lands (even those that were considered "abandoned"). Thus, spoiler attempts to construct outposts on privately owned lands have altogether failed, in what might be viewed as a positive act of the Supreme Court against spoilers. Furthermore, the success of Palestinian landowners in their legal struggles calmed other Palestinian landowners' fears, because they understood their land would not be used as a bargaining chip in negotiations. Ignoring the landowners' demands for justice might have damaged the public legitimacy of any future agreement between the parties, as it would deepen the feelings of frustration so much that it inhibits any possibility of real reconciliation between nations and individuals feeling that they have been wronged and were not granted justice as they see it.

However, the question remains, what has been the overall effect of the struggle against the settlements? From a utilitarian perspective, the legal proceedings could be seen as the cause of the authorization and advancement of the settlements (through the government's reaction to the legal struggles by authorizing additions to existing settlements or creation of new settlements), but it is important to underscore that the legal proceedings themselves only came as a reaction to an existing situation. Additionally, the legal struggle helped expose the true positions of the Israeli governments and forced them to adopt a clear policy regarding the settlement project. This issue is crucial when trying to understand the significance of the legal struggle within the general framework of the political process. It could have been assumed that the court would attempt to refrain whenever possible from intervening in the settlements issue and the question of their legality, and indeed that was the case. The judiciary didn't have much power in coping with the spoilers (the settlement project), especially when such spoilers were created (or endorsed) by other institutions of the government. The principle of justice could only exist in its narrow sense. However, when the state was forced to confront the domestic illegality of the outposts, it was forced for the first time to choose sides—not in the legal sense, but in the political and international sense. Despite the fact that Israeli governments had committed to the international community, more than once, that no new settlements would be established,[90] that unauthorized outposts would be evacuated,[91] and that existing settlements would not be expanded (except due to natural population growth), in reality new points of settlements were established,[92] and existing settlements were expanded significantly.[93] Hence, in cases where justice was not achieved, and no determination was made, the truth about the nature of the governments' actual policy was revealed.

It seems the policy of the Israeli government followed the path laid by the spoiler-generators, the settlers, which turned the government into the official sponsor of this spoiler. This was expressed mostly by the state's reluctance to implement the Supreme Court judgments in the few cases where it ruled that illegal buildings must be evacuated.[94] The Israeli governments throughout the years funded the establishment of outposts, whether directly or indirectly,[95] while in parallel to such financial and logistic assistance, the political echelon publicly disowned them. The Israeli governments favored the political interests of domestic interest groups over international obligations. In the majority of cases, the government policy was in favor of establishing additional settlements and expanding existing ones.

Are Israel's settlements building and expanding a sophisticated negotiation strategy under the disguise of restraint that is in fact only an outcome of legal proceedings? Actually, many of the disputes between Israel, the Palestinians, and the mediating parties are on the nature of the territorial compromise intended to be achieved ultimately. For instance, the majority of known peace proposals focus on leaving central settlement blocks within the framework of future peace agreements, in return for territorial exchanges in other locations (the principle of swaps).⁹⁶ When examining the actual policy of Israeli governments over decades, we can see that it has expanded these blocks.⁹⁷ This "approach," which was fully exposed only within the framework of the state's responses in legal proceedings, shows that Israeli governments used the outposts tactically, in order to reshape the boundaries of the settlement blocks. The establishment of the outposts and their retroactive authorization due to legal proceedings transformed the debate from the sphere of legality to the sphere of politics, drawing international attention to the issue. It was the ambiguity of the legal situation that allowed the various Israeli governments to stall—and act surreptitiously—while negotiations were taking place. Once the outposts became a fait accompli and were backed by political decisions made by the State of Israel, the Palestinians were urged to turn to the international political sphere.

As demonstrated by the disengagement in 2005 and the evacuation of Israeli settlements from the Sinai Peninsula in 1982, the authorized or unauthorized status of a settlement does not prevent significant political steps that the political echelon wishes to take. From a legal, public, and practical perspective, it would be easier to evacuate an unauthorized outpost (a clear law breaker) than it would be to evacuate an authorized settlement. However, if a political resolution to evacuate settlements was to be presented to the court, the court could provide legitimacy for such an act. In crucial decisions as this, the court would likely back the government's political step and would minimize its intervention in materialistic issues, as it has done previously.

Even if the legal proceedings may be viewed as ones that are eventually leading to absolute spoilers, it cannot be said that the legal proceedings are acting as spoilers to the peace process, but rather the political responses to these proceedings. The legal proceedings can, however, lead to specific improvements where a direct violation of basic rights has occurred. This does not suffice to hinder or prevent the spoilers; it may even lead, as seen above, to the exact opposite: such legal proceedings are likely to cause the retroactive authorization of outposts. Thus, the significant fruit of these proceedings is the exposure of the truth about the unauthorized outposts.

At the beginning of this section, the legal proceedings were depicted as promoters of justice and the discovery of truth. It can be said that both elements existed, yet to a limited extent. Occasionally, a legal proceeding that ended in justice on the individual level led on the political level to the establishment of new settlements, a result that may be viewed as unfair and unjust by the Palestinians. The same applies to the discovery of truth.

Legal proceedings may expose the true policies of Israeli governments, who seek to increase the Israeli presence in the West Bank through the retroactive authorizing of outposts and the expansion of existing settlements. Such intentions may be at the core of the negotiations, and, at the very least, it may be said that Israel's intentions have been made clear.

Legal Internationalization of the Conflict: An Independent Spoiler to the Peace Process?

The discussion so far has revolved around analysis of the outcomes of the legal proceedings attempting to fight the settlements. The conclusion was that such proceedings had a limited influence over the peace process. On the one hand, it led to the evacuation of outposts. On the other hand, it led to the authorization of other outposts and to the acceleration of the construction in the settlements. However, an analysis of the effect of legal proceedings regarding the settlements, and of the question of whether they can serve to either help or hinder spoilers, would be incomplete without addressing the possibility of regulation of international law regarding the Israeli-Palestinian conflict.

Previous sections have mentioned the actions leading to the advisory opinion given by the International Court of Justice regarding the legality of the separation barrier. Despite attempts to present the barrier as one serving purely security purposes, it was proven that it also bears political aspects, including shaping of the future border between the State of Israel and the Palestinian state in the West Bank,[98] and serves to expand existing settlements and their jurisdiction.[99] The Israeli government's decision to construct the barrier was perceived by the Palestinians as a one-sided attempt to resolve the conflict. This action led the Palestinians to approach the international legal institutions for them to determine the legality of the separation barrier, and, indirectly, the legality of the settlements.

The implications of this action are in dispute to this day. On the one hand, the State of Israel continued to construct the barrier despite the opinion of the ICJ, and the Israeli Supreme Court criticized the ICJ's advisory opinion.[100] The position of the Israeli governments over the years was that the ICJ proceedings were illegitimate, and therefore the advisory opinion was perceived as biased and one sided.[101] The Israeli position was strengthened by the fact that the advisory opinion was not binding and did not set a legal precedent. Ultimately, the legal ICJ proceedings had little effect on Israel's actual intention to construct the barrier, or to its delineation.[102] On the other hand, the advisory opinion was perceived by the Palestinians as a legal-diplomatic defeat for Israel, which created an arena in which Israel lacked effective tools, particularly since the barrier was delineated to enlarge the settlement blocks. The barrier was perceived as an instrument of annexation of Palestinian lands in favor of settlements, which are illegal according to international law. The advisory opinion has since cast a shadow on Israeli activities in the West Bank and created a genuine threat that the legal internationalization of the settlement issue might lead to further legal defeats.

In 2012 the United Nations Human Rights Council (UNHRC) passed a resolution to "dispatch an independent international fact-finding mission . . . to investigate the implications of the Israeli settlements on the civil, political, economic, social and cultural rights of the Palestinians throughout the Occupied Palestinian Territory."[103] The UNHRC has a reputation for having a biased approach regarding Israel, yet the fact remains that there was now another session of international legal discussion regarding the effects of the settlements on the human rights and daily lives of the Palestinians. The report, published on March 2013, was as harsh as Israel expected.[104] It determined, among other things, that the settlements and the infrastructures serving them undermined the Palestinians' ability to exercise their right to self-determination; that the settlements constituted a slow annexation of territory and were preventing any possibility of a viable Palestinian state in the future; and that the establishment of the settlements led to a methodical violation of human rights of the Palestinian population, including the freedom of movement, the right to due legal process, the right to equality, the right to freedom of speech, the right of access to holy places, the right to property, the right of access to clean water, the right to education, and more.[105] The recommendations of the report included a demand that Israel immediately cease all activities pertaining to the expansion of settlements, and that Israel initiate a process for evacuating all settlements from the occupied territories. There were also recommendations from UN member states to intervene in cases of violation of the basic norms of international law, and a call to commercial corporations to avoid business relations where these might cause a violation of Palestinians' human rights.[106]

The status of the UNHRC report is marginal in legal terms and could not serve as evidence or as a base for any operative steps of the various UN institutions. However, that was one out of many attempts to overlegalize the conflict. The way this report relied on the ICJ determinations in the separation barrier case, even though it could not serve as a binding precedent, indicates how factual and legal findings had taken root among the international legal community regarding the settlement issue. Such overlegalization entailed a binary-dichotomous resolution of the conflict, leaving very little room for diplomacy.

It is noticeable that such use of a judicial or quasi-judicial institution was employed by the Palestinians exactly when Israel took unilateral steps (specifically the construction of the separation barrier, which commenced in 2002–2003, the authorization of illegal outposts and the expansion of existing settlements as in 2008–2012, and the decision to appoint a committee headed by Supreme Court Justice [ret.] Edmond Levy), all of which led to the conclusions of the UNHRC's fact-finding mission.[107] The Security Council resolution regarding the settlements from December 2016 (UNSC No. 2334)[108] was a direct outcome of the Regularization Law mentioned above.[109] The Palestinian turn to international legal institutions was not only a response to unilateral steps taken by Israel but also a reaction to the basic disagreements in the negotiations between Israel and the Palestinians; it was designed to break free of the status quo, which in the Palestinian view only perpetuated the standstill.

At this point, the most powerful legal weapon in the fragile relationship between the parties, one the Palestinians have threatened to use, is to apply to the International Criminal Court (ICC) in Hague. The Palestinians claimed that the war that took place in the summer of 2014, known in Israel as "Operation Protective Edge," required an ICC investigation regarding Israel's alleged war crimes.[110] Among other things, the Rome treaty that established the ICC defines the transfer of a population, directly or indirectly, by the occupying party into the occupied territory as a war crime.[111] The Regularization Law that was legislated in February 2017 might also be subjected to investigation under ICC jurisdiction; whether this is legal or not depends on the Israeli Supreme Court decision.[112] The Palestinians joined the Rome Statute as a member state in 2014, which means that they might bring the issue of the settlements before the ICC. Doing so will be viewed by Israel as a hostile step and thus might prevent the advancement of the peace process, at least for as long as such criminal proceedings are pending.

Preferring the international legal path regarding the settlements would most certainly constitute an absolute and independent spoiler, indicating that the Palestinians have abandoned the diplomatic-political path and from now on would rely entirely and solely on judicial rulings. Moreover, the threat to turn to international judicial rulings or judicial institutions undermines the confidence between the parties. The use of international legal proceedings might reinforce the perception, which at the time was unfounded, that such legal proceedings could provide both justice and truth, and do so in a way that neither the Israeli courts nor negotiations had so far succeeded in providing.

It is true that international legal proceedings are commonly perceived by the weaker party as more objective, and as such, they are capable of leading to the restoration and rectification of the wrongdoings that occurred in the conflict. Such proceedings might be seen as collective justice and lead to discovery of truth, but the international legal proceedings such as the advisory opinion given in 2004 or the report of the UNHRC fact-finding mission from 2013 create a perception of reality and truth for the Palestinians that could actually delay the possibility of reaching a negotiated agreement—which most certainly would require some sort of compromise. At the same time, such proceedings, which would increase Israelis' sense of isolation, might trigger a reaction from Israel in the form of further expansion of the settlements, rather than stopping it.

Yet the effect of international criminal proceedings remains unclear regarding the possibility of reaching a peace agreement between the parties. There is no doubt that both parties fully comprehend that the use of international legal proceedings would only occur when the achievement of justice and the discovery of truth is impossible within the framework of existing negotiations, or the legal proceedings conducted in Israel. Contrary to the Israeli Supreme Court, which avoided any discussion of the legality of the settlements due to its concerns of confrontation with other governmental institutions and parts in the Israeli public, international judicial forums are considerably freer to discuss this issue. Moreover, there is a dispute over the legality of the settlement among experts of international law. The legal rulings and decisions are stacking up, and the more unilateral steps are taken by Israeli governments to expand the settlements in the West Bank, the more likely it is that more and more international legal mechanisms would come into play. The perception of the settlements as a spoiler sponsored by the Israeli government might harden Palestinian positions and will possibly lead to an increase in the number of Israeli settlements. This vicious circle might impede the progress toward an agreement.

Conclusions

The power of the Israeli Supreme Court is restricted, in part because of the two other branches of the government, which are hostile. Dorit Beinisch, former chief justice of the Israeli Supreme Court, said in the concluding hearing on the Ulpana outpost in 2011, "The Israeli-Palestinian conflict will not be resolved within the boundaries of the courtroom."[113] This hearing was held several weeks after the judgment on the Migron outpost, and Israeli public opinion was still struggling to accept the court's intervention in an issue that is perceived as purely political. However, aside from these concrete circumstances, Justice Beinisch's statement illustrates what was known to all those involved in the tense relationship between the court and the settlements: the legal system has a limitation of power. The Israeli Supreme Court was willing and able, in most cases, to assist individual Palestinians in protecting their rights; on all other issues, the court made every possible effort not to intervene and to leave such decisions to the political echelon, even at the cost of hurting the rights of Palestinian communities or the Palestinian collective, as their lands were gradually "repurposed" for the sake of Israel's settlement project.

In the early years of the occupation, the court did provide some sporadic achievements for those who turned to legal proceedings to limit or halt the settlement project. That said, these achievements did not change the landscape of the West Bank. Actually, sometimes the outcomes of legal proceedings even led to the exact opposite and increased construction. Later on, legal struggles against the outposts and illegal construction in the settlements led to a similar outcome. There were cases in which the court acted as a spoiler-enabler (by refusing to define legality or to intervene) or a spoiler-enhancer (by forcing the government to make decisions that would ultimately lead to further construction). There were, however, cases regarding construction on private lands in which the court acted as a spoiler-inhibitor. Ultimately, the court had a major role in the exposure of the true policies of the government regarding the settlements: its interest in the sanctioning of the outposts rather than their evacuation; its preference for fulfilling promises to narrow settler-interest groups rather than international obligations; and its quest for domestic political peace, even at the cost of confrontation with the judicial branch and the disregard of the rule of law. The government and the court preferred to leave the question about legality of the settlements ambiguous, refusing to address the issue even in the face of international judicial institutions' willingness and interest to do so.

The ongoing approach of "nonintervention" regarding the legality of the settlements while granting a legal umbrella to the various methods designed to increase the number of settlements had the effect of encouraging the Palestinians to seek legal solutions in the international arena. Such moves must also be seen in the context of unilateral steps by Israel, such as the building of the separation barrier, the creeping enlargement of the settlement blocks, and the hiatus of the peace process. In that context, legal internationalization could be considered a tactical step, but it jeopardizes the resumption of the negotiations and the political-diplomatic path toward a resolution of the conflict—in other words, a spoiler action on the part of the Palestinians. However, the continued avoidance of the Israeli Supreme Court to deliberate the key issues regarding the settlements constitutes, in fact, acceptance of the settlement project as a fait accompli—thereby constituting a major spoiler in any peace process.

Notes

Adv. Shlomy Zachary holds an LLB and a BA in international relations as well as an LLM in international law, all from Hebrew University in Jerusalem. The writer has represented in dozens of legal proceedings regarding Israeli activities and policies in the West Bank in the last decade, including some of the cases that are discussed in this chapter. However, the opinions and assessments appearing in this chapter are those of the author himself and do not necessarily represent the opinions of the parties to these below-mentioned proceedings. The author wishes to thank Adv. Michael Sfard, Ms. Ziv Stahl, and Mr. Nadav Sigal for their contributions and remarks on previous drafts of this chapter. Huge thanks are due to Prof. Galia Golan and Adv. Gilead Sher, as well as other editors of this book, for their keen insights and meticulous analysis while this chapter was written. Last, but not least, the author wishes to thank Ms. Deborah Shulman in her assistance during the final stages of writing. As always, any factual or legal errors are strictly the author's.

1. The demolition started minutes after the Israeli Supreme Court rejected the constructor's last petition the same day, in the High Court of Justice. HCJ 5215/15 M.D. Yehonatan Construction LTD v. Minister of Defense et.al., July 29, 2015; Chaim Levinson, "Police, Settlers Clash as Illegal West Bank Structures Demolished," *Haaretz*, July 29, 2015.

2. Barak Ravid, "Under Pressure, Netanyahu Approves New Settlement Construction," *Haaretz*, July 29, 2015.

3. HCJ 9060/08 Yassin et al. v. Minister of Defense et al., hereinafter "Ulpana Case," judgment given on September 23, 2011, and an additional decision given on May 7, 2012.

4. European Union External Action, "Statement by the Spokesperson on Recent Israel Decisions for Further Settlement Expansion," July 29, 2015, http://eeas.europa.eu/statements-eeas/2015/150

729_01_en.htm; Tovah Lazaroff, "US, EU: Israel's Authorization of 300 New Settler Homes Harmful to Peace," *Jerusalem Post*, July 30, 2015.

5. Although there is almost a consensus among the Israeli public that most of the existing settlement blocks in the West Bank will remain part of Israel if a final agreement is reached between Israel and Palestine, during recent years these blocks are being expanded rapidly by connecting isolated settlements to larger, existing settlement blocks in a way that creates a substantial fragmentation of the West Bank. See Yesh Din and The Rights Forum, "Under the Radar: Israel's Silent Policy of Transforming Unauthorized Outposts into Official Settlements," March 11, 201, http://www.yesh-din.org/en/under-the-radar-israels-silent-policy-of-transforming-illegal-outposts-into-official-settlements-2/.

6. See The Geneva Initiative, "An Israeli-Palestinian Initiative to End the Conflict," http://www.geneva-accord.org/, accessed August 8, 2017; The Clinton Parameters, Clinton's Proposal on Israeli-Palestinian Peace, "The Clinton Parameters," December 2000; the Road Map to Peace Agreement, April 2003, hereinafter "Road Map"; speech given by US President Barak Obama in Jerusalem, March 2013; see also Gilead Sher and Liran Ofek, "Dividing the Land, Not the People: Lessons from Givat HaUlpana and Migron Evacuations," *Strategic Assessment* 154 (2013): 38.

7. In a statement given at Bar Ilan University in 2009, Prime Minister Benjamin Netanyahu declared that "the territorial issues will be discussed in a permanent agreement. Till then we have no intention to build new settlements or set aside land for new settlements." The statement is considered a guiding policy since 2009. A different, yet relatively isolated, view is presented in the following paper: Eugene Kontorovich, "Unsettled: A Global Study of Settlements in Occupied Territories," *Northwestern Public Law Research Paper*, no. 16–20, September 7, 2016.

8. HCJ 302/72 Sheik Abu Hilo et al. v. The Government of Israel, PD 272 167, 180.

9. David Kretzmer and Gershom Gorenberg, "Politics, Law and Legal Proceedings: The Case of Israeli Supreme Court and Occupied Territories," *Mishpat Umimshal* (Law and Government) 17 (2016), 249. For the report of the inquiry commission of the Israeli Defense Force, see "Expulsion from Rafah Salient: The Declassified Report of the Commission of Inquiry," published by AKEVOT —the Institute for Israeli-Palestinian Conflict Research, accessed August 8, 2017, http://akevot.org.il/en/article/rafah-salient-report/.

10. HCJ 834/78 Salame et al. v. The Minister of Defense PD 331/471; HCJ 258/79 Amira et al. v. Minister of Defense PD 34 (1), 90.

11. HCJ 606/78 Ayub et al. v. The Minister of Defense et al. PD 332, 113, hereinafter "Beit El Case."

12. As one of the Supreme Court judges, Justice Miriam Ben-Porat, wrote in her concurring opinion in the Beit El case: "I have been bothered by the question whether the phrase 'permanent settlement' reflects the intentions to confiscate the lands forever, but then I came to a conclusion that the adjective 'permanent' should be read as a relative one. The settlers are not by-passers who will spend the night or guests that come for a temporary visit of few weeks or months, but rather people who will see this place as their home. It should be remembered that the State of Emergency which governs the State since it was born, 30 years ago. The chances for a comprehensive peace with all of its neighbors is viewed as aspiration hidden in the unknown future. A peace agreement with our neighbors will bring—when the day will come—the creation of prominent security arrangements. The considerations taken into account during signing peace agreements might be different from those deriving

from the reality existing today. It is clear, therefore, that the provisions and conditions of the agreement will be those which determine the faith of that settlement or any other."

13. Beit El case, leading judgment, as given by Justice Alfred Witkon.

14. Beit El case, concurring opinion by Vice Chief Justice Moshe Landau.

15. For criticism on the Beit El case, see, for example, Yoram Dinstein, "Settlements and Deportations in the Occupied Territories following HCJ 606/78 Saliman Tawfiq Ayub et al v. Minister of Defense et al.," *Iyuney Mishapt, Tel Aviv University Law Journal* 7 (1979): 188; David Kretzmer, "Agora: ICJ Advisory Opinion on Construction of a Wall in the Occupied Palestinian Territory: The Advisory Opinion: The Light Treatment of International Humanitarian Law," *American Journal of International Law* 99 (2005): 94–100.

16. HCJ 390/79 Dwiqat et al. v. The Government of Israel et al., PD 341, 1, hereinafter "Elon Moreh Case."

17. Cabinet Decision no. 145, dated November 11, 1979.

18. Menachem Hofnong, *Israel: Security Needs v. the Rule of Law—1948–1991*, in Hebrew (Jerusalem: Nevo, 1991), 307.

19. HCJ 285/81 El Nazar et al. v. Military Commander in Judea and Samaria PD 361, 701.

20. HCJ 277/84 Arreyeb v. Appellate Committee in the Judea and Samaria District et al., PD 402, 57, hereinafter "Arreyeb Case."

21. Since the second Oslo Accord Interim Agreement was signed between the State of Israel and the Palestinian Liberation Organization in 1995, the relevant area of the West Bank that is totally governed by the Israeli Military Commander comprises slightly more than 60 percent of the West Bank and is named "Area C." In this area, which includes all the settlements in the West Bank, Israel has full and sole military and civil responsibilities, unlike in Area A, in which the Palestinian Authority has full responsibility, and Area B, in which the Palestinian Authority has civil control but Israel retains control for security matters. According to the agreement, areas of C were to become B, and B eventually A, depending on the final status agreement.

22. In a freedom-of-information petition, A.D.A 40223-03/10 Bimkom—Planners for Rights in Planning et al. v. The Civil Administration in Judea and Samaria, the petitioners asked for the relevant information regarding allocations of public lands as were allocated by the Civil Administration in Area C in the West Bank. Analyzing the information received following the petition, it was found that the total amount that was allocated to Palestinians in Area C by the Civil Administration was estimated at around 0.7 percent of all the public land in this area. On the other hand, the World Zionist Organization, which is the government's long branch for settlements, granted 31 percent of the public lands in Area C; Israeli regional and municipal councils granted 8 percent of public lands; Israeli governmental offices and Israeli infrastructures companies granted approximately 12 percent of public lands in Area C. For further details regarding the petition and the documents and files that were filed in it, see The Association for Civil Rights in Israel, "Information Sheet—Allocation of State Land in OPT," April 23, 2013, http://www.acri.org.il/en/2013/04/23/info-sheet-state-land-opt/.

23. Hofnong, *Israel: Security Needs*, 307–308.

24. HCJ 4481/91 Bargil et al. v. The Government of Israel et al PD 474, 210, hereinafter "Bargil Case."

25. Ibid., 215.

26. Ibid., 220.

27. HCJ 3125/98 Iyad v. IDF Military Commander in Judea and Samaria PD 551, 913, hereinafter "Iyad Case."

28. Avigdor Feldman, who was the leading council in the abovementioned cases of Iyad, Bargil, Elon Moreh, and Arreyeb, as quoted by Moshe Gorali, "The Supreme Court of Justice—The Settlements' Babysitter," *Haaretz*, September 9, 2003.

29. David Kretzmer, "Judicial Review and the Occupied Territories: Aharon Barak's Doctrine," in *Studies in Aharon Barak Judicial Activity*, ed. Eyal Zamir, Barak Medina, and Cilia Wasserstein-Fassberg, in Hebrew (Jerusalem: Hari and Michael Sacher Institute for Comparative Studies in the Hebrew University in Jerusalem, 2009), 259–321, 303.

30. See Security Council Resolution 242 from November 1967, which declares the legal status of the territories occupied in the 1967 war as "Occupation"; Security Council Resolution 446 from March 1979, which confronts the legal argument given by Israel for the settlements; Security Council Resolution 2334 from December 2016, which states that Israel's settlement policy and actions constitute a "flagrant violation" of international law and have no legal validity. See also the following scholars' analysis regarding the illegality of the settlements: Adam Roberts, "Prolonged Military Occupation: The Israeli Occupied Territories since 1967," *American Journal of International Law* 84 (1990): 67; J.H.H. Weiler, "Israel, the Territories and International Law: When Doves Are Hawks," in *Israel Among the Nations*, ed. A. E. Kellermann et al. (The Hague: AMC Asser Institute, 1998): 381; James Crawford, "Third Party Obligations with respect to Israeli Settlements in the Occupied Palestinian Territories," January 2012, http://www.tuc.org.uk/tucfiles/342/LegalOpinionIsraeliSettlements.pdf); Eyal Benvenisti, *The International Law of Occupation*, 2nd ed. (Oxford: Oxford University Press, 2012), 70; David Kretzmer, *The Occupation of Justice: The Supreme Court of Israel and the Occupied Territories* (New York: SUNY Press, 2003), 73.

31. International Court of Justice, "Legal Consequences of the Construction of a Wall in the Occupied Palestinian Territory, Advisory Opinion," accessed August 8, 2016, http://www.icj-cij.org/docket/index.php?p1=3&p2=4&case=131&p3=4.

32. Ibid., 183–184. It should be mentioned that even the minority opinion given by Justice T. Buergenthal determined that the establishment of the settlements violates international law and that "it follows that the segments of the wall being built by Israel to protect the settlements are ipso facto in violation of international humanitarian law." Ibid., paragraph 9 of the dissenting opinion by Justice Thomas Buergenthal.

33. Statute of the International Court of Justice, June 26, 1945, *American Journal of International Law* 39 (Supp. 1945): 215.

34. HCJ 7957/04 Marabe v. The Government of Israel et al., PD 602, 477 at p. 523, hereinafter "Marabe Case."

35. Ibid.; see also Aeyal Gross, "The Construction of a Wall between the Hague and Jerusalem: The Enforcement and Limits of Humanitarian Law and the Structure of Occupation," *Leiden Journal of International Law* 26 (2006): 393–440.

36. Marabe Case, 498.

37. Krestzmer, *The Occupation of Justice*, 302–303. However, it should be mentioned that Prof. Kretzmer also criticized the International Court's different opinions, especially regarding the issue of the legitimate means to protect settlers' lives, regardless of the illegality of the settlements they live in, and even for the interim period until their evacuation.

38. Iyad Case.

39. *The Disengagement Plan from the Gaza Strip and Northern Samaria*, Cabinet Decision No. 1996, dated June 6, 2004.

40. *Implementation of the Disengagement Plan Act*, SH 1982, February 18, 2005, 141.

41. HCJ 1661/05 Gaza Coast Local Council v. Knesset (2005) PD 592, 481, Articles 15 and 119 of the leading judgment given by Chief Justice A. Barak. It is interesting that the court did not reject the petitions based on the argument that the issue is mainly political by its nature or on grounds of inadmissibility, like its previous judgments regarding the establishment of settlements. The court ruled that a decision to cancel the Israeli presence and domination in the area is soaked with national and security considerations, but since such a decision and the statutory framework that governs the evacuation also include other aspects of human rights violations, there is no ground for dismissing the petition as inadmissible. Ibid., at articles 73–75.

42. Talia Sasson, *Report Regarding Unauthorized Outposts*, March 2005, 20, hereinafter "Sasson Report." These four criteria were set for the first time by the Supreme Court, HCJ 5834/04 Amana et. al v. the Government of Israel et al. (2004) PD 59 2, 289.

43. HCJ 8287/98 Raz et al. v. Minister of Defense et al., unpublished; judgment from December 9, 1999.

44. Shlomo Tzezna, "Ten Families and Tank: A Profile of an Outpost," *Ma'ariv*, June 29, 2001.

45. See Sasson Report.

46. Ibid.

47. HCJ 6431/02 Hess et. Al v. the Government of Israel et al., unpublished; judgment from December 2, 2012.

48. Ibid.

49. Anat Roth, *Not for Any Price: From Gush Katif to Amona, the Story behind the Struggle for Eretz Israel*, in Hebrew (Yediot Ahronot Publishers House, 2014).

50. HCJ 6357/05 Peace Now v. Minister of Defense et al., unpublished, judgment given January 18, 2006.

51. HCJ 851/06 Amona Agricultural Cooperation et al. v. Minister of Defense et al., unpublished, judgment given on January 29, 2006; 1019/06 Mateh Binyamin Regional Council et al. v. Government of Israel et al., unpublished, judgment given on February 1, 2006.

52. HCJ 9051/05 Peace Now et al. v. Minister of Defense et al., petition filed in November 2005, judgment given on August 20, 2014, hereinafter "Haresha Case."

53. Haresha Case, decision given on July 12, 2009.

54. State updated in the Haresha Case, dated November 26, 2008.

55. HCJ 2295/09 Fadie'h v. Minister of Defense et al., judgment given on July 31, 2013.

56. HCJ 2962/11 Abed-EL-Jalil et al. v. Minister of Defense et al., judgment given on November 7, 2012.

57. HCJ 3091/11 Hareb et al. v. Minister of Defense et al., judgment given on September 20, 2012.

58. A decision given by the Ministerial Team headed by the prime minister, dated April 24, 2012.

59. Ulpana Case.

60. Prime Minister Netanyahu declared that "every house that will be evacuated will lead to the new building of 10 new houses." Quoted in Chaim Levinson, Barak Ravid, and Yehonatan Liss, "Netanyahu Considers Removing the *Ulpana* Houses; Official in the Ministry of Defense Argues That It Is Impossible," *Haaretz*, June 2, 2012.

61. HCJ 8887/06 *El*-Nabouth et al. v. Minister of Defense et al., petition filed in October 2006, judgment given on August 2, 2011, hereinafter "Migron Case."

62. Preliminary Response by the State in the Migron Case, December 17, 2006, available in English at http://peacenow.org.il/eng/sites/default/files/Migron_Petition_Eng_StateRespons_Dec2006.pdf/

63. Updated Responses by the State on the Migron Case, February 2, 2009, and June 28, 2009.

64. HCJ 8815/10 Bisharat et al. v. Sub-Committee for Settlement in the Supreme Planning Committee in the Civil Administration et al., judgment given on May 5, 2011.

65. *Military Order for Authorizing the Establishment without the Need for Licensee regarding Temporary Housing Sites with regional Importance*, Interim Order (Judea and Samaria) No. 1695, 2012.

66. HCJ 6130/12 Regional Council of the Village Michmas et al. v. Minister of Defense et al., judgment given on November 8, 2012.

67. HCJ 5180/12 Yehoshua Set et al. v. Minister of Defense et al., judgment given on August 29, 2012; HCJ 3905/14 El Wattan Inc. v. Minister of Defense et al., judgment given on January 6, 2015.

68. Shlomy Zachary, "Stating the Obvious: Ideological Criminality in Migron," *JURIST* 4 (September 2011), http://jurist.org/sidebar/2011/09/shlomy-zachary-migron-ruling.php.

69. Talia Sasson, *On the Brink of the Abyss: Is the Triumph of the Settlemetns the End of Israeli Democracy*, in Hebrew, (Keter Publishing House, 2015), 67–68.

70. Ibid., 71–74.

71. State response from October 19, 2010, in a petition filed by Peace Now demanding the evacuation of six outposts in the West Bank. HCJ 7891/07 Peace Now et al. v. Minister of Defense et al.

72. The idea behind this path of thought was that in exchange for freezing the building in the settlements and evacuating outposts, the United States would be more tough and aggressive with Iran's nuclear program, and maybe would turn a blind eye toward any Israeli attacks on Iranian nuclear facilities. See "Barack Obama on Brink of Deal for Middle East Peace Talks," *Guardian*, August 25, 2009, available at http://www.theguardian.com/world/2009/aug/25/barack-obama-middle-east-peace; Aluf Ben, "US to Cut a Deal: A Permit for Israeli Attack in Iran for Settlement Freeze-Out," *Ha'artez*, August 28, 2009.

73. HCJ 5023/08 Shehada et al. v. Minister of Defense et al., judgment given on February 8, 2015, hereinafter "Ofra Case."

74. State response in Ofra Case, October 25, 2009.

75. Ofra Case, paragraph 16.

76. See Ido Tamari, "Homesick for Nine Houses: On Masquerade, Property Rights and Rule of Law following HCJ 5023/08 Shehade v. Minister of Defense," in Hebrew*Hamishpat Online—Human Rights* 43 (May 2015): 5–16, in Hebrew, https://www.colman.ac.il/sites/college.stage.linnovate.net/files/43_may_2015_5_tamari.pdf.

77. Nahum Barn'ea, "The Holy Concrete," *Yediot Ahronot*, July 29, 2015.

78. HCJ 9949/09 Miryam Hammed et al. v. The Minister of Defense et al., judgment given on December 25, 2014.

79. HCJ 9949/08, request by the State from 30 October; see also Tovah Lazaroff, "State to Ask Court to Delay Amona Evacuation," *Jerusalem Post*, October 13, 2016.

80. HCJ 794/17 Wae'l Ziada et al. v. IDF Commander in the West Bank et al., petition filed on January 23, 2017; see also Barak Ravid, "MFA: Relocating Amona to Abandoned Palestinian Lands Will Damage Israel in the International Arena," *Ha'aretz*, October 30, 2016.

81. HCJ 794/17 Ziada Case, judgment from February 1, 2017.

82. Barak Ravid, "Israel Approves First New West Bank Settlement in Over 20 Years for Amona Evacuees," *Ha'aretz*, March 31, 2017.

83. The Judea and Samaria Settlement Regulation Law, S.H. 2604, February 13, 2017.

84. "Britain Joins International Condemnation of Israel's Settlement Law," *Telegraph*, February 7, 2017; Barak Ravid, "Germany's Merkel Cancels Summit with Israel in Wake of Palestinian Land-Grab Law," *Ha'artez*, February 13, 2017; Elior Levy, "France to Israel: Cancel the Regularization Law, It leads to Annexation," Ynet News, February 7, 2017; Elior Levy, "The EU Condemns Israel Due to Regularization Law: 'It Crosses Dangerous Line That Will Lead to One State,'" Ynet News, February 7, 2017.

85. HCJ 2055/17 Mayor of Ein Yabroud et al. v. Knesset et al., filed on March 5, 2017. The attorney general has declared that since the law is illegal and unconstitutional, he will not defend it and will not represent the government in the coming hearings. See Tamar Pileggi, "Attorney General Won't Defend Contentious Outpost Law in Court," *Times of Israel*, March 1, 2017.

86. See, for example, HCJ 6821/09 Peace Now et al. v. Minister of Defense et al., judgment given on October 24, 2011, in which following a petition asking for enforcement regarding twelve houses, it has been decided to promote a new master plan for the entire settlement; the abovementioned cases in HCJ 2295/09, HCJ 2962/11 and HCJ 3091/09, which led to a decision on the establishment of three new settlements; HCJ 1813/11 Peace Now et al v. Minister of Defense et al., judgment given on October 5, 2011, regarding the outpost of Shvut Rachel, which led to the annexation of the outpost to the nearby settlement of Shilo and legalized the entire illegal building that was within its boundaries; and HCJ 3047/11 Iyad et al v. Minister of Defense et al., judgment given on June 27, 2013, which challenged parts of the illegal building in the settlement of Ofra and led in the end of it all to the approval of the settlement's jurisdiction and master plan, for the first time since it has been erected.

87. See HCJ 8171/09 The Mayor of the Village El-Jania v. the Supreme Planning Council in the Civil Administration et. al., judgment given on November 20, 2011; HCJ 7590/14 Bimkom—Planners for Human Rights in Planning v. Sub Committee for Opposing for Master Plans in the Supreme Planning Committee in the Civil Administration et al., judgment given on August 10, 2015.

88. Aharon Barak, "On Law, Judging and Truth," *Mishpatim, the Hebrew University Law Review* 28 (1995).

89. See Migron Case; Ofra Case; Ulpana Case; see also the analysis of Sher and Ofek, "Dividing the Land, Not the People."

90. Sasson, *On the Brink of the Abyss*, 129–137.

91. See *A performance-based roadmap to a permanent two-state solution to the Israeli-Palestinian conflict*, April 30, 2003 (available at: https://2001-2009.state.gov/r/pa/prs/ps/2003/20062.htm); Letter From Dov Weisglass to NSA Condoleezza Rice, April 19, 2004, available at: https://www.haaretz.com/1.4782863.

92. According to a report published by the Israeli NGO Yesh Din in March 2015, "since 2011, alongside the official, well-known track for government approval and advancement of building plans in the settlements, Israel has been advancing the establishment of new settlements and expanding the areas under its control in the West Bank using a secret parallel track of retroactively approving dozens of illegal outposts, sparing no effort along the way. Currently, approximately a quarter of the outposts (25 out of about 100 outposts in the

West Bank) have either been approved or are undergoing approval processes, pursued under government instructions." See Yesh Din and The Rights Forum, *Under the Radar*.

93. The official data backing these assumptions: according to the Israeli Central Chamber of Statistics, in 1992 there were approximately 90,000 settlers in the West Bank; in 2004 there approximately 240,000 settlers in the West Bank; and in 2015 there were approximately 400,000 settlers.

94. Ulpana Case and HCJ 1217/15.

95. Sasson Report.

96. See, for example, The Geneva Initiative, "An Israeli-Palestinian Initiative."

97. Recently it has been disclosed by the state archives that the "settlements blocks" were an official goal promoted by Israeli governments: after the Elon Moreh Case, in a cabinet meeting, a map of a "desirable" West Bank was presented by some of the ministers in the cabinet "The Elon Moreh Case: Responses and Reactions within the Government of Israel to the Judgement Given on 22 October, 1979," Israeli State Archives, published on October 16, 2012, in Hebrew, http://www.archives.gov.il/ArchiveGov/pirsumyginzach/HistoricalPublications/ElonMore/. This map contained several visual definitions of "blocks" for settlements. Comparing this map with the current geographical spread of the settlements and outposts reflects that this goal has been achieved, more or less. On the critical approach regarding these blocks, their developments and their potential influence, see Shaul Arieli, "Abandon the Blocks' Fixation," *Haaretz*, March 10, 2016.

98. Shaul Arieli and Michael Sfard, *The Wall of Folly*, in Hebrew (Tel Aviv: Yediot Ahronot, 2008).

99. See, for example, HCJ 2732/05 The Mayor of the Municipality of Azun et al. v. The Government of Israel et al., judgment given on June 15, 2006; HCJ 8414/05 Yasin et al. v. The Government of Israel et al., judgment given on September 4, 2007.

100. See the Marabe Case.

101. Israeli Ministry of Foreign Affairs, *Unofficial Summary of State of Israel's Response Regarding the Security Fence*, February 28, 2005, http://mfa.gov.il/MFA/AboutIsrael/State/Law/Pages/Summary%20of%20Israels%20Response%20regarding%20the%20Security%20Fence%2028-Feb-2005.aspx. For criticism of this point of view and response, see Yuval Shany, "Head Against the Wall? Israel's Rejection of the Advisory Opinion on the Legal Consequences of the Construction of a Wall in the Occupied Palestinian Territories," *Yearbook of International Humanitarian Law* 7 (2004): 352–372.

102. It should be mentioned, however, that following the International Court Advisory Opinion and the Supreme Court rulings regarding the separation barrier, the route of the wall has been changed due to some of these rulings.

103. A/HRC/RES/19/17, "Israeli Settlements in the Occupied Palestinian Territory, Including East Jerusalem, and in the Occupied Syrian Golan," April 10, 2012, http://daccess-dds-ny.un.org/doc/RESOLUTION/GEN/G12/130/13/PDF/G1213013.pdf?OpenElement.

104. *Report of the Independent International Fact-Finding Mission to Investigate the implications of the Israeli Settlements on the Civil, Political, Economic, Social and Cultural rights of the Palestinian People throughout the Occupied Palestinian Territory, Including East Jerusalem*, http://www.ohchr.org/Documents/HRBodies/HRCouncil/RegularSession/Session19/FFM/FFMSettlements.pdf.

105. Ibid., paragraphs no. 100–111.

106. Ibid., paragraphs no. 112–119.

107. *Report on the Legal Status of Building in Judea and Samaria*, published July 9, 2012 ("the Levy Report"); its goals were to examine ways to sanction illegal construction in the outposts and other contiguous issues. This report drew huge criticism: Juan Pedro Schaerer, "The Levy Report v. International Law," *Haaretz*, November 4, 2012; Frances Raday and Ido Rosenzweig, "The Status of the West Bank Settlements under International Law: A Review of the Conclusions of the Levy Committee," The Israel Democratic Institute, August 15, 2012, http://en.idi.org.il/analysis/articles/the-status-of-the-west-bank-settlements-under-international-law/; Yesh Din, *Unprecedented: A Legal Analysis of the Report of the Committee to Examine the Status of Building in Judea and Samaria (the Levy Committee)*, May 19, 2014, http://www.yesh-din.org/postview.asp?postid=278.

108. United Nations Security Council Resolution No. 2334, Adopted by the Security Council at its 7853rd meeting, December 23, 2016, S/RES/2334 (2016), http://undocs.org/S/RES/23342016.

109. See "Recent Resolutions," *Harvard Law Review* 130, 2269.

110. "Palestine Declares Acceptance of ICC Jurisdiction since 13 June 2014," International Criminal Court Press Release, January 5, 2015, https://www.icc-cpi.int/en_menus/icc/press%20and%20media/press%20releases/Pages/pr1080.aspx.

111. Article 82)b)viii) of the Rome Statute states as follows:
> For the purpose of this Statute, "war crimes" means: . . .
>
> b) Other serious violations of the laws and customs applicable in international armed conflict, within the established framework of international law, namely, any of the following acts:
>
> . . .
>
> viii) The transfer, directly or indirectly, by the Occupying Power of parts of its own civilian population into the territory it occupies, or the deportation or transfer of all or parts of the population of the occupied territory within or outside this territory.

112. Pnina Sharvit-Baruch, "The Regularization Law and the Role of the Legal System," *INSS Insigh*, no. 894, February 10, 2017; Barak Ravid and Chaim Levinson, "Netanyahu Warns Cabinet: Outpost Legalization Bill Could Lead to International Probe Against Israeli Officials," *Ha'aretz*, November 28, 2016; Yonah Jeremy Bob, "Dershowitz: ICC Will Go After Israel if Settlement Bill Passes," *Jerusalem Post*, December 16, 2016.

113. Ulpana Case, hearing from September 21, 2011.

SHLOMY ZACHARY is an Israeli lawyer, representing domestic and international human rights and peace organizations, and works in the areas of International Law and International Humanitarian Law.

4

THE AMERICAN JEWISH DIASPORA AS A SPOILER

Ofira Seliktar

Introduction

In the first decades of Israel's existence, the American Jewish community was fully mobilized to defend the new state. This unquestioning and unflinching loyalty inspired scholars to describe the relations as a model of diaspora–home country linkage. By early 1980s, the right-wing shift in Israeli foreign policy created cracks in the relationship. Initially, only marginal left-wing groups voiced their condemnation of Israel's occupation of the Palestinians and its conduct in the first Lebanon war. Following the First Intifada in the late 1980s and early 1990s, more mainstream sectors of the community joined in the criticism. This prompted the leading communal organizations to try to restore the perception of model unity, a task that proved a failure as American Jewry split along the same fault lines as the home country. The left and liberal wings of the Diaspora supported reaching a peace agreement with the Palestinians while the right wing and the Orthodox segments vehemently objected to giving up territory.

Not surprisingly, the decision of the Labor government of Yitzhak Rabin to embrace the Oslo peace process exhilarated the former and embittered the latter. More astounding, however, was the fact that opponents of Oslo turned into spoilers of the peace process. That a relatively small and marginal sector of the community, estimated at some 10 percent, emerged as a full-fledged peace spoiler reflected the paradigmatic shift in the relations between the community and Israel.

The Demise of the "Sacred Unity": From Mobilization to Direct Engagement

Shortly after the creation of the State of Israel, mainstream American Jews adopted the so-called mobilization model of diaspora-homeland relations. Israel was said to form the core of the modern American Jewish identity, a virtual "civil religion" for the secular and assimilation-prone Jews. To put it differently, defending the Jewish state from its many enemies was said to strengthen Jewish identity and prevent out-marriage and other forms of ethnic defection. Many described the relation as a "sacred unity," a theme that Melvin I. Urofsky, a noted scholar, celebrated in his popular book, *We Are One!: American Jewry and Israel*.[1] The organizational infrastructure of relations with Israel reflected the mobilization model. To amply the voice of American Jewish advocacy, a large number of smaller groups consolidated into the umbrella group of the Conference of Presidents of the Major Jewish Organizations in 1956, and the American-Israel Political Affairs Committee (AIPAC) was incorporated in 1963. These two so-called defense organizations dealt with all issues pertaining to Israel, and AIPAC assumed the role of the official lobby in Congress.

But the postmodern dynamics in the community had eroded the mobilization model and its top-to-bottom command structure. The sociologist Pierre Bourdieu theorized that in the postmodern period diasporans organize their relations to the homeland in distinctive fields, each creating its own organizations, professional networks, and communication channels. Most important, the new paradigm emphasized direct engagement that bypassed or defied the central defense institutions. In the words of one analyst, "the centralized, consensus-oriented advocacy and philanthropy model is weakening. American Jews directly connect to Israel by expressing their political views, and targeting donations for their favorite cause."[2] While the Conference and AIPAC were still standing, they were flanked by the "sentinels" of the right and the left wing, a configuration that turned them into an arena of dissention and ugly public squabbling.

If the postmodern, direct-engagement model explained the emergence of the peace spoilers, old fashioned wheeling and dealing played a role as well. Settlers raised funds in the United States, and Likud politicians tried to review the tiny network of Revisionist stalwarts. During his years as Israel's ambassador to the United Nations, the American-educated Benjamin Netanyahu created an extensive network of donors and activists. In the early 1990s, visits by right-wing Israeli politicians became de rigueur.

The pace accelerated after Israel and the Palestinians signed the Declaration of Principles (DOP) in the White House on September 13, 1993. A few days later, Netanyahu, by then the head of Likud, traveled to the United States to rally opposition against the agreement, followed by settlers and other Israeli opponents of the deal.

But Netanyahu's bold proclamation that "I will lobby [against Oslo] in America and American Jews will lobby in Israel" was more rhetoric than reality.[3] Polls of the Jewish community conducted at the time indicated an overwhelming support for the DOP. A survey of the American Jewish Committee (AJC) found that 84 percent of the respondents backed the agreement, and only 9 percent opposed it. Sixty-four percent believed that Oslo would lead to a Palestinian state, and some 57 percent favored such an option. Many commentators noted that for the dominant liberal sector, the peace accord came as a great relief. After years of dissonance created by Likud's policies in the occupied territories, the "community could embrace the Jewish state without compromising either their liberalism or their fealty to Israel."[4] With communal sentiments overwhelmingly in favor of peace, it was imperative for the right wing to translate their misgivings into action.

The Spoiler's Coalition: Advocates of Greater Israel and Warriors against Armageddon

Steven Stedman suggested that those with deeply held beliefs and a matching commitment should be considered total spoilers. By all accounts this category fits the religious and secular-nationalist components of the spoilers' coalition.[5]

The religious spoilers encompassed the entire Orthodox spectrum—the Union of the Orthodox Jewish Congregations in America, the Rabbinical Council of America (RCA), Agudat Israel, Young Israel, the Rabbinical Alliance of America (RAA), and the Chabad-Lubavitch Hasidim, among others. Taking an early lead, on September 19, 1993, the National Council of Young Israel decided to launch a major struggle against the Oslo process. The Lubavitch followed up with a multi-million-dollar campaign of their own. Many Orthodox Jews withdrew their donations to the American Jewish Appeal, the umbrella group of American Jewry, in order to contribute to settlement-oriented charities like Operation Hizuk and the Committee for the Preservation of the Holy Land, One Israel Fund/Yesha Hartland Campaign, Operation Kiryat Arba, and the Jerusalem Reclamation Project.

As Orthodox Jews saw it, the land-for-peace Oslo formula was a huge affront to the sanctity of *Eretz Israel*. But the perceived threat of giving up the West Bank was also personal, since some 15 percent of the settlers were Orthodox American Jews. The journalist Yakov Kornreich wrote of the horror of watching "as the homes of 130,000 Jews [in the territories] were, potentially, signed away with a stroke of pen."[6] Rabbi Moshe Gorelick, president of the RCA, explained that Labor policies were putting Jewish settlers at a grave risk. Just six days after the White House ceremony, on September 19, an emergency meeting of East Coast rabbis organized by the National Council of Young Israel launched a call to defeat Oslo. In February 1994 the Orthodox community organized a large rally in New York under the slogan "adopt a settlement." Local synagogues were encouraged to form an alliance with a settlement and, by implication, protect it from the dangers of Oslo.[7]

Rabbi Abraham Hecht, a prominent leader in the community and the president of the RAA, went further. Quoting Maimonides's Code of Jewish Law, Hecht proclaimed that Rabin may have been the cause of Jews murdered in the territories; as one responsible for the shedding of Jewish blood, he could be declared a *rodeph*—a person who was likely to be executed during the Jewish kingdom. In August 1995 he published a letter to American rabbis in the *Jewish Press,* an Orthodox publication in New York, reiterating that "the Torah permits the most extreme action against those who harm our fellow Jews." He repeated the statement in an interview with *New York* magazine in October. The magazine pointed out that "Hecht's is not the voice of a lone, crazy extremist, but that of one of a growing chorus of Jewish militants who have crossed the line of legitimate debate and dissent into calls for violence—and into violence itself."[8]

While the secular spoilers were less cohesive, they were equally vehement in denouncing the alleged ills of Oslo. Americans for Safe Israel (AFSI) was created in 1971 by Herbert Zweibon, a self-proclaimed disciple of Zeev Jabotinsky, and Shmuel Katz, one of the founders of the Herut party and the Movement for Greater Israel. Katz, who served as an adviser for information abroad in the government of Menachem Begin, used AFSI to publicize Revisionist ideas in America, positioning the group for an early opposition to Oslo. Less than a month after the White House ceremony, on October 10, 1993, Zweibon organized the American Leadership Conference for a Safe Israel. In an opening statement, he paraphrased President Roosevelt: "Thirteen of September is a date that will live in infamy. A great people prostrated themselves before a thug."[9] Bernard J. Shapiro founded the Freeman Center for Strategic Studies in Houston in 1992; the *Maccabean*, its online publication, opposed territorial concessions to the Palestinians. The Zionist Organization of America (ZOA) under the leadership of Morton Klein had emerged as a leading member of the total spoilers.

Three themes united the secular spoilers. The security threat posed by the potential creation of a Palestinian state formed the first theme. Israel's tenuous geopolitical position, the strategic shortcoming of the Green Line border, and the fragility of its existence were constantly emphasized. The notion that the Oslo formula of land for peace was untenable because the Palestinians were not reliable partners informed the second theme. As Zweibon contended, "The 'land for peace' concept is rooted in the reliability of Arab promises. Israel is the only party that is being pressed to make physical concessions, that is, the surrender of vital territory. The Arabs are expected to make verbal concessions, in the form of promises to be peaceful."[10]

Arguably the American Jewish spoilers were not the only ones to voice concerns, but before Arafat won a landslide election (to head the Palestinian Authority) in 1996, terrorism did not feature prominently in the discourse. Oslo supporters were willing to give the PA chief the benefit of the doubt and assume that he could not control the violent dissenters. But as the level of terror had grown, doubts about the reliability of the Palestinians had increased too. Many skeptics on both sides of the Atlantic struggled with the same issue but, eager to achieve peace, were willing to hope for the best.

For the spoilers, however, those who tended to frame the entire conflict as a zero-sum game, experienced a lack of hope. In this narrative Yasser Arafat was an unreconstructed terrorist, who, having failed in his terrorist strategy, switched to the alternative peace strategy to weaken Israel from within. According to this so-called Trojan Horse theory, the territories regained from Israel would be used to build a Palestinian state on the ruins of the Jewish one. In the words of one analyst, "The hallmark of right-wing discourse, in the focus groups, was its utter rejection of the possibility of reaching a secure, enforceable, and reliable settlement."[11]

The third theme was built around the apocalyptic-sounding argument that the Arabs in general and the Palestinians in particular were committed to physically eliminating Israel from the Middle East. Using infamous Arab statements about "pushing the Jews into the sea," secular spoilers warned that Oslo would lead to an inevitable Armageddon. By framing their opposition in security terms, the nationalist spoilers could describe their actions as saving Israel from a catastrophe akin to a new Holocaust.

Dramatic claims aside, spoilers need a range of capabilities to effectively undermine the process they target. Arguably, the most important was funding, as neither of the religious or secular sectors could compete with the wealth of the mainstream Jewish establishment.

Funding the Spoiler Coalition: The Right-Wing Donors Club

Both the religious and secular rejectionists could count on a number of dedicated donors to sponsor their activities. Irving I. Moskowitz, a philanthropist who sponsored settlement activities, especially in East Jerusalem, emerged as a leading donor. His Irving I. Moskowitz Foundation contributed to AFSI, the Freeman Center, and the ZOA, among others. Moskowitz once described the peace process as a "slide toward concession, surrender, and Israeli suicide" and compared Rabin to Chamberlain. Rose Mattus of the Haagen-Dazs ice cream fortune was another important donor. She stated that "everything changed when Yitzhak Rabin signed the Oslo accord." Describing it as an "act of appeasement," she added that "American Jews had learned from the Holocaust [that appeasement] is the sure road to war." Mattus sat on the board of the ZOA, and Klein supported her candidacy to the World Zionist Congress. Not incidentally, Mattus was close to the Likud leader Benjamin Netanyahu, who befriended her and her husband while serving as Israel's envoy in the United States. Sam Domb, a New York–based businessman and philanthropist with close ties to the Chabad-Lubavitch Hasidim, was a veteran Likud supporter. His distaste for the Oslo process was palatable, leading him to personal attacks on its leaders. Domb described Rabin as "a man seemingly devoid of honor, self-respect, compassion, common sense and a sense of history" who was "spiritually destroying the Jewish people." Morris Baily, another businessmen-philanthropist based in New York, had close ties with the Syrian Jewish community in Brooklyn and one of its leaders, Jack Avital. Like Domb, Baily took a dim view of the peace process.[12]

Manfred R. Lehmann, a Miami-based businessman, philanthropist, and scholar, was an early opponent of the peace process who called Rabin and his Labor colleagues "mischief makers." Lehmann wrote that "if Rabin continues to put Jewish lives at risk, delivers Israel to the PLO, and dismantles Israel, he may end up being compared with French hero Marshal

Philippe Petain, who saved France in World War I, but betrayed France by delivering his country to Hitler and the Nazis." Morton Klein gave Lehmann an honorary position for his contribution to the ZOA. Lehmann was the founder of the World Committee for Israel (WCI), which was heavily involved in advertising against Oslo and organizing rallies. On December 13, 1993, in a rally sponsored by WCI and attended by Domb and Hecht, some participants described Rabin as "Hitler" and demanded that he be killed.[13]

In what was a classic force multiplier, the contribution of major donors helped to establish a large number of groups that one observer described as "letterheads and advertising budgets and nothing else." In addition to the WCI, the Coalition for Secure US-Israel Friendship, Pro-Israel, and Jewish War Veteran of America, among others, created the impression of a large grassroots presence and solicited for donations in national and local venues.[14] Making their opposition to the peace agreement in paid advertisements, conferences, and public rallies was only one way to demonstrate capability. Another highly effective way to undermine the peace process was lobbying Congress.

Fighting Oslo in Washington: Congress as a Battleground

For virtually all of its existence, the Conference of Presidents and AIPAC were careful not to violate their two rules: present a unified voice of the community in Congress and support the elected government of Israel. To lobby for Israeli opposition parties was unthinkable, and openly dissenting from the policy of an elected government was, in the words of one observer, "sordidly painful."[15]

But the deep schism created by Oslo trumped this self-imposed rule. Leading the way, the ZOA launched a separate lobbying effort in Congress that, in effect, contradicted the policy of the Rabin government. Klein was among the first to reach out to the segment of the Evangelical community, whose support for the State of Israel is grounded in dispensationalist theology. Known as Christian Zionists, they have created several "defense" organizations in the United States under the leadership of prominent Evangelical leaders like John Hagee, Pat Robertson, and Jerry Falwell. Christians United for Israel (CUFI), Unity Coalition for Israel, and others were behind the Third International Christian Zionists Congress in 1996 that came out against giving back land and recognizing a Palestinian state.

The poor record of Palestinian compliance with the Oslo provisions gave the spoilers an opening to paint Arafat as a convert to public diplomacy who had learned to appease his interlocutors in English, while making radical statements in Arabic. Likud activists obtained tapes of the PLO chief praising jihadists, which were disseminated in the United States. In addition, on December 13, 1994, the Israeli Defense Force (IDF) Advocate-General Office released a sixteen-page report listing dozens of violations of the DOP by the Palestinian Authority (PA). Citing these and other incidents of noncompliance, the spoilers urged Congress to stop the Clinton administration's funding of the PA, a key element in the ongoing peace negotiations. Klein persuaded Senator Arlen Specter, a Republican from Pennsylvania, to include compliance as a condition for funding. Cosponsored by the Democratic senator from Alabama, Richard Shelby, the Spector-Shelby amendment to the Foreign Aid Act took effect on July 29, 1994. Specter went on to cochair the ZOA-inspired Peace Accord Monitoring Group (PAM) in the Senate. Congress added the compliance provision to the PA aid, stipulating that the PA needed to be certified as compliant with the 1993 agreement or risk having its aid cut.[16]

In yet another clever maneuver, the spoilers launched a campaign to relocate the American embassy from Tel Aviv to Jerusalem. Jerusalem was a highly sensitive issue in the negotiations with Arafat, and both the Rabin government and the Clinton administration felt that such a hugely symbolic step would complicate matters. But the spoilers calculated that Rabin would be in no position to oppose the initiative in public and, with the help of Likud operatives in the United States, pushed the issue. American domestic politics played into their hands. Anticipating a presidential run against Clinton, Senator Bob Dole signed on to the initiative, helped by Newt Gingrich, then Speaker of the House. Although Martin Indyk, the American ambassador to Israel, warned that the move would "explode the peace process," Congress passed the Jerusalem Embassy Act in November 1995, but allowed for a loophole that enabled the White House to postpone the actual transfer of the embassy as part of the presidential foreign policy prerogative.[17]

The Oslo Custodians versus the Diaspora Spoilers: The Limits of Influence

As the custodians of the Oslo project, it was up to the Israeli Labor Party to offer a response. Having read the opinion polls showing widespread support for Oslo, Labor was taken by surprise by the vehemence of the protest. Belatedly, it created an "American desk" to oversee the outreach to the Jewish community. Yet Rabin and his colleagues had few options to thwart the spoiling efforts. Stedman had suggested using the strategy of convincing the spoilers to join the process. If this strategy failed, then one should try to marginalize them or use the defense organizations to discipline them.

Labor officials who traveled to the United States to calm the waters made virtually no impact on the rejectionists. In fact, these visits seemed to inflame their passions. Shimon Peres and Yossi Beilin, who were perceived as the true architects of the Oslo accords, were favorite targets. Peres was described as a "ridiculous buffoon" and a "hired defense attorney for Yasser Arafat." Beilin was depicted as a "flamboyant and reckless sloganeer and posturer." Shulamit Aloni, the Minister of Education from the leftist Meretz party, was allegedly physically assaulted when she tried to speak at an Israel Day Parade sponsored by the WCI. Itamar Rabinovitch, the Israeli ambassador to Washington, was heckled in some synagogues, and Colette Avital, Israel's counsel general in New York, was called a "traitor." More generally, the spoilers considered the narrow Oslo vote in the Knesset as suspect because the Arab parties supported it. Even though the Arabs were Israeli citizens, in their view, they did not have enough legitimacy to cast a ballot for an issue as weighty as Oslo.[18]

Attempts to marginalize the spoilers did not fare any better. Rabin called the Orthodox rabbis "ayatollahs" and disparaged the credentials of other critics to question his policies. In 1995, the prime minister singled out the spoilers when he complained, "Never before have we witnessed an attempt by US Jews to pressure Congress against the policies of a legitimate, democratically elected government." He described such attempts as unacceptable and "loathsome." AFSI's *Outpost* responded in kind, accusing Rabin of cowardice, alcoholism, and a lifetime "of psychological and military retreats." When a large group of Orthodox rabbis met in New York and issued a halachic ruling forbidding Israeli soldiers to withdraw from bases and settlements in the West Bank, Rabin lashed out, stating, "Those who don't send their sons and daughters to the army have no moral right to take action against the policy of a democratically elected government."[19]

Under normal circumstances, Labor's appeals to the Conference and AIPAC to curb the "privatization" of congressional lobbying would have been a logical step to take. But the hard-won coherence of the defense organizations had been gravely challenged by Oslo. Both forums were spilt between supporters and spoilers, making a consensual policy difficult to achieve. Although AIPAC picked Steve Grossman, a liberal Democrat, as its president in 1992, the pro-Likud faction—Larry Weinberg, Robert Asher, Edward Levy, and Meyer Mitchell—retained considerable power. The "gang of four," bolstered by Howard Khor, the managing director and a conservative Republican, overruled Grossman, who wanted to fight the "peace obstructions." Rabbi Alexander Schindler, the leader of the large Reform movement, complained in the *New York Times* that "unreconstructed hawks" in AIPAC did not support the peace process. In yet another sign of international strife, Thomas Dine, AIPAC's long-time executive director, was forced out in 1993, ostensibly because of a slur against Orthodox Jews reported by a journalist. His successor, Neal Sher, did not fare any better. He resigned after two years apparently because he was not "right-wing enough." Morton Klein, who had criticized Sher, welcomed his departure. Sher responded in the *Jerusalem Post* by calling Klein a "Jewish Thought Policeman."[20]

Still, the struggle to contain the divisions within AIPAC paled in comparison to the frenzied debates in the Conference. Some of the Conference members took issue with the ZOA ad in the *New York Times* criticizing the Israeli government. Lester Pollack, a past chair, stated, "It was outrageous and unacceptable . . . for a conference member to buy full-page ads . . . against the policy of Israel's government." ZOA's separate lobbying efforts, in conjunction with the Christian Zionists, were of particular concern. Malcom Hoenlein, the executive vice chairman, emphasized the danger of speaking with many voices, stating that the lawmakers "may just throw their hands up and say 'forget all of you clowns.'" But the ZOA refused to attend a special meeting with the Conference and AIPAC, exposing the defense organizations' failure to corral wayward actors.[21]

The Labor government and its supporters pressed Hoenlein to address the vilification of Israel and lack of civility during Conference meetings. He responded by drafting a statement on "civil discourse" to be signed by all fifty-two presidents, stating that "we are distressed . . . that irresponsible individuals and groups resort to name-calling, incitement, misinformation, and disinformation." Hoenlein added that "for four decades it has been the position of the Conference of Presidents that we support the democratically elected government of Israel. It is the people of Israel who have the right to make decisions that affect their lives and security." But several members refused to sign the document because of the "right to decide" reference; after another acrimonious debate, a much-diluted version was signed by fifty out of the fifty-two presidents. The final declaration spoke of "community and unity" and respect for "differences of view born of genuine concern."[22]

Far from being an exercise in semantics, the two versions of Hoenlein's draft attested to the real difficulties of the Oslo custodians in fighting the spoilers. By all accounts, the latter took it upon themselves to monitor the conduct of the Palestinians and the Israeli response to it. For instance, during a Conference meeting in Jerusalem, Morton Klein demanded to know why the government had not cracked down on Palestinian violations. This prompted a visibly irritated Beilin to respond, "It's none of your business.... It's none of AIPAC's business. It's none of Congress's business. It's the business of the government of Israel." Similarly, the "right to decide" phrase had been suggested by Rabinovitch at the request of the Labor government; when it failed, the dismayed ambassador stated that "we are the democratically elected government of Israel."[23]

But the Orthodox circles took exception to the view that a democratically elected government was entitled to give away the land. Drawing on what they saw as a divine mandate, they asserted that the land is under *Hashem*'s sovereignty, God's sovereignty. As a result, the "land is held in perpetuity as a covenant between G-d and Abraham and cannot be traded for some temporary false 'peace.' *Eretz Israel* belongs to the whole of Am Yisrael (People of Israel for all eternity)." Adding his considerable weight, the revered Lubavicher spiritual leader Rabbi Menachem Mendel Shneerson declared that the [Israeli] prime minister "has no right to give away the Land of Israel because it does not belong to him." Though the secular nationalists did not explicitly claim a divine mandate, ZOA, AFSI, and others were all too happy to agree with their Orthodox peers.[24]

Israeli officials found themselves stumped by what they considered outrageous interference in Israeli affairs. Ambassador Rabinovitch wryly noted that "from this novel perspective, the Land of Israel was no longer seen as a sovereign, unchallenged decision-maker. The land of Israel and Jerusalem were seen as the sacred property of the Jewish people, temporarily managed by the government of Israel." But, like the Labor officials who had arrived to sell the agreement to the spoilers, Rabinovitch made little headway. Routinely heckled and occasionally pelted with eggs and tomatoes when speaking to spoiler audiences, he was reduced to lobbying Congress members against the spoilers' legislative proposals.[25]

The assassination of Rabin by an Israeli nationalist in November 1995 delivered a temporary blow to the spoilers, but there was little healing between the rival camps. Rabbi Sholom Klass, the publisher of the *Jewish Press*, the Orthodox organ of Brooklyn, expressed sadness at the death of the prime minister, but added that "the peace process violates the commandments of our Holy Torah." When Israeli officials and propeace advocates organized a memorial service to the slain leader in Madison Square Garden, there was a real threat that it would be boycotted by the Orthodox and the secular right. Indeed, the ZOA and the Council for Young Israel took out an ad the *New York Times* complaining about the partisan nature of the event. Twelve former Conference chairs responded by calling the ad "unacceptable" and "censurable." After lengthy negotiations about the content of speeches, many in the Orthodox community attended, but ZOA and AFSI declined.[26]

Alignment and Misalignment: Between Benjamin Netanyahu and Ehud Barak

When Shimon Peres lost the election to Benjamin Netanyahu in May 1996, spoilers felt that their anti-Oslo stand had been vindicated. Morton Klein declared that Likud's 9 percent margin among Jewish voters proved that the ZOA "was representative of the Jewish mainstream all along." AFSI's *Outpost* described the result as a fulfillment of an "ardent hope." Freeman Center for Strategic Studies titled its editorial "Victory at Last—Israel Saved."[27]

Visiting in July, the newly elected prime minister declared that Israel was committed to the peace process, but he promised to hold the Palestinians accountable to the DOP. Speaking on behalf of the spoiler coalition, Klein expressed satisfaction that "Arafat's violation of the peace accords" would become a "central theme for achieving a real and durable peace." But the honeymoon between Netanyahu and the rejectionists proved short lived. In line with the Oslo timetable, in the fall of 1996 Israel entered negotiations on withdrawing the IDF from most of Hebron, a move that greatly displeased the right wing. During an October ZOA fundraiser, Eliyahu Ben Elissar, Netanyahu's new ambassador to Washington, was heckled for noting that under the DOP "not everything can be saved." Signed in January 1997, the Hebron Agreement ruffled the spoilers further. Activists protested outside the Israeli consulate in New York, demanding that the Likud reveal "its true self." The Freeman Center published an article asking, "How does a government, elected on a platform guaranteeing continued Jewish development in Hebron, literally strangle the existing Jewish community?!"[28]

Unhappiness with Netanyahu's performance on Hebron aside, the spoilers mobilized again to act against renewing aid to the PA under the Middle East Facilitation Act, due to expire in August 1997. This time around, the spoilers could produce a long list of noncompliance examples, starting with a string of ferocious suicide bombings that brought Israel to its knees. They publicized an audit on May 25, which indicated waste and corruption in the PA and pointed out that Arafat advocated imposing a death sentence on Palestinians selling land to Jews. Under a new version sponsored by Jesse Helms, the influential chair of the Senate Foreign Relations Committee, a number of stiff compliance conditions were added. The Clinton administration, the Labor government, and mainstream Jewish organizations pushed back, claiming that such steps would doom the peace process. The new legislation was defeated, but the intercommunal tension remained high. Anticipating a rancorous debate, the Conference decided to forgo a vote on the issue, but the general discourse was nothing but vitriolic. A widely publicized case involved Thomas Freedman, a *New York Times* columnist invited to address the ADL's annual dinner in December 1996. Morton Klein, who considered Tom Friedman a leading Oslo booster, called on ADL chief Abraham Foxman to cancel the speech. When the latter refused, Klein urged the Jewish public to protest, prompting Foxman to call Klein the "attack dog of the thought police."[29]

Shocking as this exchange was, it was just a prelude to what turned into a virtual guerilla war between the Oslo boosters and the rejectionists over the next phase of the peace negotiations. The rejectionists were infuriated by the administration's efforts to push the reluctant Netanyahu to give up more territory. They attacked US secretary of state Madeleine Albright (who made a number of trips to Israel to pressure Netanyahu) and Martin Indyk, by then assistant secretary of state for Near East affairs. The ZOA criticized Indyk's "insulting, demeaning, and patronizing statements about Israel" and his alleged eagerness to twist Netanyahu's arm. Oslo advocates responded by encouraging more pressure by the administration. The New York–based liberal Israel Policy Forum (IPF) defended Indyk as a "devoted public servant," and Americans for Peace Now (APN) thanked him for showing concern on behalf of Israel. S. Daniel Abraham, a top Democratic donor, urged Clinton to press the Israeli government for more concessions. Prior to one of Albright's visit to Jerusalem, forty prominent Jewish leaders, including Alexander Schindler, Eric Yoffie, and Ismar Schorsch, issued a statement to the same effect.[30]

Taking a page from the spoilers' playbook, peace activists targeted Irving Moskowitz, who had increased his profile by sponsoring a group buying up property in the Muslim Quarter in East Jerusalem. In December 1996, CBS's *60 Minutes* ran an expose on Moskowitz, prompting some peace activists to call for a formal investigation. They pointed out that much of the money came from the Bingo Club in Hawaiian Gardens, an impoverished Latino neighborhood in California. Rabbi Gerald Serota, the head of a Coalition for Justice in Hawaiian Gardens and Jerusalem, noted that most of the funds from the bingo operation went overseas "to do damage to the Jewish people and the future of Israel." The Central Conference of American Rabbis (CCAR), the organizational arm of the Reform movement, issued a scathing condemnation of the use of gambling money to fund "activities that cause agitation and threaten peace in the holy city of Jerusalem."[31]

The spoilers' growing alliance with Christian Zionists was another bone of contention between the two camps. By the time Netanyahu came to power, the modest outreach to the Evangelicals initiated by the ZOA had blossomed into a powerful political alliance against Clinton. In April 1997 Netanyahu addressed some three thousand Christian Zionists at the annual conference of Voices United for Israel. The organizing committee featured Pat Robertson, Jerry Falwell, Ralph Reed, and other leading figures of the Evangelical movement. When in January 1998 Netanyahu snubbed Clinton by visiting Falwell immediately on his arrival, the mainstream community took it as a personal affront. Foxman implied that some of Falwell's pronouncements were either anti-Semitic or "crude." Using the anniversary of the Oslo agreement, on September 13, 1998, more than four hundred representatives from a variety of Jewish groups joined Rabin's widow, Leah, to pledge their steadfast support for the peace process.[32]

Reassured by the support of the mainstream Jewish community, the Clinton administration forced the reluctant Netanyahu to proceed with the Oslo process. The Wye Memorandum signed on October 23, 1998, obligated Israel to withdraw from additional territory in exchange for a Palestinian promise to curtail terrorism and stop incitement. Oslo boosters were elated; the Jewish Council for Public Affairs (JCPA), a coordinating body for a large number of Jewish organizations, described the Wye accord as "an important achievement . . . [that] renews our hope that the ultimate vision of Oslo . . . can yet be realized."[33]

What delighted the peace camp, however, displeased the spoilers. Even before Wye, a group calling itself Israel Support Network placed an advertisement in the *New York Post* warning Netanyahu not to give up land. It described any withdrawal as a "fundamental breach of trusts"—a trust placed on him by "Republicans in Congress, the fundamentalist Christians and 2 million right-wing American Jews." Echoing the earlier campaign against Rabin, three prominent Orthodox rabbis, Aaron Soloveichik, Moshe Tendler, and Herschel Reichman, stated in a *New York Post* ad that Jewish law prohibits the ratification of an agreement that gives up land. AFSI and the Freeman Center joined Joseph Frager from the Jerusalem Reclamation Project to call for political change in the Likud. As Frager put it, the new leadership needs to "be loyal to the Jewish people, to the land of Israel, and the Torah of Israel." According to some sources, Moskovitz was ready to finance seven Likud members who broke with Netanyahu, as they looked to create a new right-wing party.[34]

In the end, however, plans to unseat Netanyahu proved unnecessary. Plagued by internal division and defection by coalition partners, the government collapsed in December 1998. In the May 1999 elections, Labor, under Ehud Barak, another military hero, won the election. In a repeat of the previous cycles, the peace camp was elated but the spoilers responded with a series of threats. AFSI warned Barak not to cross "red lines," and Frager promised to accelerate the settlement drive in East Jerusalem and beyond. Morton Klein reserved the right to monitor PA compliance, and he lobbied Congress to condition aid to Palestinians on the extradition of twenty-three Palestinians allegedly implicated in the killing of American citizens in terror attacks. On the day that Barak was elected, Moskowitz unveiled plans to construct a two-hundred-unit development in the East Jerusalem suburb Abu Dis, an area rumored to be site of a future Palestinian capital.

Undaunted, in his first meeting with President Clinton on July 15, Barak unveiled an ambitious plan to conclude a peace treaty with the PA, Syria, and Lebanon. On September 5, Israel and the PA signed an agreement dubbed Wye II; in exchange for a further withdrawal from the territories, Congress was asked to approve a $1.9 billion aid package, originally mentioned in Wye I. The package included $1.2 billion for Israel, $400 million for the PA, and $300 million for Jordan. The Clinton administration was also keen to advance Israeli negotiations with Syria over an Israeli withdrawal from the Golan Heights in exchange for a peace treaty. The White

House considered stationing American troops on the Heights to bolster the credibility of an accord.

Both proposals riled the spoilers. AFSI declared that Wye II was tantamount to the "cleansing" of Jews from the West Bank and the Golan. The ZOA reiterated charges that financing the Palestinians was synonymous to subsidizing a "brutal regime" that "tramples on the principles of freedom and democracy that Americans cherish." Helped by the Christian Zionists, the spoilers launched a lobbying campaign to stop Congress from approving the aid package. AFSI argued that if "Israel chooses to take perilous risks for peace," American taxpayers should not "foot the bill." Esther Levens from the National Unity Coalition urged members to write to their congressmen protesting the "flagrant misuse of American tax dollars." Top Republicans in Congress, engaged in a bitter struggle with President Clinton, were all too happy to help trounce the Wye II funding.[35]

The defeat of the Wye aid enraged the Israeli government and the Jewish mainstream. Deputy Defense Minister Ephraim Sneh accused Jewish spoilers and their Christian allies of sabotaging the bill. Foxman accused right-wing activists of using Congress to win a fight they had lost in Israel. He and others worried that the spectacle of Jewish groups lobbying against the mainstream Jewish community and the Israeli government would erode the political clout of American Jewry on Capitol Hill. A senior Jewish source close to the White House complained that by failing to stand up to the spoilers, the Jewish community abandoned Congress to right-wingers. The intercommunal strife over Wye II became so deep that Ariel Sharon, who had taken over the leadership of the Likud Party (now in opposition) from Netanyahu, promised to end all lobbying against a sitting government. AIPAC mobilized its extensive assets to engineer a bipartisan majority to support a bill restoring the Wye aid, which passed in November 1999.

However, the newly found goodwill lasted only a short time. In January 2000, Prime Minister Ehud Barak embarked on a round of formal negotiations with the Syrian government in Shepherdstown, a historic site in Virginia. The Clinton administration was keen to see a peace agreement in exchange for Israeli withdrawal from the Golan Heights. As noted above, the White House considered stationing American troops in the Golan to bolster the credibility of the treaty and promised financial aid to Syria and Israel.

Both proposals generated an intense pushback from the spoilers and their Christian allies. Individually and together, they launched a number of initiatives to block the proposed deal. An organization called the International Coalition for Missing Israeli Soldiers demanded Syria collaborate on finding Israeli soldiers missing since the 1982 war in Lebanon. Morton Klein raised Syria's prominent role in the Holocaust-denial movement, a highly emotional issue in the community. Elie Wiesel, the Nobel Prize laureate and a leading spokesman on the Holocaust, joined other prominent leaders to condemn Syria's Holocaust-denial record in a letter published by ZOA in the *New York Times* on February 9, 2000. Other spoilers prevailed on Michael Forbes, a Republican Congressman, to introduce legislation conditioning any deal with Syria on its withdrawal from Lebanon.[36]

Lobbying Congress on the issue was intense. ZOA's Klein urged lawmakers to sign a letter stating that Syria was linked to many terror groups in the Middle East. On February 8, more than a hundred volunteers from AFSI, ZOA, and the Christian groups came to Capitol Hill to explain that implementing the agreement would cost some $10 billion and would endanger American soldiers. Republican lawmakers shared such sentiments. Senator Jesse Helms wrote that "the peace between Israel and Syria must come on its own terms—not because the countries believe that they can temporarily push aside their fundamentalist bilateral problems in return for US dollars." As for the stationing of American troops on the Golan, the proposal was virtual anathema in Congress.[37]

Trying to help Barak, AIPAC urged members of Congress not to sign the ZOA letter, noting that the timing would jeopardize the delicate negotiations. Debra DeLee, president of Americans for Peace Now, accused "hardline Jews" of stoking isolationism in order to torpedo the talks with Syria. The Israel Policy Forum and other propeace groups echoed this theme and complained that the spoilers had collaborated with the most reactionary forces in America, a pact that upset the mainstream Jewish community, in their view. But the spoilers were unrepentant. AFSI's Zweibon stated, "It's irrelevant what American Jews think. It is relevant what Congress thinks. If I want to convince anybody, it would be the Christian community."[38]

If Wye II and the Syrian deal brought Jewish unity to the brink, the issue of Jerusalem and other territorial concessions pushed it over the edge. Even before Camp David II commenced on June 30, 2000, spoilers had begun a massive campaign against the anticipated concessions. In scores of speeches, articles, press releases, editorials, and paid advertisements, they attacked Barak for his willingness to make far-reaching territorial concessions to the Palestinians. The *Jewish Press* called the Israeli Prime Minister "pathetic" and the Friends and Families of Victims of Oslo described Barak, Arafat, and Clinton as a "dastardly trio." The Center for Security Policy called Camp David II the "assisted suicide of Israel" and a new organization, Victims of Arab Terror International (VATI) vowed to physically fight the removal of settlers. Rumors about the division of Jerusalem and plans to create a Palestinian capital in Abu Dis were met with vehement opposition by the rejectionists, who invoked the doctrine of limited Israeli sovereignty over the entire Land of Israel and its eternal capital, Jerusalem. The ZOA recruited thirty prominent leaders to sign an ad that read, "Israel Must Not Surrender Judaism's Holiest Site. . . . And no Israeli leader has the right to give away the essence of the Jewish people that is embedded in the Temple Mount."[39]

As before, peace proponents responded by questioning the right of the spoilers to sabotage a democratically elected Israeli government. They were particularly incensed by Klein's insistence that American Jews had opposed the peace process all along. Theodor Mann from the American Jewish Congress and IPF's Seymour Reich noted that "recent assertions that American Jews oppose the Prime Minister's efforts to reach an agreement with the Palestinians are inaccurate." To prove that the right-wingers were not representatives of the Jewish community, IPF organized a letter signed by 384 leaders, including six former chairs of the Conference of Presidents, twenty-four AIPAC officials, and leaders of scores of Jewish organizations.[40]

The exchange between the ZOA and the propeace groups triggered another round of recriminations and more questions as to who speaks for the American Jewish community. But the failure of Camp David II, the outbreak of the Second Intifada, and the collapse of the Labor coalition made the point moot. Ironically, the refusal of Arafat to accept what was considered by many as exceptionally generous offers united the community in criticizing the PA. In many ways, the new Intifada bolstered the credibility of the spoilers, who had for years cast doubts on the willingness or ability of the Palestinians to conclude a deal and, more importantly, to abide by its terms.

Evaluating the Impact of the Oslo Spoilers: A Net Assessment

One of the problems hindering the discussion of the spoilers is the difficulty of evaluating the impact of an individual spoiler or a coalition of spoilers. Stedman offers a good description of the spoiling process and its various actors, but his treatment of the potential impact of spoilers is somewhat deficient. For instance, Stedman asserts that violent spoilers tend to inflict fatal injuries on the negotiating process, but he is less clear about the effect of nonviolent measures such as civil resistance or political sabotage.

Arguably, grading the individual impact of a large number of actors in a highly dynamic, competitive, and synergistic process is not easy. A modified net assessment technique can help with this task. Net assessment is a practice developed by Andrew Marshall, the head of the Net Assessment Office in the Pentagon in the 1950s, to tackle the evaluation of complex strategic problems. Marshall contended that, when tackling complex strategic problems, bureaucracies break them down to smaller, manageable pieces that fit their bureaucratic security structure. This decomposition skews the weight of the components in relation to other components in way that distorts the whole picture. By reinterpreting the fragments and integrating them into an intellectual whole, the net weight of a component in its interactions with other components in a particular time span can be assessed.[41]

As applied to the Oslo process, net assessment needs to integrate the multifaceted competition among Israeli custodians, potential spoilers, and total spoilers on both the Israeli and Palestinian sides. The time span is divided into three subperiods covering the tenure of Rabin, Netanyahu, and Barak. In each period, the impact of the spoilers is assessed, based on several criteria: the performance of the Palestinian Authority, the response of the Israeli custodians, the gap between the spoilers and the mainstream organizations, and the degree to which opinion polls reflect the spoilers' position.

Few who had watched the White House ceremony in September 1993 could have imagined that the peace process would soon be violently disrupted by Palestinian (albeit Islamist) terror. The Islamic Jihad (PIJ) carried out the first bombing in Afula in April 1994, soon to be followed by Hamas and dissident elements in the PLO. By the end of December, fifteen Israelis had been killed and scores of others wounded. The year 1995 brought no respite; on January 22, an attack at the Bet Lid junction claimed the lives of twenty IDF soldiers and one civilian. Under intense pressure from Israel, Arafat took some steps to clamp down on the violent spoilers, but it became clear that he could not control the Islamists. It hardly helped that the Palestinian Authority, eventually created and presided over by Arafat, was both chaotic and corrupt, a fact that was increasingly discussed in the Israeli press.[42]

The growing terror and mismanagement of the PA, which distressed the Israeli custodians and their American Jewish supporters, had given the spoilers some leverage, but they had no free hand at AIPAC and the Conference, which as noted, was still willing to work with the Labor government and the Clinton administration. Opinion polls indicated that the Jewish community was still largely supportive of the peace process. A May 1995 poll revealed that 76 percent of the respondents were in favor of negotiations and 18 percent objected, even though 61 percent reported having "no trust" or "little trust" in Arafat. In other words, the terror did not undermine the deep support for peace. Ironically, the spoilers' premier achievement, the Embassy Relocation Act, mattered little to the community. An AJC survey in August 1995 found that only 20 percent of the sample favored moving the embassy to Jerusalem right away; 45 percent echoed the Labor (and US) government position to postpone the relocation to some future time.[43]

Netanyahu, who coasted to victory on the promise of dealing decisively with terror, did not fare better than his predecessor in this regard. To the contrary, some of his policies in fact provoked a strong reaction from the Palestinians. In September 1997 Netanyahu ordered the Hasmonean Tunnel under the Temple Mount in Jerusalem secretly opened. The event touched off a wave of violence in which scores of Palestinians and fourteen Jews, mostly IDF soldiers, were killed. Together with the decision to approve a hundred housing units in the controversial East Jerusalem Har Homa settlement, the Likud government's policy was criticized by high-ranking officials in the Clinton administration. To showcase the support of the Jewish community, the administration organized a White House meeting with dozens of key leaders, but they also urged the president to push both Netanyahu and Arafat to continue with the peace process.

Community-wide public opinion was likewise interested in seeing the Oslo process go on, in spite of the vigorous opposition of the spoilers. The American Jewish Committee's (AJC) American Jewish Population Survey of February 1997 indicated that 59 percent supported the Hebron agreement and 24 percent opposed it. When asked how optimistic the respondents were about the peace process compared to the year before, some 58 percent reported the same level of optimism, 17 percent felt more optimistic, and 23 percent felt less optimistic. Labor had a 60 percent popularity rating compared to 41 percent for Likud.[44]

These numbers indicate that Arafat's failure to stop terror and improve compliance during the Netanyahu time span did not resonate as much as would have been expected given Stedman's contention that violence tends to turn skeptics into spoilers. In this case, another issue has interfered with the mainstream community assessment of Netanyahu. Analysts have pointed out that the Likud's Orthodox coalition partners' effort to "roll back" the Israeli Supreme Court ruling opening the door to non-Orthodox conversions played a significant role. The Sephardi-Orthodox Party Shas, in particular, was determined to use its executive power to marginalize the position of Conservative and Reform Jews. Shlomo Benizri, an influential Shas politician, declared that the Reform and Conservative movements were a "new religion" with which there should be no compromise, and the Sephardi Chief Rabbi Eliyahu Bakshi Doron stated that Reform Judaism had done more harm than the Holocaust. The backlash in America was so extreme that Netanyahu was forced to devise a compromised solution in 1997, but the bulk of the Reform and Conservative movements remained nonplussed. As one commentator put it, "the Netanyahu government represented to American Jews someone different—not the familiar European Ashkenazi Jews that Jewish Americans have grown accustomed to. Rather, they have risen from the ranks of the dark-skinned Sephardi Jews, its recent Russian immigrant and the black-coated ultra-Orthodox." Visiting Labor officials reminded their audiences that the fight for the peace process was also a fight for an enlightened, pluralistic Israel.[45]

The return of a Labor government in 1999 eased the religious tensions between Israel and the Conservative and Reform diasporans, but subsequent developments in the peace process were hardly encouraging. Just prior to but especially following the failed Camp David II talks, the PA, under the increasingly erratic leadership of Yasser Arafat, seemed to be in a virtual free fall while Hamas and the Islamic Jihad once again employed violence to challenge the core of the DOP. Indeed, the situation was so chaotic after Camp David that the Israeli intelligence services engaged in a heated debate on whether Arafat was actually colluding with the Islamists or being overrun by them. Against this background what had been proclaimed as Barak's far-reaching concessions turned many in the Diaspora into skeptics and, ultimately, spoilers.[46]

Nowhere was the change more visible than among mainstream Jewish leadership. Malcom Hoenlein, the executive vice chairman of the Conference, stated that "the position of the Jewish community remains the same as it always has been—a unified Jerusalem, the capital of Israel." On June 23, 2000, thirty leaders—including two past chairs of the Conference; top officials of AIPAC, ADL, and Israel Bonds; and other moderates—warned Labor about dividing Jerusalem and other concessions. Even before the Second Intifada exploded, opinion polls showed the narrowing of the gap between the spoilers and the mainstream community.

Members of the peace camp were notably rattled by the failure of Camp David and especially the extraordinary violent Second Intifada. The dovish John Ruskay, the CEO of the United Jewish Appeal-Federation, expressed the sentiments of many of his peers: "If Oslo had shattered the fantasies of Greater Israel, the events of the last three weeks have certainly challenged if not shattered the fantasies of an early, quick, peaceful coexistence between Israelis and Palestinians." The commentator Hillel Halkin was even blunter when describing the Palestinian society that "in the form of street mobs, its politicians, or its supposed intellectuals, seems so easily incitable . . . so incapable of distinguishing between truth and falsehood or subjecting itself to the slightest degree of self-criticism or self-analysis."[47]

Conclusion

By the fall of 2000, with former peace proponents sounding like ardent spoilers, it was easy for the ZOA and other rejectionists to claim vindication. More to the point, the rejectionist coalition took credit for the paradigmatic change in the community. Measured on its own, however, the input was rather negligible compared to their large investment in fighting Oslo. Arguably, the shift occurred only after the breakdown of the peace process and the unprecedented violence of the Second Intifada when, as noted above, peace supporters-turned-skeptics gradually drifted into the spoilers' realm.

Whatever the initial dynamic, the long-term balance of power showed the paradigmatic impact of Oslo. Peace advocates virtually disappeared from the public square, and their funding dried up. Conversely, the ZOA and other spoilers came to occupy a prominent position in the discourse, aided by the hefty contributions of right-wing megadonors like the billionaire Sheldon Adelson. The defense organizations have reflected this right-wing makeover as well. The Conference, still ostensibly an arena for communal voices, is indicative of the new trend. In 2014, J-Street, a relatively new peace group, was denied membership after a stormy debate. Opponents like ZOA and other right-wingers asserted that J-Street was not sufficiently "pro-Israeli," an argument that carried the day.

Yet the new Israeli-based litmus test comes at a cost. The Pew Survey and other polls reveal that a majority of American Jews are not comfortable with the policies of the Likud government. Rather than engaging with Israel in general and the peace process in particular, large numbers of the diasporans have opted for cognitive and organizational withdrawal. Despite the much-touted Birthright Israel and similar programs designed to build attachment, Israel has become too divisive to reverse the postmodern path that leads from direct engagement to disengagement.

Notes

1. Melvin I. Urofsky, *We Are One!: American Jewry and Israel* (New York: Anchor Books, 1978).
2. Theodore Sasson, *The New American Zionism* (New York: New York University Press, 2013), 145.
3. Ibid., 35.
4. Ofira Seliktar, *Divided We Stand: American Jews, Israel and the Peace Process* (Westport, CT: Praeger, 2002), 123–125; Sasson, *New American Zionism*, 35.
5. Stephen John Stedman, "Spoiler Problems in Peace Processes," *International Security* 22, no. 2 (1997), 5–53.
6. Seliktar, *Divided*, 127.
7. Ibid., 127.
8. Michael I. Karpin and Ina Friedman, *Murder in the Name of God: The Plot to Kill Yitzhak Rabin* (New York: Metropolitan Books, 1998), 133, 148–150; Gershon Tannenbaum, "My Machberes," *Jewish Press*, January 9, 2013, accessed June 1, 2015, http://www.jewishpress.com/sections/community/my-machberes/my-machberes-51/2013/01/09/0/; "The Rabbi who Sentenced Yitzhak Rabin to Death," *New York Magazine* 28, no. 40 (October 9, 1995), 24, accessed June 1, 2015, https://books.google.co.il/books?id=DuUCAAAAMBAJ.
9. Seliktar, *Divided*, 126.
10. Herbert Zweibon, "Are the Arabs Reliable Partners for Peace," Americans for a Safe Israel, January 1993, accessed June 5, 2015, www.afsi.org/Outpost/1993/Outpost_1993_01.pdf.
11. Sasson, *New American Zionism*, 122.
12. Seliktar, *Divided*, 128; Edward Alexander, *The Jewish Wars* (Carbondale: Southern Illinois University Press, 1996), 173, 179.
13. Seliktar, *Divided*, 136.; Manfred R. Lehmann, "'Peace Breakers' and 'Mischief Makers' or 'Peace Makers' and 'Mischief Breakers'?" accessed June 5 2015, http://www.manfredlehmann.com/sieg435.html.
14. Barton Gellman, "At the Crossroads," *Washington Post,* May 26, 1996, accessed June 2015, http://www.washingtonpost.com/archive/lifestyle/magazine/1996/05/26/at-the-crossroads/c5b197c6-a5e3-400b-ab33-7d009af6ac47/.
15. Jonathan Jeremy Goldberg, *Jewish Power: Inside the American Jewish Establishment* (Boston, MA: Addison-Wesley: 1997), 206.

16. Goldberg, *Jewish Power*, 54–57; Ofira Seliktar, *Doomed to Failure?: The Politics and Intelligence of the Oslo Peace Process* (Santa Barbara, CA: ABC-CLIO, 2009), 85, 97.

17. Katharine Q. Seeley, "Relocating Embassy in Israel: Move Could Backfire on Dole," *New York Times,* May 18, 1995.

18. Alison Mitchel, "Rabin Rebukes U.S. Jewish Groups on Lobbying," *New York Times,* September 30, 1995, accessed June 1, 2016, http://www.nytimes.com/1995/09/30/world/rabin-rebukes-us-jewish-groups-on-lobbying.html; Seliktar, *Divided,* 128–129; Karpin and Friedman, *Murder,* 157.

19. Seliktar, *Divided,* 129; Karpin and Friedman, *Murder,* 160; Sasson, *New American Zionism,* 36; Gellman, "Crossroads."

20. Seliktar, *Divided,* 134; Thomas Friedman, "Jewish Lobbyist Ousted for Slur," *New York Times,* June 20, 1993; Matthew Dorf, "AIPAC Head of 2 Years Resigns Amid Mystery Over Reason Why," *Jewish Weekly,* March 31, 1996; Neal Sher, "A Jewish Thought Policeman," *Jerusalem Post,* January 17, 1997.

21. Sasson, *New American Zionism;* 36; Gellman, "Crossroads."

22. Gellman, "Crossroads."

23. Gellman, "Crossroads"; Seliktar, *Divided,* 144.

24. Seliktar, *Divided,* 144; Bernard J. Shapiro, "Personal Note & Response to Pro-Appeasement Ad," Freeman Center for Strategic Studies, *Maccabean Online* 8 (July–August 2000), 7–8, accessed June 5, 2015, http://www.freeman.org/m_online/Augusto0/.

25. Gellman, "Crossroads"; Itamar Rabinovich, "Zionism and the Arab World," in *Zionism, Liberalism and the Future of the Jewish State: Centennial Reflections on Zionist Scholarship and Controversy,* ed. Ernest S. Frerichs and Steven J. Zipperstein (Providence, RI: Dorot Foundation: 2000), 67.

26. Goldberg, *Jewish Power,* 373; Lawrence Grossman, "Jewish Communal Affairs," in *American Jewish Year Book* 96 (New York: American Jewish Committee, 1996), 187.

27. Seliktar, *Divided,* 151; Lawrence Grossman, "Jewish Communal Affairs," in *American Jewish Year Book* 96 (New York: American Jewish Committee, 1996), 175–215; *Maccabean,* June 1996.

28. Seliktar, *Divided,* 153, 154; David Wilder, "Impending Disaster?" Hebron Blog, October 30, 1996, accessed June 1, 2015, http://davidwilder.blogspot.co.il/1996_10_01_archive.html.

29. Seliktar, *Divided,* 156; Michael Shapiro, "U.S. Envoy to Israel Slated for Top Mideast Job in D.C." *Washington Jewish Week,* July 25, 1997, accessed June 1, 2015, http://www.jweekly.com/article/full/6215/u-s-envoy-to-israel-slated-for-top-mideast-job-in-d-c/.

30. Seliktar, *Divided,* 158; Douglas M. Bloomfield, "Lonesome Dove Flies Bibi's Coop," *Washington Jewish Week,* January 15, 1998.

31. Seliktar, *Divided,* 159; Christopher D. Cook, "The Bingo Connection," *Mother Jones,* September/October 2000.

32. Seliktar, *Divided,* 158-160; Debra Nussbaum Cohen, "Evangelicals Voice Solid Support for Israel." *Washington Jewish Week,* April 17, 1997.

33. Seliktar, *Divided,* 170.

34. Seliktar, *Divided,* 170; Forward Staff, "Irony at AIPAC as Feud over Dissent Widens," *Forward,* July 7, 2002.

35. Seliktar, *Divided,* 183–184; AFSI ad, *Jewish Voice,* Nation Unity Coalition for Israel, Press Release, November 1, 1999.

36. Michael Shapiro, "No Troops, No Money Declared Opponents of Israel-Syria Deal," *Jewish Telegraphic Agency*, February 13, 2000; Eli Lake, "Battle Brews over Aid to Syria," *Forward*, March 3, 2000; Seliktar, *Divided*, 186.
37. Shapiro, "No Troops"; Lake, "Battle"; Seliktar, *Divided*, 186.
38. Seliktar, *Divided*, 186–187; APN Release, February 3, 2000; Lake, "Battle."
39. Sasson, *New American Zionism*, 38.
40. Seliktar, *Divided*, 192; "No Time for Mourning," *Forward*, July 28, 2000; Melvin Salberg, "American Jewish Critics of Barak Should Pipe Down," *Jewish Exponent*, July 6, 2000; Marilyn Henri, "The Battle for the Hearts and Minds of US Jewry," *Jerusalem Post*, July 16, 2000.
41. Paul Bracken, "Net Assessment: A Practical Guide," *Parameters*, Spring 2006, 90.
42. Seliktar, *Doomed*, 84–98.
43. Seliktar, *Divided*, 124–125; *American Jewish Attitudes toward Israel and the Peace Process: A Public Opinion Survey* (New York: American Jewish Committee, 1995), 1–10.
44. Seliktar, *Divided*, 158–159; American Jewish Committee, American Jewish Population Survey, February 1997.
45. Seliktar, *Divided*, 163; *Jewish Exponent*, January 7, 1999; *Jewish Exponent*, February 4, 1999.
46. Seliktar, *Doomed*, 128.
47. Elli Wohlgelernter, "A Sobering Experience" *Jerusalem Post*, October 27, 2000; Hillel Halkin, "Intifada II: Israel's Nightmare," *Commentary*, December 2000, 44–48.

OFIRA SELIKTAR is Professor Emerita of Political Science at Gratz College. Her latest book (with Farhad Rezaei) is *Iran, Israel, and the United States: The Politics of Counter-Proliferation Intelligence*.

5

VISUAL SPOILERS?
PEACE AND CONFLICT IN ISRAELI
POLITICAL CARTOONS

Tamir Shaefer, Ilan Danjoux, Shira Dabir-Gvirsman,
and Shaul Shenhav

> Cartoonists have a big influence on the way different groups of people look at each other. They can encourage us to look critically at ourselves, and increase our empathy for the sufferings and frustrations of others. But they can also do the opposite.
> —United Nations Secretary-General
> Kofi Annan, *2006*

Introduction

News media coverage informs public perception of conflict. Its potential to undermine popular support for peace is often harnessed by parties opposed to a negotiated end to conflict. Staged acts of violence exploit the medium's sensationalist and negative bias to "confirm" popular fears and undermine the emergent trust between adversaries. Research into the media's influence on support for peace tends to treat media framing as institutionally consistent. Media outlets are presumed to reflect an internally coherent framing of events. This paper tests this uniformity by examining the depiction of peace in Israeli political cartoons, as compared to the news media coverage, during the Oslo peace process.

The decision to examine political cartoon depictions of peace originates with the medium's long association with violence. Political cartoons have been described as the "merger of caricature to political conflict" whose production reflects the "conflictfulness" of an era.[1] The cartoon's association with conflict is reinforced by a history of being used to galvanize populations to war, revolution, and genocide. Paul Revere used caricatures to fuel the American Revolution; William Hearst commissioned cartoonists "to whip up support for a war against Spain"; governments on both sides of the Second World War deployed cartoons to mobilize domestic support for war; and rebels in Benghazi posted political cartoons on the outer walls of their headquarters.[2] Nazi and Hutu dehumanization of their Jewish and Tutsi populations in cartoons were also precursors to both the Holocaust and the Rwandan genocide, respectively.[3]

The use of cartoons to mobilize support for war, delegitimize adversaries, and dehumanize victims of violence explains the fear and foreboding felt by those whose image cartoonists ridicule, demonize, and ostracize. Protests and outrage against the 2006 *Jyllands Posten* Mohammed cartoon contest and Iran's Holocaust cartoon contents reflect the sense of concern that can accompany political cartoon depictions. The 2014 murder of *Charlie Hebdo* cartoonists and the ongoing police protection for *Jyllands Posten* staff are testaments to the violence cartooning can summon.

The artistic techniques used by cartoonists to condense complex politics into a single visual image often accentuate their offensiveness by exacerbating political fault lines and xenophobic fears, even against the wishes of their creators. Cartoons personify perceived threats in the bodies of culprits, making no distinction between actors and their actions. This suggests that their behavior is innate, implying that the elimination of, rather than negotiation with, perpetrators is the only reasonable approach to neutralize a threat.

With little room for written descriptors, physical appearance, such as facial features and stereotypical attire, is often used to identify actors. While this eliminates the need to label actors, it can exacerbate conflict by implicating entire ethnic, cultural, or religious communities in the actions of select members. The use of kilts, kippahs, and kefiyahs as visual identifiers can easily be (mis)construed as indictments of the entire Scottish, Jewish, or Arab population, respectively.

The need for visual austerity also compels cartoonists to strip their depictions of all superfluous information. This often means that conflict is distilled into a binary clash of interests with outsiders clearly demarcated.

Even when not graphically vilified, these polarizing depictions designate entire groups as dangerous or foreign. This does little to promote coexistence. Finally, with no room to develop argument or provide evidence, cartoon commentary is an ideal forum for voicing the unsubstantiated and uncorroborated claims that can accentuate the most tenuous and dubious of conspiracy theories and prejudices. Combined, these elements lend cartoons to the coverage of conflict.

It is perhaps unsurprising, then, that cartoon research disproportionately focuses on conflict.[4] For many, the medium appears ill suited, even incompatible, with the aspirations of peace. Hogan contends that cartoons "reinforce almost completely the negative images of politics and politicians, with almost no countervailing positive images."[5] Brinkman calls them a "destructive art."[6]

Peace and the Political Cartoon

This chapter examines the depiction of peace in Israeli cartoons during the Oslo peace process to test whether political cartoons act as peace spoilers. The prolonged, public, and contested nature of these negotiations and the countervailing forces of violence and diplomacy that characterized these talks make it an ideal context within which to understand the relationship between political cartoons and peace.

For this study, we examined every cartoon published in two leading Israeli newspapers, *Ha'aretz* and *Yediot Ahronot*, between July 1, 1995, and March 31, 2003. These papers were selected because they appeal to different demographic cross sections of Israeli society. *Ha'aretz* is a broadsheet that offers a leftist elite perspective on politics, while *Yediot Ahronot* caters to the popular center. The period chosen for this investigation covers several rounds of negotiations that took place as part of the Oslo peace process, such as the Oslo II talks, the Camp David 2000 negotiations, and the Taba talks; waves of suicide bombings by Palestinian militants against Israeli civilians; the outbreak of the Second Intifada; and the reoccupation of the West Bank territories by Israeli forces.

A comparison of the prominence and tone of Israeli cartoon coverage of the Oslo peace negotiations between 1995 and 2003 with newspaper articles, surveys, and changes in the security situation at the time was used to determine not only whether cartoons are predisposed to conflict and negative coverage but also to understand how their images correspond to real and perceived insecurity. Three questions form the focus of this inquiry: (a) Do political cartoons favor conflict? (b) Are cartoons pessimistic on peace? and (c) How do political cartoons respond to changes in public support for peace?

Do Political Cartoons Favor Conflict?

The cartoon's long-standing association with conflict suggests that its coverage will orient itself toward violence. To test whether violent encounters with Palestinians were more prominent in Israeli cartoons than diplomatic initiatives, we needed first to identify every caricatured interaction between Israelis and Palestinians. Every image of Palestinian leaders, citizens, or symbols that appeared in the Israeli editorial cartoons was coded as an Israeli-Palestinian interaction. The presence of Israelis or Israeli symbolism was not deemed necessary for this coding as their publication in an Israeli newspaper was considered indicative enough of an Israeli perspective. Of the 4,129 cartoons examined, a total of 945 cartoons (23%) addressed Israeli-Palestinian relations, with slightly more appearing in *Ha'aretz* (524) than were published in *Yediot Ahronot* (421).

A secondary coding was then applied to distinguish cartoon depictions of peace from violence. Any image of Israelis or Palestinians taking part in negotiations, whether sitting at conference tables or discussing terms of an agreement, was given a *peace-oriented* coding. This was applied irrespective of whether the actors were shown to be conciliatory, antagonist, or frustrated with the process; or whether the cartoon satirized, criticized, or scrutinized negotiations. What was deemed important was that the cartoon focused attention on diplomacy. Conversely, any cartoon where Palestinians or Israelis were seen preparing, sanctioning, or initiating violence against each other was coded as *security-focused* interactions. It did not matter whether the threat of violence was credible or comical. What was important was that the cartoon focused on the threat of force. A March 12, 2003, cartoon (fig. 5.1) published in *Ha'aretz* depicts a family picnic taking place under a missile-defense launcher used by the Israeli army to intercept rockets fired into Israeli territory. The relaxed demeanor and the sense of security conveyed by the family did not alter its security-focused coding. In an attempt to reduce bias, only explicit visual references to peace and violence were included in the dataset. Cartoons that contained neither diplomatic symbols nor violence imagery were coded as *indeterminate* in focus.

Any cartoons that contained symbolic references to both violence and diplomacy also received a security-focused coding because of the destructive

Figure 5.1. Caricature of "families in a field" by Amos Biderman (*Ha'aretz*, March 12, 2003). Reprinted courtesy of the artist.

impact that violence has on diplomacy. A July 25, 1995, cartoon (fig. 5.2), for example, published in *Yediot Ahronot* shows a determined Yitzhak Rabin, prime minister of Israel at the time, driving a bus with the word "peace" written on its side. Despite its overt reference to diplomacy, the mangled metal, shattered windows, and charred exterior of the bus, presumably the result of a suicide bombing, are at the core of the cartoon's message.

The findings of our examination challenge the presumption that cartoons orient themselves to conflict. Over the eight-year period examined—amid waves of suicide attacks, the assassination of Israeli Prime Minister Yitzhak Rabin, the outbreak of the Second Intifada, and the reoccupation of the West Bank territories—Israeli cartoon coverage of Israeli-Palestinian relations was disproportionately focused on the Oslo peace talks. Our analysis shows that 51 percent of the cartoons coded in both *Yediot Ahronot* and in *Ha'aretz* (482/945) were depictions of diplomacy. A total of 58 percent of *Ha'aretz* cartoons that addressed the Israeli-Palestinian relations (303/524)

Figure 5.2. Caricature of "Rabin driving a bus" (*Yediot Ahronot*, July 25, 1995) © Meir Ronnen, reprinted with permission.

were focused on the peace process. In *Yediot Ahronot*, 43 percent (179/421) depicted peace negotiations. Conversely, only 30 percent of the cartoons (286/945) in both papers focused their attention on the security situation. This imagery was more balanced between the two newspapers than may be expected. Of the *Ha'aretz* cartoons that depicted interactions between Israelis and Palestinians, 29 percent were concerned with security (154/524). In *Yediot Ahronot*, this figure was 31 percent (132/421). What this means is that far from a conflict-obsessed medium, Israeli cartoons were much more concerned with the prospects of peace.

The reason for the Israeli cartoon preference for peace was unclear. Curiosity over whether shifts between the prominence of peace and conflict were related to changes in political reality led us to examine whether the *conflictfulness* of Israeli cartoons corresponded with flare-ups in violence. A real-world security variable, generated by combining Israeli military deaths, civilian fatalities, and terror incidents (as reported by the Ministry of Defense and the Israeli Social Security office) with the key peace talks that took place between Israeli and Palestinian negotiators (e.g., Camp David, Wye, Taba), was compared with the prominence of both diplomacy and violence in cartoons. What we found was that changes in the number of security-focused and peace-oriented cartoons correlated positively and significantly with changes in the security situation. Increases in civilian/military casualties and the breakdown of peace talks resulted in a greater number of security-focused political cartoons (Pearson's r = 0.59). When the security situation improved, the number of cartoons focusing on the peace negotiations also increased (Pearson's r = 0.61).

Are Cartoons Pessimistic on Peace?

Finding a correlation between cartoons' themes and the security situation led us to examine whether changes in the security situation also affected the tone of cartoon coverage. More specifically, did increased violence result in growing pessimism in the coverage of the peace talks? Mood resonates deeply in cartoons. Historic, cultural, and religious analogies make connotative connections to collective memories of hope, dread, and despair. With no space for detailed analysis, the "mood tells us how we should feel over what is happening" is central to the cartoon's message.[7] The caricatured dishonesty of negotiators and incompetence of terrorists is a direct comment on viability of peace or the seriousness of threat. Giarelli and Tulman go so far as to argue that the cartoon's tone is more important than its content.[8]

To examine the impact of violence on cartoon depictions of peace, we compared the tone of political cartoons to changes in real-world security. Each cartoon was coded as either a *positive* or *negative* image of peace. A negative coding was applied to cartoons that showed outbreaks of violence as either imminent or inevitable, or that depicted diplomacy as irrelevant or ineffective. A positive coding was applied to cartoons in which Israeli and Palestinian negotiators appeared genuinely committed to peace, diplomatic progress was being made, and/or threats of violence were negligible. A *neutral* coding was given to depictions of peace that had indeterminate connotations or in which negotiators were seen as benign.

Two cartoons by Israeli cartoonist Meir "Mike" Ronnen illustrate the connotative differences between cartoon depictions of peace. Despite the presence of identical actors in similar artistic style in the same newspaper within a year of each other, the tone of these caricatures is notably different. The first cartoon was published on July 18, 1995, in *Yediot Ahronot* (fig. 5.3). It shows Palestinian leader Yasser Arafat carrying a smiling newborn child who is seen waving a small Palestinian flag. A bedridden Shimon Peres looks contently at the recently birthed Palestinian State. Smiles on the faces of both men, coupled with the joy associated with childbirth, infuse this

Figure 5.3. Caricature of "Peres and Arafat with baby" (*Yediot Ahronot*, July 18, 1995). © Meir Ronnen, reprinted with permission.

cartoon with an optimistic view of the peace process. This cartoon was coded as a positive depiction of the peace process.

Less than a year later, on February 26, 1996, a cartoon of these same actors depicted by the same artist in the same newspaper conveys a notably different sentiment. Both Arafat and Peres are seen seated at opposite ends of what appears to be the remains of a public transit bus (fig. 5.4). The middle of the vehicle is mangled by what one can only assume to be a suicide attack. The concerned look on the faces of both leaders, in addition to the heartbreak accompanying terror attacks, infuse this scene with pessimistic overtones. Neither leader seems sure how to respond. As a result, this cartoon was coded as a negative depiction of peace and the leadership's inability to contain violence.

A majority of Israeli cartoons examined were pessimistic in coverage, with 55 percent (520/945) of the 945 cartoons examined pessimistic in tone. Only 14 percent (137/945) conveyed any sense of optimism. These were consistent in both depictions of peace and conflict. Of the 482 cartoon depictions of diplomacy, 49 percent (235/482) were negative in tone. Diplomacy

Figure 5.4. Caricature of "Peres and Arafat sitting in a bus" (*Yediot Ahronot*, February 26, 1996). © Meir Ronnen, reprinted with permission.

cartoons were more pessimistic in *Ha'aretz* (52% of diplomacy cartoons in this newspaper) than in *Yediot Ahronot* (43% of diplomacy cartoons in this newspaper). Only 16 percent (79/482) of these cartoons were optimistic on the prospects or progress of the peace process. The difference between the two newspapers is rather unexpected, with only 14 percent of the diplomacy cartoons in *Ha'aretz* being coded as optimistic compared with 21 percent of the diplomacy cartoons in *Yediot Ahronot* receiving an optimistic coding. The majority of the 286 security-focused cartoons were also negative in tone, with 80 percent (228/286) pessimistic and only 12 percent (33/286) optimistic on conflict. While this corresponds with the characterization of cartoons as a negative art with a penchant for critical coverage of current affairs, it remained unclear whether this negativity was the result of the medium itself or was reflective of the country's security situation.[9]

A comparison between the evaluative tone of Israeli cartoon depictions of peace and changes in the country's security situation found no correlation between the two. Increased levels of violence did not result in a more negative depiction of peace; nor did a reduction in violence between parties result in a more positive mood in Israeli cartoons. Israeli cartoonist assessments of peace were not driven by changes in violence, suggesting a degree of latitude in the framing of peace.

We sought to understand if the apparent autonomy of cartoonists from political reality was consistent with news media coverage in general, or if this was particular to Israeli political cartoons. We compared the tone of the news media coverage with the change in the security climate by a sampling of every third day of front-page articles published in both *Yediot Ahronot* and *Ha'aretz*, generating a dataset of 2,915 items that spanned a seventy-nine-month period (1995 to March 31, 2005). News coverage was coded as positive if it presented an improving state of security or improvements in the peace process, and negative if the security situation was seen in decline.[10] What we discovered was a positive correlation between changes in the tone of media coverage and the actual security situation (Pearson's $r = 0.51$; $p \leq .01$). An even stronger correlation was found with the number of monthly terror incidents (Pearson's $r = 0.78$; $p \leq .01$). This stood in contrast to the absence of a relationship between cartoon tone and the security climate. There was no significant correlation between the tone in news coverage of the peace process and the tone in cartoons. Cartoonists demonstrated not only an autonomy from political reality, but also from the representation of reality by their newspaper.

How Do Political Cartoons Respond to Changes in Public Support for Peace?

The media play a central role in the ways citizens perceive, understand, and legitimize peace processes. They often serve as the primary source of information for many readers, allowing journalistic analysis to influence public support for diplomacy. Negative media coverage has been shown to harden foreign policy preferences, granting journalists, and their publishers, a disruptive influence on peace talks.[11] A sustained focus on violence and negative depictions of diplomacy can undermine the viability and logic of negotiations.

With their inclination for negative coverage, the centrality of mood to their message, and their polarizing depictions of politics, political cartoons might be especially potent spoilers of peace. However, political cartoons also differ significantly from news media coverage in their inability to inform or analyze. Space limitations prevent them from developing arguments or providing evidence to persuade readers. Instead, they use symbolic fusion to visually analogize current events to historic precedent, fictitious narrative, or religious parable. They can insinuate nefarious motives, hidden agendas, and looming danger, but they cannot prove their claims or substantiate their allegations. Cartoons have little influence on readers who are either unfamiliar with the logic of their associations or doubt the validity of the comparisons. It is difficult to imagine that a sinister depiction of trusted leaders in a political cartoon will sway audiences to reconsider their support and affection. This limits cartoon influence to the reiteration and reinforcement of opinion "already partially framed" in the public sphere.[12] Thus, cartoons are better understood as the chroniclers, rather than determinants of public opinion.[13]

To understand the relationship between cartoon images of peace and domestic support for diplomacy, we looked for a correlation between the cartoons' imagery and public opinion. The tone of cartoon coverage was compared with surveys conducted by the Tami Steinmetz Center for Peace Research at Tel Aviv University. Monthly telephone interviews asked respondents: "Do you believe or do you not believe that the Oslo Agreement between Israel and the PLO will lead to peace between Israel and the Palestinians in the coming years?" This analysis found no correlation between the tone of cartoons and faith in the Oslo peace process. This was surprising given the use of cartoons to gauge public opinion, first proposed by Press, who saw cartoons as an important tool for relaying popular sentiment to leaders.[14] This is the understanding that underpins cartoon insight into the popularity of electoral candidates both during and after elections and their policies.[15]

We decided to test whether changes in the public mood toward the Oslo peace process was visible in the focus of cartoons. Did changes in the prominence of diplomacy and conflict correspond with perceptions of the Oslo peace process? As single-issue commentary, cartoonists select a single issue of focus, making prominence indicative of the perceived importance of an issue.

Our analysis found a significant and positive association between the prominence of diplomacy in Israeli cartoons and public expectations toward the Oslo peace process (Pearson's $r = .65$; $p \leq .01$). Likewise, a significant and negative association was discovered between the salience of security cartoons and declining public expectations of the peace process (Pearson's $r = -.64$; $p \leq .01$). As their public grew more optimistic about peace, Israeli cartoons shifted coverage to diplomacy. When faith in peace dwindled, cartoons focused their attention on violence. Yet this topic-oriented association with public opinion does not necessarily mean that cartoonists have looked for public opinion when deciding the focus of their cartoons. What strengthens this assessment is the complete lack of a significant correlation between public mood toward the peace process and the tone toward the peace process depicted in the cartoons.

Discussion

Political cartoons appear well poised to be peace spoilers. Their binary depictions of current events are naturally divisive. Space limitation and spartan imagery make for speculative analysis and baseless accusation. The exaggeration characteristic of caricature easily offends. It was not surprising, then, that a majority of the cartoons examined (55%) depicted a pessimistic outlook on the peace process. From this perspective, one might conclude that cartoons function as peace spoilers.

Yet considering the negative nature of the genre, we believe that the characterization of cartoons as "peace spoilers" is premature. If cartoons truly acted as peace spoilers, one might expect cartoons to focus readers more often on security and violence rather than diplomacy and peace, as was clearly the case for the news coverage of the peace process.[16] Yet the cartoons examined were more focused on talks between Israelis and Palestinians than on the violence that took place between them. Their negative depictions of diplomacy might be indicative of disappointment in the peace process, rather than opposition to a negotiated settlement. Israeli cartoons also proved to be more negative in their depiction of conflict than they were of negotiations. From this perspective, cartoonists play a much less destructive role toward the peace process than one might expect.

Our comparison of cartoon coverage with both changes in the security and public opinion further substantiate this conclusion. Where cartoons determined to undermine support for peace, one might expect more negative depictions of peace or greater attention to violence when levels of security improved and the public grew more hopeful on peace. Efforts to derail peace talks, by highlighting violence and negatively depicting peace, would be expected to strike hardest when the reconciliation appeared most likely. Yet we found no relationship between changes in the tone of cartoons, on the one hand, and either public perception of peace or changes in security, on the other hand. What we did find was that cartoons paid more attention to diplomacy as the security situation improved. When violence flared and pessimism grew, cartoons returned their gaze to conflict. Cartoonists then followed events quite closely. At the same time, the lack of significant correlation between cartoons' tone and either developments in the peace process, news media presentation of the peace process, or public opinion toward the peace process, suggests that political cartoons provide a unique and independent coverage of peace.

Notes

1. Charles Press, *The Political Cartoon* (New Jersey: Fairleigh Dickinson University Press, 1981), 34; and William A. Coupe, "The German Cartoon and the Revolution of 1848," *Comparative Studies in Society and History* 9, no. 2 (1967): 137–167.

2. Paul Martin Lester, *Visual Communication: Images with Messages* (Boston: Wadsworth, 1995); and Fatima Göçek, *Political Cartoons in the Middle East: Cultural Representations in the Middle East* (Princeton, NJ: Markus Wiener, 1998), 5.

3. Ilan Danjoux, *Political Cartoons and the Israeli-Palestinian Conflict* (Manchester, UK, Manchester University Press, 2012), 8.

4. Victor Alba, "The Mexican Revolution and the Cartoon," *Comparative Studies in Society and History* 9, no. 2 (1967): 121–136; Harry Amana, "The Art of Propaganda: Charles Alston's World War II Editorial Cartoons for the Office of War Information and the Black Press," *American Journalism* 21, no. 2 (2004): 79–111; Jonathan A. Becker, "A Disappearing Enemy: The Image of the United States in Soviet Political Cartoons," *Journalism and Mass Communication Quarterly* 73, no. 3 (1996): 609–619; Palmira Brummett, "Dogs, Women, Cholera, and Other Menaces in the Streets: Cartoon Satire in the Ottoman Revolutionary Press," *International Journal of Middle East Studies* 27 (1995): 433–460; Lucy Shelton Caswell, "Drawing Swords: War in American Editorial Cartoons," *American Journalism* 21, no. 2 (2004): 13–45; Joan Conners, "Hussein as Enemy: The Persian Gulf War in Political Cartoons," *The Harvard International Journal of Press/Politics* 3, no. 3 (1998): 96–96; Danjoux, *Political Cartoons*; John Darby, *Dressed to Kill: Cartoonists and the Northern Ireland Conflict* (Belfast: Appletree, 1983); Klaus Dodds, "The 1982 Falklands War and a Critical Geopolitical Eye: Steve Bell and the If . . . Cartoons," *Political Geography* 15, no. 6–7 (1996): 571–592; Göçek, *Political Cartoons*; Chang-Tai Hung, "War and Peace in Feng Zikai's Wartime Cartoons," *Modern China* 16, no. 1 (1990): 39–83; J. G. Lewin and P. Huff, *Lines of Contention: Political Cartoons of the Civil War* (New York: HarperCollins/Smithsonian, 2007); Afar Lutfia al-Sayyid Marsot, "The Cartoon in Egypt," *Comparative Studies in Society and History* 13 (1971): 2–15; Richard Minear, *Dr. Seuss Goes to War: The World War II Editorial Cartoons of Theodor Seuss Geisel* (New York: New Press, 2001); Yesheyahu Nir, *The Israeli-Arab Conflict in Soviet Caricature* (Tel Aviv: Tcherikover, 1976); Mohamed Salah Omri "Gulf Laughter Break: Cartoons in Tunisia during the Gulf War," in *Political Cartoons in the Middle East*, ed. Fatima Göçek (Princeton, NJ: Wiener, 1998), 133–156; Susan Slyomovics, "Cartoon Commentary: Algerian and Moroccan Caricatures from the Gulf War," *Middle East Report* 180 (1993): 21–24; Kristen M. Smith, *The Lines Are Drawn: Political Cartoons of the Civil War*, (Athens, GA, Hill Street, 1999); Asia Tunç, "Pushing the Limits of Tolerance: Functions of Political Cartoonists in the Democratization Process: The Case of Turkey,"

International Communication Gazette 64, no. 1 (2002): 47–62; Fred Vultee, "Dr. FDR & Baby War: The World through Chicago Political Cartoons before and after Pearl Harbour," *Visual Communication Quarterly* 14, no. 3 (2007):158–175; and Helen Yu-Rivera, *A Satire of Two Nations: Exploring Images of the Japanese in Philippine Political Cartoons* (Diliman, Quezon City: University of the Philippines Press, 2009).

5. Michael Hogan, "Cartoonists and Political Cynicism," *Australian Review of Public Affairs* 2, no. 1 (2001): 29

6. Del Brinkmann, "Do Editorial Cartoons and Editorials Change Opinions?" *Journalism Quarterly* 45 (1968): 242.

7. Charles Press, *The Political Cartoon* (New Jersey: Fairleigh Dickinson University Press, 1981), 62.

8. Ellen Giarelli and Lorraine Tubman, "Methodological Issues in the Use of Published Cartoons as Data," *Qualitative Health Research* 13, no. 7 (2003): 947.

9. Chris Lamb, *Drawn to Extremes: The Use and Abuse of Editorial Cartoons* (New York: Columbia University Press, 2004), 4; Joan Edwards, "Running in the Shadows in Campaign 2000: Candidate Metaphors in Editorial Cartoons," *American Behavioral Scientist* 44 (2001): 2140–2140; William Koetzle and Thomas Brunell, "Lip-Reading, Draft-Dodging, and Perot-Noia: Presidential Campaigns in Editorial Cartoons," *Harvard International Journal of Press/Politics* 1, no. 4 (1996): 94–115; William Gamson and David Stuart, "Media Discourse as a Symbolic Contest: The Bomb in Political Cartoons," *Sociological Forum* 7, no. 1 (1992): 55–86; Thomas Patterson, *Out of Order: An Incisive and Boldly Original Critique of the News Media's Domination of America's Political Process* (New York: Vintage, 1993); and Tamir Sheafer and Shira Dvir-Gvirsman, "The Spoiler Effect: Framing Attitudes and Expectations toward Peace" *Journal of Peace Research* 47, no. 2 (2010): 205–215.

10. For more information see Sheafer and Dvir-Gvirsman, "The Spoiler Effect."

11. Alison Astorino-Courtois, "Transforming International Agreements into National Realities: Marketing Arab-Israeli Peace in Jordan," *Journal of Politics* 58, no. 4 (1996): 1035–1054; Claude Berrebi and Esteban F. Klor, "On Terrorism and Electoral Outcomes: Theory and Evidence from the Israeli-Palestinian Conflict," *Journal of Conflict Resolution* 50, no. 6 (2006): 899–925; Shana Kushner-Gadarian, "The Politics of Threat: Threat, Media and Foreign Policy Opinion," *Proceedings from American Political Science Association* (2006); Mark Peffley and Jon Hurwitz, "International Events and Foreign Policy Beliefs: Public Responses to Changing Soviet-US Relations," *American Journal of Political Science* 36, no. 2 (1992): 431–461; and Sheafer and Dvir-Gvirsman, "The Spoiler Effect."

12. William Gamson, "News as Framing: Comments on Graber," *The American Behavioral Scientist* 33, no. 2 (1989): 157–161.

13. Danjoux, *Political Cartoons*; Peter Duus, "Presidential Address: Weapons of the Weak, Weapons of the Strong—the Development of the Japanese Political Cartoons," *The Journal of Asian Studies* 6, no. 4 (2001): 965–997; Giarelli and Tubman, "Methodological Issues"; Patricia Gilmartin and Stanley D. Brunn, "The Representation of Women in Political Cartoons of the 1995 World Conference on Women," *Women's Studies International Forum* 2, no. 5 (1998): 535–549; Press, *Political Cartoon*; Ria Wiid, Layland Pitt, and Ann Engstrom, "Not So Sexy: Public Opinion of Political Sex Scandals as Reflected in Political Cartoons," *Journal of Public Affairs* 11, no. 3 (2011): 137–147.

14. Press, *Political Cartoon*, 11.

15. Jody Baumgartner, "Polls and Elections: Editorial Cartoons 2.0: The Effects of Digital Political Satire on Presidential Candidate Evaluations," *Presidential Studies Quarterly* 38,

no. 4 (2008): 735–758; Sushmita Chatterjee, "Framing the Obama Political Cartoons: Injury or Democracy?" in *Doing Democracy: Activist Art and Cultural Politics,* ed. Nancy S. Love and Mark Mattern, (Albany: State University of New York, 2007): 53–74; Edwards, "Running," 2140–2140; Ofer Feldman, "Political Reality and Editorial Cartoons in Japan: How the National Dailies Illustrate the Japanese Prime Minister," *Journalism & Mass Communication Quarterly* 72, no. 3 (1995): 571–580; Hayden Manning & Robert Phiddian, "Where Are the Clowns? Political Satire in the 1998 Federal Election Campaign," in *Howard's Agenda: The 1998 Federal Election,* ed. Marian Simms and John Warhurst (Brisbane: University of Queensland Press 2000), 48–63; Hayden Manning and Robert Phiddian, "Two Men and Some Boats—the Cartoonists and the 2001 Election," in *The Centenary Election,* ed. John Warhurst and Marian Simms (Brisbane: University of Queensland Press, 2002), 41–62; Janette Kenner Muir, *Political Cartoons and Synecdoche: A Rhetorical Analysis of the 1984 Presidential Campaign* (Amherst: University of Massachusetts–Amherst, 1986); Mustafa Kabha, "The Palestinian Press and the General Strike, April–October 1936: Filastin as a Case Study," *Middle Eastern Studies* 39, no. 3 (2003): 169–189.

16. Sheafer and Dvir-Gvirsman, "The Spoiler Effect."

TAMIR SHEAFER is Professor of Political Science and Communication at the Hebrew University of Jerusalem.

ILAN DANJOUX is a lecturer at the University of Toronto. He is author of *Political Cartoons and the Israeli-Palestinian Conflict.*

SHIRA DVIR-GVIRSMAN is Senior Research Associate Lecturer of Communication at Tel Aviv University.

SHAUL SHENHAV is Associate Professor of Political Science at the Hebrew University of Jerusalem. He is the author of *Analyzing Social Narratives.*

6

THE PSYCHOLOGICAL EFFECTS OF FORCED EVACUATION

The Case of Jewish Settlers in the West Bank

Sivan Hirsch-Hoefler, Tamar Saguy, and Gilad Hirschberger

IN THE COMING YEARS, THE STATE OF ISRAEL will have to make fateful decisions regarding the future of the West Bank; Israel will have to decide whether to withdraw from these territories, and if it chooses to do so, it will face an inevitable massive evacuation of Jewish settlements, one of unprecedented magnitude. Twice before Israel has evacuated Jewish settlements following political decisions, from the Sinai Peninsula in 1982 and from the Gaza Strip in 2005, but in both cases only a few thousand residents were evacuated and resettled within Israel's borders. These previous experiences indicate that Israel is able to implement such evacuations on a practical level, both in terms of managing the evacuation event itself and, at least to a certain extent, integrating evacuees into new homes and communities. At the same time, however, the psychosocial implications of forced evacuation have been relatively neglected in spite of the fact that in previous evacuations a large percentage of evacuated settlers exhibited and continue to exhibit prolonged distress and posttraumatic reactions, significant difficulties in adjusting to their new lives at their new place of residence, family problems, and an overall deep sense of frustration after the withdrawal.[1] In past withdrawals that involved a relatively small number of people, these problems primarily impacted individual lives, and had little effect on Israeli society as a whole. In the event of an evacuation of settlers from the West Bank, the psychosocial effects of forced evacuation can no longer be considered an individual or community problem. An evacuation that would affect an approximated one hundred thousand settlers is a momentous event,[2] a veritable earthquake, and the implications for Israeli society as a whole are likely to be substantial.

To prepare for massive evacuation of unprecedented scale, an understanding of the likely reactions during and after the evacuation is needed. The extant theoretical and practical knowledge, however, on socioemotional coping under conditions of forced evacuation is scarce. Case studies of previous evacuations suggest that an important balance exists between the role of the judiciary branch (the Supreme Court) and the executive branch (the government) in carrying out a forced evacuation of settlers. The judiciary branch sets the legal limits, but these limits intensify the political debate over the evacuation. The government may reduce the likelihood of violent resistance by (a) planning the details of the evacuation in advance and not withdrawing haphazardly; and (b) negotiating with the leaders of the settlers, allowing them to be involved in decisions regarding the fate of their community, and expressing empathy toward them.[3] Most other research is based primarily on theoretical studies and surveys,[4] with no empirical investigation of the possible factors that may influence the emotional reactions, coping mechanisms, motivations, and behaviors of the affected settler population. The present research represents a first step in filling this gap in the literature. In particular, we aim to supply insights and tools that may help in future efforts to support evacuated populations and promote their integration into their new homes and communities during a period of collective trauma and emotional and ideological upheaval.

In addition to understanding the factors that contribute to the well-being of evacuees, we were also interested in understanding the immediate reaction to forced evacuation and, specifically, identifying the factors that may provoke aggression, resistance, and violence in response to a possible evacuation. Past experience suggests that the failure to address the severe psychological implications of forced evacuation may contribute to violent resistance against the evacuation. In our research, we differentiate between normative protest within the boundaries of the law, and acts of violence that are not part of the democratic process and violate the law,[5] and examine whether different factors predict these reactions. Our overarching goal in this research was to better understand the cognitive, emotional, and motivational processes affecting settlers. In addition, our objective was to establish an appropriate set of psychosocial strategies in the period leading up to the evacuation to address both immediate reactions to the evacuation and long-term coping and adjustment in the aftermath of this event.

Forced Evacuation: Psychological Effects

Massive evacuation of a population from their place of residence may involve consent or coercion, may be temporary or permanent, and may come in the wake of natural disasters or political decisions.[6] When an evacuation is forced, it is often accompanied by a subjective sense of existential threat, reflected in and arising from a significant disturbance in the evacuees' way of life, a collapse in their social and community systems, a loss of material resources, and—perhaps most important—a perceived attack on fundamental religious and moral beliefs.[7] Such significant and multifarious losses (of resources, community, security, core beliefs) can lead to traumatic reactions, especially to the extent that the evacuees resist the process and/or have little control over it.[8] Studies conducted on populations evacuated under coercion due to political decisions point to a series of emotional and physical symptoms seen in the short and long terms after evacuation. These include pain, mourning, anger, anxiety, depression, adjustment problems, marital and parental problems, loss of self-confidence, and feelings of uncertainty about the future.[9]

When a coerced evacuation also includes the transfer of territory to a foreign entity, dealing with the evacuation is likely to be particularly difficult.[10] In such a case, opposition to leaving will be even stronger, and the settlers will likely show less openness to formal (psychologists, social workers) and informal (friends, family) systems of support.[11] Studies investigating the effects of forced evacuation on Israeli society have found that evacuated settlers show high levels of posttraumatic symptoms and symptoms of depression, in comparison both to settlers from the same areas who were not evacuated, and to the general Israeli population.[12]

Thus far, Israel has experienced two large-scale evacuations of populations resulting from political decisions: the 1982 evacuation of the Sinai Peninsula in the framework of the peace treaty between Israel and Egypt, and the 2005 evacuation of the Gaza Strip and northern West Bank in the framework of Israel's unilateral disengagement from those areas. Studies of the Sinai evacuees showed that the settlers suffered emotional distress on personal, family, and community levels during the evacuation and for a long time thereafter. In addition, the evacuees experienced greater physical morbidity, a rise in divorce rates, a sense of alienation from the state and from fellow citizens, and a diminished sense of belonging to the state.[13] The evacuation from Gush Katif in the Gaza Strip also proved to be a traumatic event,[14] and in this case as well, high levels of emotional distress were found both during and following the evacuation.[15] These were expressed in symptoms such as invasive thoughts, increased arousal, mourning, and depression.[16] A study conducted during the first year after the disengagement found that the emotional reactions of about 40 percent of the evacuees fit the clinical criteria of posttraumatic stress syndrome.[17] Moreover, the sense of loss among the evacuees involved not only the loss of a physical place, but also loss of a sense of belonging to Israeli society and loss of faith in state institutions.[18]

Predicting Reactions to Forced Evacuation

Threats to material, psychological, and sociological resources engender significant stress, according to the theory of conservation of resources (COR).[19] Indeed, a great deal of research shows that levels of stress rise significantly regardless of whether or not resources are actually reduced; the mere threat of resource loss is sufficient to affect the individual's ability to cope.[20] On the other hand, contextual variables can soften or mitigate the harmful effects of such threats; for instance, studies that followed evacuees from Gaza found that those who were married, who were better educated, or who did not lose their employment due to the evacuation showed relatively lower levels of posttraumatic symptoms.[21] In particular, connections to family strongly moderated evacuees' emotional distress,[22] as did a sense of connection to the community, such that evacuees reporting a strong connection to the community showed relatively low levels of traumatic symptoms.[23] In addition, among evacuees who identified strongly with the state and believed that the state was taking responsibility for their situation, the state was perceived as a resource that moderated their emotional reaction.[24] Sense of connection to the state, to one's new place of residence, and to fellow citizens predicted reductions in pathological reactions among the settlers of Gush Katif.[25]

Other theories explaining reactions to forced evacuations focus on ideology, arguing that the trauma that follows forced evacuations does not necessarily relate to the loss of physical resources, but rather to the *symbolic* significance of the event.[26] While studies of reactions to extremely stressful situations show that ideological belief is likely to help in coping with crises by granting significance to the event,[27] studies on the evacuation of settlers for political reasons show the exact opposite—that strong ideological belief is linked to higher reactions of distress and depression.[28] This apparently stems from the fact that the evacuation itself significantly undermines the ideology.

The disintegration of ideology in the face of withdrawal from areas with deep historical and religious significance constitutes a formidable existential crisis, according to terror management theory (TMT).[29] Ideologies are an important element of people's worldview and identity that grant meaning to human life and serve to elevate humans above their animal, mortal nature. Forced evacuation, from this perspective, does not only threaten material resources or constrain choice, it taps into the very essence of human existence and threatens to leave the evacuees with a profound sense of emptiness and disillusionment, rendering them devoid of any meaning. In the face of this impossible threat, people facing the possibility of forced evacuation may choose to deny reality—a defense mechanism that offers short-term refuge from the threat, but it is precisely those individuals who initially deny reality that are most likely to respond with violence when the evacuation is set in motion and denial is no longer possible.[30]

TMT provides a theoretical framework to understand the potential for political violence[31] and the high prevalence of posttraumatic reactions[32] following forced evacuation. From this perspective, the evacuation represents first and foremost a crisis of faith in which all of the individual's basic assumptions and beliefs are cast into doubt, and this shattering of assumptive worldviews is a main predictor of posttraumatic reactions.[33] The fact that right-wing ideologies are characterized by greater ideological rigidity,[34] cognitive closure, opposition to change, and low tolerance of uncertainty[35] places adherents of these ideologies in an especially vulnerable position. High ideological commitment is, therefore, a risk factor for violent resistance to forced evacuation and poor adjustment in the aftermath of the evacuation. There are, however, mitigating factors that may temper reactions even among the ideologically committed. Research has shown that greater preparedness for an evacuation may reduce posttraumatic symptoms following the evacuation,[36] and that commitment to the superordinate group—the state or the nation—is associated with lower long-term levels of distress among those committed to the ideology compared with those exclusively committed to the ideology and not to the superordinate group.[37]

A Prospective Experimental Approach

The existing studies in the literature have investigated emotional reactions to forced evacuation either just before the evacuation date or after the evacuation had already taken place. The present study seeks to examine expected reactions to evacuation of West Bank settlements even *before* any such decision has been made. Such prospective research not only enables an investigation of vulnerability factors and predispositions of maladaptive functioning at the time of the evacuation, but also enables us to preempt these adverse outcomes by formulating research-based interventions, policies, and strategies that may increase the success of the process and decrease individual and collective psychological costs.

There is a paucity of information on how West Bank settlers are likely to react in the event of a forced evacuation, and the little existing knowledge about their expected reactions is based primarily on nonempirical sources, such as interviews with leading public figures. One main source of information is a 2005 report drafted by the Israel Democracy Institute, which examined a number of key parameters that are likely to moderate reactions to a forced evacuation (e.g., compensation to evacuees, public legitimacy for the evacuation).[38] According to Sheleg, three features of any future evacuation can be expected to moderate settlers' reactions.[39] First, settlers will more positively accept an evacuation that takes place in the framework of a peace agreement with the Palestinians compared with a unilateral action. This counterintuitive conclusion is based on the notion that although settlers distrust the Palestinian leadership and do not believe in the feasibility of peace, a formal agreement will enable them to define the evacuation as a partial achievement, and to claim that their steadfastness enabled Israel to achieve a peace agreement under more favorable terms (e.g., the annexation of large settlement blocks to Israel). By construing a peace agreement as a partial victory for the settler movement, settlers avoid facing the more devastating possibility of conceding that the entire settler enterprise was futile, and that all of their losses and sacrifices were in vain. Second, an agreement that is perceived as legitimate—one that enjoys broad unequivocal support in the Knesset, or in a national referendum—will be perceived as expressing the will of the people and is thus less likely to be met with violent opposition. The issue of legitimacy has been overshadowing negotiations with the Palestinians since the 1993 Oslo accords, as many crucial decisions were passed with a bare majority. Violent resistance to a process that clearly reflects the will of the people will be difficult to justify, and most settlers will reluctantly accept the majority vote. Finally, in previous evacuations of setters, the antipathy they experienced from the state and from many of the people changed their status from pioneers to pariahs. The successful execution of a large-scale resettlement plan requires an ability to show empathy and appreciation toward the settlers even at a time when their movement is in direct clash with the interests and policies of the state. Insincere and manipulative empathy, however, could backfire, producing greater frustration, alienation, pathological symptoms, and even violence.

Based on Sheleg's extensive report, the research reported here examined among West Bank settlers whether emotional and motivational responses to the possibility of an Israeli withdrawal from the West Bank would be influenced by potential political gains—the perception that the evacuation is taking place unilaterally or in return for substantial benefits such as peace, recognition, and security; legitimacy—the perception that the evacuation reflects the unequivocal will of the Israeli public, expressed in a national referendum or a vote in the Knesset; and messages of support and empathy toward the settlers and their ongoing sacrifices for the state and for the people.[40]

West Bank settlers are a diverse group comprising various subgroups that differ in terms of religiosity, lifestyle, education, income, country of origin, and motives for settlement. While the settler population as a whole is heterogeneous, individual settlements tend to support homogenous communities based around either a national-religious vision of "land redemption" or a desire for a better quality of life with no particular religious ideology attached.[41] The "quality-of-life" settlers are mostly young couples who were drawn to the settlements by highly subsidized mortgages for single-family homes within driving distance of the center of the country, where most of them work and have family and friends. The ideological settlements, on the other hand, were not established for the sake of material benefits (though they too received great material advantages), but rather to realize the ideal of resettling the ancient land of Israel. That is, ideological settlers, most of whom are deeply religious, are motivated by the goal of redeeming the land of their forefathers, and fulfilling the biblical promise of the return of the people of Israel to the land of Israel.[42] Keeping these important differences in mind, the present research compared ideological settlers and quality-of-life settlers because we predicted that there would be substantial differences between these populations in how they would cope with a forced evacuation, and in their willingness to adjust to a new life within the recognized borders of the State of Israel.

An Experimental Survey of West Bank Settlers

Our research was conducted in the format of face-to-face interviews that took place at people's homes in the West Bank. Between April and November of 2013, we surveyed 590 Jewish settlers,[43] half from ideological settlements and the other half from quality-of-life settlements.[44] The interviews were held in Hebrew by trained interviewers who either resided in the settlements or had the necessary background to act comfortably and naturally in this environment. Of the entire set of participants, 440 were randomly selected to participate in an experimental study that had two goals. The first goal was to examine reactions to different evacuation scenarios that vary on two dimensions: legitimacy—whether or not the decision to withdraw from the territory enjoyed an overwhelming majority or passed by a hairbreadth—and gain—whether the decision to withdraw was unilateral (with no gain) or bilateral in the context of a comprehensive peace agreement. The combination of these two dimensions yielded four scenarios: (a) unilateral withdrawal passed with support of a marginal majority; (b) unilateral withdrawal passed with support of a large majority; (c) bilateral agreement passed with support of a marginal majority; (d) bilateral agreement passed with support of a large majority. The second goal was to examine whether collective self-enhancement (i.e., "the settlers are the spearhead of the Jewish people") or emphasizing the importance of national unity ("unity among the people of Israel is the most important value") would moderate the effects of the scenarios on measures of aggression and adjustment among quality-of-life and ideological settlers.

The results of this research validate the distinction between ideological and quality-of-life settlers and indicate that these two populations significantly differ in their reactions to a possible evacuation from the West Bank.[45] Both groups showed a high motivation to adjust to the new reality after the evacuation, with quality-of-life settlers being slightly higher than ideological settlers in their intent to continue to be law-abiding citizens and in their trust of the government. Although both populations are high in the willingness to adjust, this comes at a considerable cost for the ideological settlers. For them, the mere thought of an evacuation from the West Bank elicits a motivation to use various coping mechanisms such as prayer, family and social support, and, for some, denial of the impending crisis. Ideological settlers also show higher levels of negative emotions compared with quality-of-life settlers when contemplating an Israeli withdrawal from the West Bank. They show particularly high levels of anger, fear, and sadness that may be associated with both resistance to the evacuation as well as poor adjustment following the evacuation. These differences between settler groups in emotional reactions and coping mechanisms are also reflected in the motivation to take action and try to stop the withdrawal from taking place. Ideological settlers show a higher inclination to actively oppose the evacuation than quality-of-life settlers within the confines of the law. They also exhibit higher levels of implicit aggression assessed with a lexical decision task—a cognitive task designed to measure the accessibility of aggression-related cognitions—compared with quality-of-life settlers. Interestingly, support for illegal violent resistance is extremely low in both groups of settlers. This may either reflect their sense of loyalty to the state, or it may be due to impression management concerns that implicit measures of aggression are impervious to.

A purely economic perspective on the psychosocial consequences of forced evacuation might suggest that these are problems that are resolvable with money, and that if settlers are offered generous compensation, their level of resistance to a withdrawal will be lower and their level of adjustment higher. To examine this possibility, we measured settler willingness to adjust if offered compensation that is equivalent to their current net worth, 25 percent higher, 50 percent higher, or 75 percent higher. Our results refute the assumptions of the economic perspective and indicate that for quality-of-life settlers, offering higher compensation had no significant effect on their motivation to adjust. For ideological settlers, however, higher compensation had a paradoxical effect; for them, the higher the compensation, the lower their motivation to adjust.

These findings can be understood from the perspective of cognitive dissonance theory.[46] Accordingly, the potential for substantial economic gain created dissonance between ideological and religious values and economic self-interest, and as cognitive dissonance would predict, this dissonance was not resolved by abandoning long-held ideologies, but rather by abdicating self-interest and sacrificing for the cause. From this perspective, ostensibly lucrative economic offers to a highly idealistic population are likely to backfire and only further intensify their commitment to the cause. Recent research in political psychology indicates that not all values were created equal, and that some values are considered sacred and are treated as inviolable and absolute.[47] Sacred values are processed as deontological principles rather than for their utilitarian value,[48] and any attempt to treat sacred values as fungible with secular goods is regarded as a violation of a taboo and elicits strong protest. Thus, when negotiators offer economic incentives in return for compromises on sacred values, this attempt will likely backfire.[49] Our results align with this analysis and indicate that settlers regard their ideology as a set of sacred values that are not for sale, and that policy makers should be extremely cautious of making economic assumptions about the motivations of extremely ideological populations.

Reactions to Different Withdrawal Scenarios

The core of this research was to examine whether the two groups of settlers, ideological settlers and quality-of-life settlers, would differ in their reactions to evacuation scenarios from the West Bank. In addition, we examined whether enhancing settlers' collective self, or reminding settlers that the most important value is the unity of the people of Israel would moderate the effects of evacuation scenarios. We initially postulated that because ideological settlers are vehemently opposed to any territorial compromise in the West Bank and to any concession of land to the Palestinians, the scenarios would have no effect on them as they would consistently show strong and unyielding opposition. We hoped the self-enhancing and group-unity messages would somewhat soften their position and lead to more pragmatic reactions. The evacuation scenarios, we thought, would have an effect only on quality-of-life settlers who are more pragmatic, less ideologically committed, and thus more open to examining the possible gains of an Israeli withdrawal from the West Bank, and more attuned to the legitimacy of the process leading to the decision to withdraw. The results of this research, however, indicate that reality on the ground is more complex.

First, ideological settlers were influenced by the evacuation scenarios just as much, but in a different way, than quality-of-life settlers, in spite of the former group's strong commitment to Jewish presence and sovereignty over this land. Both groups of settlers showed more support and more constructive and adaptive reactions to an evacuation within the framework of a peace agreement passed by a large majority (66% of the Knesset, in our scenario). However, for ideological settlers a peace agreement that is passed by a small majority of the Knesset (51% in our scenario) elicits strong opposition. Quality-of-life settlers seem to be less sensitive to the legitimacy of the evacuation, and they exhibit less negative emotions and more positive emotions to a withdrawal within the framework of a peace agreement, regardless of the size of the majority. The one effect that a large majority seemed to have on these settlers is that it also aroused feelings of pride. These findings suggest that a formal agreement with the Palestinians is important for both groups of settlers, but reaching such an agreement without the clear unequivocal support of the people elicits opposition among ideological settlers.

A peace agreement seems to be the preferred option among both groups of settlers, but it may not be a feasible option at this point. The Arab Spring and the disintegration of nation-states in the Middle East and the radicalization and Islamization of Arab societies may render such an agreement impossible at present. The alternative to an agreement would be a unilateral Israeli withdrawal from large portions of the West Bank to a line that offers maximum security and minimum control over the Palestinian population.

The ideological settlers, while responding favorably to a clear majority decision to sign a peace treaty with the Palestinians, responded in a dialectically opposite manner to a clear majority decision to withdraw unilaterally. In this case, ideological settlers exhibited the most extreme reaction: a unilateral withdrawal from the West Bank with a decisive majority increased their support for all forms of protest and resistance, including taking the law into their own hands and using violence. Ideological settlers in this scenario also expressed a reduced readiness to adapt or receive monetary compensation, and were prone to using denial-based coping strategies that were characteristic of settler coping in the disengagement from Gaza in 2005—a coping strategy that was found to be linked to violent resistance.[50] The unilateral withdrawal scenario in our study is strongly reminiscent of the disengagement from the Gaza Strip, which was a unilateral process that enjoyed overwhelming public support. The evacuation from Gaza is remembered as a collective trauma by ideological settlers, and they often attribute the government's success in implementing this plan to the denial and inaction of the settlers and their supporters.

The Road to Hell Is Paved with Good Intentions: The Case of Backfiring Messages

Part of our reasoning prior to this project was that a successful withdrawal from the West Bank and massive evacuation of settlers requires a genuine effort to reach out to settlers, show appreciation and support for their efforts and sacrifices over the years, and welcome them back into the larger Israeli public. We used biblical and religious texts to convey messages that reflected these ideas. The first was to recognize the settlers as the vanguard of the people of Israel, the spearhead, those who have the special role to lead and show the direction to others. We believed that settlers exposed to this message would feel the admiration and appreciation of the Israeli public, and this would increase their motivation to react constructively and in a cooperative manner with a possible evacuation. The second message emphasizing national unity taps into an ancient Jewish notion that the unity of the people of Israel is a value that surpasses all other values. We reasoned that at a time when another central value—the settlement of the land of Israel—is in jeopardy, it is important to shift settlers' attention toward superordinate values that may enable them to see the big picture—namely, that the unity of the people is more important than redeeming the land. We hoped that shifting attention from the land to the people would moderate negative reactions to the evacuation and promote positive and constructive adaptation.

Quality-of-life settlers conformed with our expectations and responded to national unity messages with an increased motivation to adapt and cope constructively with the evacuation. Ideological settlers presented a more mixed picture. For them, national unity messages worked in the expected direction only when presented in the context of a peace agreement that enjoys a substantial majority. In this case and only in this case, national unity messages decreased negative emotions. Surprisingly, national unity messages backfired when ideological settlers were exposed to a unilateral withdrawal that enjoys a clear majority. To begin with, ideological settlers responded to this scenario with unrestrained hostility. Then they were presented with messages of unity, and these only further exacerbated their negative emotions and their refusal to adapt and receive compensation, and increased their reliance on maladaptive coping mechanisms such as denial. It seems that messages of national unity at a time when the majority is willing to uproot them from their land and communities for no clear reason seem manipulative and disingenuous. Majority support for their forced evacuation could be perceived as an act of aggression by the majority against their group and ideology, and even as an act of treason against Zionism and the Jewish faith. It is then not surprising that they would react with great hostility to insincere attempts to embrace them.

The spearhead message also had unintended and paradoxical effects among ideological settlers. Rather than eliciting a positive reaction to their affirmation as the vanguard of the Jewish people, it generated greater anger, greater support for legal means of protest against the evacuation, and less openness to monetary compensation. This message may have backfired for similar reasons to the backfiring of the unity message—both may have been perceived as devious and hypocritical. But the spearhead message may have gone awry for other reasons as well. When affirming a group's leadership role and historical calling, members of this group may indeed want to lead, and may show stronger opposition to dictates from the majority. From this perspective, it is quite absurd to proclaim the settlers leaders of the people and then expect them to succumb to the government and passively follow.

Discussion and Conclusions

This research on settler groups and their reactions to a possible withdrawal from the West Bank emphasizes the centrality and importance of psychological reactions to forced evacuation—an aspect of human experience often ignored in political scholarship. We argue that, in any given scenario, settlers *differ* in their experiences of the evacuation and the resulting psychological ramifications. We show that merely imagining a future evacuation arouses significant distress among settlers, with the specific nature of their response affected by three factors: (a) the character of the settlers (quality-of-life settlers versus ideological settlers); (b) the way the decision is taken (unilaterally or in the framework of a peace treaty, with broad or narrow support); and (c) the messages conveyed by decision-makers to the settler public (collective self-enhancement or national unity).

Using an experimental survey design, our analyses provide powerful evidence that ideological settlers differ from quality-of-life settlers in many important respects when it comes to adapting to and coping with a forced evacuation. Moreover, the two groups react differently, and sometimes even in opposing ways, to different evacuation scenarios and expressions of support or empathy from the government and policy makers. Politicians must take these differences into account and offer responses to the specific needs of each group.

Interestingly, we found that ideological settlers *do not* comprehensively and unequivocally reject withdrawal from areas of the West Bank. This conclusion stems primarily from the fact that the ideological settlers among our respondents reacted differently to the various evacuation scenarios. Had they completely rejected any possibility of withdrawal, their reactions to all four scenarios would have been more or less identical. It is notable that most of the settlers we surveyed, including the ideological settlers, even expressed a certain degree of willingness to adapt to the new reality after the withdrawal and to accept compensation for their material losses. However, our findings also make clear the psychological price of any future evacuation for ideological settlers, reflected in their coping strategies and their expression of negative emotions such as fear, sadness, anger, and even hatred.

One important determinant of settler reactions to the evacuation scenarios was the degree of support the withdrawal enjoyed from the Israeli parliament, the Knesset. On the one hand, the fact that West Bank settlers, including the most devout and ideologically committed, were sensitive to the democratic process and to the will of the people suggests that settlers are, for the most part, law-abiding citizens who respect the majority vote, even when it goes against their most treasured beliefs. However, this simple relationship between degree of support and settler reactions proved true only among quality-of-life settlers, who clearly preferred a peace agreement to unilateral withdrawal and a large majority over a narrow majority. The ideological settlers, conversely, showed a different pattern of reactions, one characterized by ambivalence to both a peace treaty and to Knesset support for withdrawal. For them, a peace treaty, as highly undesirable as it may be, provides an opportunity to capitulate on their losses and save as much of their investment as they can. Because a peace treaty would be a lesser of two evils compared with a unilateral withdrawal, political legitimacy works in the expected direction in this case, and when exposed to a large majority in support of an agreement, ideological settlers decrease their resistance to such an outcome. Political legitimacy, however, is not seen as such among ideological settlers in the case of a unilateral withdrawal. In this specific case, a withdrawal decisively backed by the people's representatives would not be perceived as legitimate, but as quite the opposite—as treacherous, leading ideological settlers to harden their resistance.

Another interesting difference between the ideological and quality-of-life settlers was their readiness to accept compensation for their losses following a forced evacuation. As expected, we found a significant difference between the two, with quality-of-life settlers showing a higher willingness to comply with the evacuation in return for monetary compensation, but even ideological settlers did not reject the idea out of hand, and actually showed a relatively high willingness to leave their homes in return for a basic level of compensation. The current research not only shows that ideological settlers are more pragmatic and reasonable than many would assume, but that the level of compensation offered to settlers must not exceed their net worth at the time of evacuation. For quality-of-life settlers, providing compensation that would increase their wealth is an ineffective incentive, as it has no significant impact on their psychosocial adjustment—a finding that is perhaps surprising for a population ostensibly motivated by economic rather than ideological considerations. For ideological settlers, as our research shows time and again, good intentions may backfire, and providing more may result in less. Indeed, for this ideologically committed population, offering higher compensations has a paradoxical effect and lowers all indices of adjustment. This finding emphasizes the care that must be taken when granting material compensation to an ideologically motivated population. As long as compensation can be seen as directly replacing a family's material losses on a dollar-for-dollar basis, there is no dishonor and no dissonance in accepting such compensation. Once the notion of profit is introduced, however, the meaning of compensation changes. The possibility of profiting from their own tragedy is akin to selling their soul, and the dissonance between immediate economic benefits and timeless, eternal ideologies can only be resolved by intensifying commitment to the cause. Hence, higher rates of compensation will not only fail to tempt an ideological population, but are likely to backfire, thereby increasing their resistance.

Our findings also show the importance of experimental research in providing the information and tools to inform policy making. Specifically, our findings show that efforts to reach out to a settler population cannot be based on intuition alone, as these well-intentioned efforts may prove to be ineffective and may even backfire. In the case of West Bank settlers, it is vitally important to consider the differences between groups of settlers and to custom tailor specific messages to each group. Quality-of-life settlers responded well to messages of support and empathy, and these messages increased their motivation to cooperate and adjust. The same messages, however, led to unexpected and in some cases paradoxical reactions among ideological settlers. These settlers also seemed to understand the spearhead message as a call to arms and not as a pat on the back as intended, and responded to this message with greater opposition, less willingness to accept compensation, stronger feelings of anger, and greater readiness to engage in (legal) forms of resistance to the withdrawal.

From a public health perspective, it seems abundantly clear that the direct and indirect psychological costs associated with a forced evacuation of settlers from the West Bank will be staggering if nothing is done to preempt these effects. The forced evacuation of settlers constitutes a significant identity crisis, in particular for ideological settlers, that is akin to significant trauma. As previous evacuations have demonstrated, evacuated populations suffer from high levels of posttraumatic reactions, depression and other mental health problems including family dysfunction, and substantial difficulties in adjusting to new workplaces and schools. Forestalling the development of significant social and psychological problems is of primary interest to Israeli society. Our research suggests that directing attention to these potential costs of forced evacuation is vitally important and no less urgent than addressing concrete concerns such as monetary compensations, housing, and future employment of evacuees.

The research reported here provides but an initial glimpse into the complex psychological ramifications of forced evacuation, and more than it offers clear-cut answers, it opens the door to further contemplation and investigation of the factors that may facilitate the evacuation and relocation of large populations against their will. This research places the spotlight on ideological settlers who are deeply committed to the land and to its historical, cultural, and religious meaning. Our research, more than it has provided clear guidelines on how to deal with this population, has identified the potential pitfalls and mistakes that could take a bad situation and make it worse. This is a population that cannot be bought with money or with sweet talk but is responsive to the will of the people and to the reasons underlying the withdrawal. Future research should focus on this population and try to identify factors that may ease reactions to the disintegration of their worldview. One possibility is to find a new cause that is in line with their belief system, such as settling on land that is not in dispute or channeling this constructive energy toward a social or educational cause. These alternative causes, termed *ideological compensation*, provide new goals that may fill the void and offer meaning that could mitigate reactions in the aftermath of substantial loss.[51]

Notes

1. Orit Nuttman-Shwartz, "From Settlers to Evacuees: Is Forced Relocation a Traumatic Event?" *Group* 31, no. 4 (2007): 265–279; Lior Oren, and Chaya Possick, "Is Ideology a Risk Factor for PTSD Symptom Severity among Israeli Political Evacuees?" *Journal of Traumatic Stress* 23, no. 4 (2010): 483–490.

2. This estimate is based on the 2008 Annapolis summit between Israelis and Palestinians wherein negotiations were based on the 1967 border as a basis for land swaps on a 1:1 ratio. Recently, however, there have been reports that Netanyahu wishes to keep settler enclaves in a future Palestinian state. Amir Tibon and Barak Ravid, June 11, 2007, "Netanyahu Demanded Settlers Be Allowed to Remain in Palestine After Future Peace Deal, Document Reveals," *Haaretz*, retrieved from http://www.haaretz.com/israel-news/.premium-1.794973.

3. Gilead Sher and Liran Ofek, "Dividing the Land, Not the People: Lessons from the Givat HaUlpana and Migron Evacuations," *Strategic Assessment* 15, no. 4 (2013).

4. Daphna Canetti, Eran Halperin, Stevan E. Hobfoll, Oren Shapira, and Sivan Hirsch-Hoefler, "Authoritarianism, Perceived Threat and Exclusionism on the Eve of the Disengagement: Evidence from Gaza," *International Journal of Intercultural Relations* 33, no. 6 (2009): 463–474; Yair Sheleg, *The Political and Social Ramifications of Evacuating Settlements in Judea, Samaria and the Gaza Strip* (Jerusalem: Israel Democracy Institute, 2004).

5. Nicole Tausch, Julia Becker, Russell Spears, Oliver Christ, Rim Saab, Purnima Singh, and Roomana N. Siddiqui, "Explaining Radical Group Behaviour: Developing Emotion and efficacy Routes to Normative and Non-Normative Collective Action," *Journal of Personality and Social Psychology* 101 (2011): 129–148.

6. Ellen T. Gerrity and Peter Steinglass, "Relocation Stress following Catastrophic Events," in *Terrorism and Disaster: Individual and Community Mental Health Interventions*, ed. Robert J. Ursano, Carol S. Fullerton, and Ann E. Norwood (Cambridge: Cambridge University Press, 2003), 259–286; Art Hansen and Anthony Oliver-Smith, *Involuntary Migration and Resettlement* (Boulder, CO: Westview, 1982).

7. Miriam Billig, Robert Kohn, and Itzhak Levav, "Anticipatory Stress in the Population facing Forced Removal from the Gaza Strip." *Journal of Nervous and Mental Disease* 194 (2006): 195–200; Brian K. Hall, Steven E. Hobfoll, Patrick A. Palmieri, Daphna Canetti-Nisim, Oren Shapira, Robert J. Johnson, and Sandro Galea, "The Psychological Impact of Impending Forced Settler Disengagement in Gaza: Trauma and Posttraumatic Growth," *Journal of Traumatic Stress* 21 (2008): 22–29; Louis M. Najarian, Armen K. Goenjian, David Pelcovttz, Francine Mandel, and Berj Najarian, "Relocation after a Disaster: Posttraumatic Stress Disorder in Armenia after the Earthquake," *Journal of the American Academy of Child and Adolescent Psychiatry* 35 (1996): 374–383; Orit Nuttman-Shwartz, Efrat Huss, and Avital Altman, "The Experience of Forced Relocation as Expressed in Children's Drawings," *Clinical Social Work Journal* 38, no. 4 (2010): 397–407; Lior Oren and Chaya Possick, "Religiosity and Posttraumatic Stress Following Forced Relocation," *Journal of Loss & Trauma* 14, no. 2 (2009): 144–160; Peter Steinglass and Ellen Gerrity, "Forced Displacement to a New Environment," in *Stressors and the Adjustment Disorders*, ed. Joseph D. Noshpitz and R. Dean Coddington (New York: Wiley, 1990), 399–417.

8. Stevan E. Hobfoll, "Conservation of Resources: A New Attempt at Conceptualizing Stress." *American Psychologist* 44, no. 3 (1989): 513–524.

9. Barbara B. Brown and Douglas D. Perkins, "Disruptions in Place Attachment," in *Place Attachment*, ed. Irwin Altman and Setha M. Low (New York: Plenum, 1992), 279–304; David, Daniella et al., "Psychiatric Morbidity following Hurricane Andrew," *Journal of Traumatic Stress* 9 (1996): 607–612.

10. Rachel Lev, "I-vada'aut, akira me'ones, vetafkid hakehila behitmodedut im dahak" (Uncertainty, forced relocation, and the role of the community in coping with stress) (Unpublished PhD diss., Hebrew University of Jerusalem, 1995, in Hebrew).

11. Hall et al., "Psychological Impact," 22–29.

12. Avraham Bleich, Marc Gelkopf, and Zahava Solomon, "Exposure to Terrorism, Stress-Related Mental Health Symptoms, and Coping Behaviors among a Nationally Representative Sample in Israel," *JAMA* 290 (2003): 612–620; Stevan E. Hoboll and Daphna Canetti-Nisim, "Rates of Probable PTSD in Occupied Territories during the Second Al Aqsa Intifada, August 17, 2004–September 7, 2004," unpublished data, 2004.

13. Haim Dasberg and Gabriel Sheffler, "The Disbandment of a Community: A Psychiatric Action Research Project," *Journal of Applied Behavioral Science* 23 (1987): 89–101; Nurit Kliot, "Here and There: The Phenomenology of Settlement Removal from Northern Sinai," *Journal of Applied Behavioral Science* 23 (1987): 35–51; Joseph Toubiana, Noah Milgram, and Hertzel Falach, "Stress and Coping among Sinai Settlers," *Megamot* 31 (1988): 65–82.

14. Rachel Dekel and Rivka Tuval-Mashiach, "Multiple Losses of Social Resources following Collective Trauma: The Case of the Forced Relocation from Gush Katif," *Psychological Trauma: Theory, Research, Practice, and Policy* 4 (2012): 56–65.

15. Billig et al., "Anticipatory Stress," 195–200; Hall et al., "Psychological Impact," 22–29.

16. Nuttman-Shwartz, "From Settlers to Evacuees," 265–279.

17. Oren and Possick, "Is Ideology a Risk Factor?" 483–490.

18. Canetti et al., "Authoritarianism," 463–474; Dekel and Tuval-Mashiach, "Multiple Losses of Social Resources," 56–65.

19. Jan Breckenridge and Kerrie James, "Educating Social Work Students in Multifaceted Interventions for Trauma," *Social Work Education* 29 (2010): 259–75.

20. Orit Nuttman-Shwartz and Rachel Dekel, "Ways of Coping and Sense of Belonging to the College in the Face of a Persistent Security Threat," *Journal of Traumatic Stress* 22 (2009): 667–670.

21. Orit Nuttman-Shwartz, Rachel Dekel, and Rivka Tuval-Mashiach, "Post-Traumatic Stress and Growth Following Forced Relocation," *British Journal of Social Work* 41, no. 3 (2011): 486–501.

22. Rinat Galili and Rachel Lev-Wiesel, "Tehushat hamakom bekerev bogrim shene'ekru begil hahitbagrut memakom megurim: Pinui Sinai bemabat leahor," *Society and Welfare*, 27 (2007): 37–53, in Hebrew.

23. Dekel and Tuval-Mashiach, "Multiple Losses of Social Resources," 56–65; Bonnie M. Hagerty, and Arthur R. Williams, "The Effects of Sense of Belonging, Social Support, Conflict, and Loneliness on Depression," *Nursing Research* 48 (1999): 215–219.

24. Nuttman-Shwartz, Dekel, and Tuval-Mashiach, "Post-Traumatic Stress and Growth," 486–501.

25. Dekel and Tuval-Mashiach, "Multiple Losses of Social Resources," 56–65.

26. Iyzhak Schnell and Shaul Mishal, *Uprooting and Settlers' Discourse: The Case of Gush Katif* (Jerusalem, Israel: Floersheimer Institute for Policy Studies, 2005).

27. Raija-Leena Punamäki, Samir Qouta, and Eyad El-Sarraj, "Resiliency Factors Predicting Psychological Adjustment after Political Violence among Palestinian Children," *International Journal of Behavioral Development* 25, no. 3 (2001): 256–267.

28. Julia Elad-Strenger, Zvi Fajerman, Moran Schiller, Avi Besser, and Golan Shahar, "Risk-Resilience Dynamics of Ideological Factors in Distress after the Evacuation from Gush Katif," *International Journal of Stress Management* 20, no. 1 (2013): 57–75; Nathaniel Laor, Leo Wolmer, Moshe Alon, Joanna Siev, Eliahu Samuel, and Paz Toren, "Risk and Protective Factors Mediating Psychological Symptoms and Ideological Commitments

of Adolescents Facing Continuous Terrorism," *Journal of Nervous & Mental Disease* 194 (2006): 279–286; Avital Laufer, Mally Shechory, and Zahava Solomon, "The Association between Right-Wing Political Ideology and Youth Distress," *Child & Adolescent Social Work Journal* 26 (2009): 1–13.

29. Tom Pyszczynski, Sheldon Solomon, and Jeff Greenberg, *In the Wake of 9/11: The Psychology of Terror* (Washington, DC: APA, 2003).

30. Gilad Hirschberger and Tsachi Ein-Dor, "Defenders of a Lost Cause: Terror Management and Violent Resistance to the Disengagement Plan," *Personality and Social Psychology Bulletin* 32 (2006): 761–769.

31. Gilad Hirschberger and Tom Pyszczynski, "An Existential Perspective on Ethno-Political Violence," in *Understanding and Reducing Aggression, Violence and Their Consequences*, ed. Mario Mikulincer and Phillip R. Shaver (Washington, DC: APA, 2011), 297–314.

32. Tom Pyszczynski and Pelin Kesebir, "Anxiety Buffer Disruption Theory: A Terror Management Account of Posttraumatic Stress Disorder," *Anxiety, Stress, & Coping* 24, no. 1 (2011): 3–26.

33. Ronnie Janoff-Bulman, *Shattered Assumptions: Towards a New Psychology of Trauma* (New York: Free Press, 1992).

34. Ruthie Pliskin, Daniel Bar-Tal, Gal Sheppes, and Eran Halperin, "Are Leftists More Emotion-Driven Than Rightists? The Interactive Influence of Ideology and Emotions on Support for Policies," *Personality and Social Psychology Bulletin* 40, no. 12 (2014): 1681–1697.

35. Laufer, Shechory, and Solomon, "Youth Distress," 1–13; John T. Jost, Jack Glaser, Arie W. Kruglanski, and Frank J. Sulloway, "Political Conservatism as Motivated Social Cognition," *Psychological Bulletin* 129, no. 3 (2003): 339–375.

36. Dekel and Tuval-Mashiach, "Multiple Losses of Social Resources," 56–65.

37. Elad-Strenger et al., "Risk-Resilience Dynamics," 57–75.

38. Sheleg, *Political and Social Ramifications*.

39. Ibid.

40. Ibid.

41. Sivan Hirsch-Hoefler, Daphna Canetti, and Ehud Eiran, "Radicalizing Religion? Religious Identity and Settlers Behavior," *Studies in Conflict & Terrorism* (in press), doi: 10.1080/1057610X.2015.1127111.

42. Sivan Hirsch-Hoefler and Cas Mudde, "Right-Wing Movements," in *The Wiley-Blackwell Encyclopedia of Social and Political Movements*, ed. David A. Snow et al. (Hoboken, NJ: Wiley-Blackwell, 2013), 1116–1124.

43. The research did not include ultra-Orthodox settlements. In addition, settlements likely to be annexed to Israel in any future peace agreement were not included in the sample.

44. We employed a probability sample combining cluster and stratified sampling procedures. In the first stage (stratified sampling), the Jewish settlements beyond the Green Line were divided into two strata, according to whether they were quality-of-life settlements or ideological settlements. During the second stage (multi-stage cluster sampling), we randomly sampled the settlements within each stratum based on municipal jurisdiction (e.g., Gush Etzion, Shomron, Benyamin, Har Hevron, Ariel) in accordance with settlement size as per the Central Bureau of Statistics. In the last stage, family homes in each settlement were systematically sampled. The response rate was 42 percent.

45. Sheleg, *Political and Social Ramifications*.

46. Leon Festinger, *A Theory of Cognitive Dissonance* (Stanford, CA: Stanford University Press, 1962).

47. Philip E. Tetlock, "Thinking the Unthinkable: Sacred Values and Taboo Cognition," *Trends in Cognitive Sciences* 7, no. 7 (2003): 320–324.

48. Jeremy Ginges, Scott Atran, Sonya Sachdeva, and Douglas Medin, "Psychology Out of the Laboratory: The Challenge of Violent Extremism," *American Psychologist* 66, no. 6 (2011): 507–519.

49. Jeremy Ginges and Scott Atran, "Humiliation and the Inertia Effect: Implications for Understanding Violence and Compromise in Intractable Intergroup Conflicts," *Journal of Cognition and Culture* 8, no. 3 (2008): 281–294.

50. Hirschberger and Ein-Dor, "Defenders of a Lost Cause," 761–769.

51. Sheleg, *Political and Social Ramifications*.

SIVAN HIRSCH-HOEFLER is a senior lecturer in the Lauder School of Government, Diplomacy, and Strategy at the Interdisciplinary Center (IDC) Herzliya.

TAMAR SAGUY is Associate Professor of Psychology at the Baruch Ivcher School of Psychology at the Interdisciplinary Center (IDC), Herzliya.

GILAD HIRSCHBERGER is Associate Professor of Psychology at the Baruch Ivcher School of Psychology at the Interdisciplinary Center (IDC), Herzliya.

7

COPING WITH SPOILERS

A Comparative Analysis

Galia Golan

COPING MEASURES OBVIOUSLY DEPEND ON THE SPECIFIC CIRCUMSTANCES of a peace process, including the nature of the political system, the actors in the conflict, the local (also regional and international) environment, and many, many more factors, in addition to the nature of the spoilers themselves. Equally obvious is the fact that not all coping measures will work in all situations or for all conflicts. In view of this, it is also difficult to weigh or rank the various methods. The most one can suggest is a range of measures designed to minimize the spoilers' chances to fatally disrupt the process, by avoiding or overcoming spoiler efforts, neutralizing them or actually winning them over to support. This involves two tasks: not only addressing the spoilers directly but also addressing those who might be influenced by them and thereby contribute to jeopardizing the process.

Most discussions of spoilers conclude with a recommendation to bring spoilers into the process so that they become stakeholders, developing loyalty to the process.[1] However, there is some question that this can be done with regard to total spoilers or if it is even preferable in the case of total spoilers. It may be argued that ideologically motivated total spoilers cannot be changed; they will simply continue spoiling efforts once inside the process, assuming the role of veto player (and devious actor).[2] One way of avoiding this might be close monitoring, accompanied by the threat of expulsion from the process should their spoiling efforts continue. There is the additional problem that rewarding total spoilers by including them in the process may send a harmful message to the adversaries on the other side of the conflict. It may also strengthen the hand of other or potential spoilers while weakening the hands of moderates—on both sides. The strength, capacity, and resources of the total spoilers will ultimately determine whether leaving them out would be more dangerous than bringing them in. In either case, however, the effort should be to minimize, if not completely neutralize, their capacity—or will—to spoil (possibly through coercion).[3]

In dealing with any type of spoiler (total or more limited), a key coping measure is that of demonstrating fully committed, determined, consistent, and cohesive leadership by the "custodians" of the process. Hesitation or uncertainty about the steps taken, or divisions within the leading group, could provide an opportunity for spoiling (manipulating the divisions at the top). It might also lead to the conviction that such action might ultimately succeed. In addition, apparent custodian weakness, inconsistency, or uncertainty would augment the spoilers' efficacy with regard to skeptics and the general public. More specifically, many of the measures for minimizing or completely neutralizing total spoilers could be applied also to other types of spoilers. Yet it should be easier to deal with limited and greedy spoilers, as distinct from total spoilers, since presumably they are not opposed to the process as such. A path might be found to bring them (carefully) into the process, possibly at some stage of decision-making or in connection with some issue that they can support. It may be possible to accommodate their grievances and interests and to allay their fears, although doing so might run the risk of encouraging greedy spoilers at least to demand still more.

Moreover, there is the problem of balance. Balance does not mean neutrality or impartiality. Rather, balance refers to an awareness of how measures taken with regard to any kind of spoiler can affect supporters, potential allies, and adversaries. The last might well include potential spoilers on the other side of the conflict. Bringing spoilers into decision-making, for example, or a coping measure such as according incentives or concessions, could discourage moderates and aggravate rather than alleviate differences among supporters or potential supporters. Thus, assurances to spoilers regarding their interests, even confidence building measures designed to dissipate opposition or mistrust, must be measured with an eye toward how these may affect negotiations and the ultimate agreement. They must be viewed not only in connection with what one can in fact deliver in the future, but also how such measures will be viewed by one's own supporters and the public at large, as well as spoilers on the adversary's side.

There are also parliamentary and diplomatic measures that may dissipate opposition or placate spoilers on one's own side, at least partially. The promise of a referendum or election at the end of the process may be sufficient to suspend spoilers' actions against the process, as well as increase the legitimacy of the process. The level of the vote (referendum, government, parliament, party or parties, or group) would make a difference, the higher level usually offering greater predictability and therefore an avenue for avoiding spoiling. A variation of this would be the promise of a vote of some kind (parliamentary approval, for example) for the more controversial parts of an agreement or a separation of issues in the negotiating process itself. This might be taken a step further in the form of actually adopting a gradual, step-by-step approach during which time spoilers may, presumably, be brought along or won over. This might be accomplished by dealing issue by issue, finding what one observer has called "islands of agreement."[4] Demonstration of success in at least part of the process can help weaken spoilers (just as apparent failures can strengthen them), although there is the risk of preventing trade-offs if negotiations lock in partial settlements.

In theory, a gradual approach would allow for the breaking down of barriers and building trust in the process, something of socialization toward a more positive approach to ending the conflict. Thus tactics in this period might include those already mentioned (offer of incentives, concessions, CBMs, and the like), or other measures to "sell" the process that we shall discuss below. Yet the gradual approach still runs the risk of allowing more time for spoilers to organize and augment their efforts. The longer the process continues without a clear end in sight, the harder it may be to insulate supporters from the arguments and actions of the spoilers (and justify the process to one's own public).[5] Spoilers may have increasing chances—and opportunities—for disrupting a process that has lingered or at least been prolonged in the absence of clear signs of final, insipient resolution (even assuming that the adversary to the conflict also has not been discouraged by the partial and prolonged process).

Uncertainty regarding the end product of a process often feeds mistrust and fear.[6] The opposite strategy is a relatively swift, secret process that allows neither time nor opportunity for spoiler action (nor supporter fatigue, frustration, or discouragement).[7] Secrecy can lead to rumors, conspiracy theories, and fears that can be exploited by spoilers; it also runs the risk of failing to mobilize the support necessary for the implementation of an agreement. Yet a secret approach has the advantage of dealing with issues without constant interference and challenges from spoilers. It makes it possible to offer, ultimately, a clear and complete product which counters the arguments of naysayers. In either case—step by step with great consideration for spoilers or swift, virtual disregard for spoilers—the implied approach is to apply, at some point, the departing train tactic. The process is nearing its close; one is either on the train or left behind.

To reach the point of effective use of the departing train approach toward spoilers, there are still other possible measures (of a negative nature). Instead of seeking to co-opt or win over spoilers, custodians should attempt to isolate them, aim at their base, challenge their loyalty or credibility, employ covert action to hurt them among their constituents, or limit the resources at their disposal, even employ coercion. Such measures, of course, would depend on whether one is dealing with a democratic society or not and, therefore, on the methods that can actually be employed, for example, in relation to spoiler access to media, freedom of association, and the like. However, spoilers' resources can be weakened by less draconian steps. Something close to a carrot-and-stick approach but more in the nature of a cost/benefit proposition can be used. This would be compatible with the incentive but also the departing train approach if spoilers were to see the benefits of joining/supporting as distinct from the losses they would endure if left behind. "Prospect" theory holds that individual decision-makers ascribe greater importance to possible losses than to potential gains, with the reference point for losses usually being the status quo. So in the case of conflict resolution, spoilers, if left behind, presumably would "lose" such things as attention to their interests or needs (for example, compensation, special rights, or power sharing).

A major issue from the point of view of spoilers, but also skeptics and even the general public, is often that of legitimacy—of the process itself or those conducting it. This is often accompanied by the credibility issue, particularly with regard to the adversary and to the sustainability of whatever agreement is reached. One tactic for addressing these issues is coalition building or the use of "helpers." These may come from society itself—for example, past victims of the conflict (or their families) or former militants who can be engaged as advocates. Coming from those groups directly affected by or involved in the conflict, and more likely than not to be counted among the ranks of spoilers, such advocates can provide a powerful token of legitimacy to the process. Civil society groups can be used for advocacy as well, particularly since they can reach publics or project credibility that political leaders often cannot. Moreover, by bringing in diverse groups from civil society, varied constituencies can be assured that their views are represented. This may not only break down resistance or skepticism but may even accord a sense of ownership of the process and therefore cooperation. Adding an element of what may be perceived as accountability, this inclusion may provide greater legitimacy.[8] There is, however, the problem of which groups to cooperate with, and how to choose. There is also the risk that groups will add issues and interests of their own (for example, environmental demands or women's rights) that might complicate or prolong the process.

Nonetheless, by expanding the circle of stakeholders, these groups may reduce and weaken those who might be drawn into the ranks of the spoilers. Civil society, including grassroots groups, can engage in dialogue, track two, and public efforts at persuasion and advocacy. Moreover, activities by civil society can strengthen the sense of popular support, possibly even demonstrating the existence of pressure for resolution. Similarly, popular individuals—for example, entertainers, sports figures, artists, "heroes," and "heroines"—may also be engaged to make the case and even to directly address spoilers or skeptics. From the top, the custodians may themselves engage with or address civil society or at the grassroots level; they may speak through "peace emissaries," peace councils, or forums. These are often presented as consultations with the public or even with spoilers, on a regular, even formal basis. Public gestures and signs of empathy from custodians can also break down resistance.

Many of these efforts can be strengthened by the use of supporters or "custodians" from the other side of the conflict. This tactic would be of particular importance in dealing with the matter of credibility, with regard to both the process and the trust or belief in the durability of an agreement. Only the individuals or groups which are chosen from the adversary's side for such tasks are of importance, as they themselves have to present (represent) sufficient authority or standing to be believable. Generally it is thought that former combatants or militants from the other side can contribute most to generating credibility. However, one research project has found that explanation of the process or presentation of a settlement by women figures from the adversary's side evokes greater credibility than that of their male colleagues. This is attributed to stereotypical beliefs that women are more fair and empathetic than men, thereby evoking greater trust for the interlocutor from the adversary's side.[9]

This basically psychological tactic is directly linked to the aspect of "selling" the process or agreement to spoilers as well as potential spoilers, including the general public. Coping with such key matters as legitimacy and creditability (countering mistrust), often the key issues raised by the spoilers, can be countered by the manner in which the promise of resolution is framed. Relying on social psychology and public relations techniques, rhetoric, images, and various types of communication can be of critical importance. However, there is little agreement on just what "works" in specific circumstances.

To counter spoilers' often "doomsday" claims (when the expected agreement, even the process itself, is portrayed as equal to an existential threat), identity issues may have to be addressed. These are issues related to the way in which individuals or groups view themselves (or their society) and what attributes or conditions they see as inherent to their very identity. If, for example, victimhood is an essential part of their identity, an attempt may be made to demonstrate that circumstances have changed and so too their own status or situation as victims. Alternatively, it may be argued that there now exists a greater threat to be confronted—as potential victims—than in the past, constituting a need for settlement.

There is a basic resistance to change due to the unpredictability of a different path, particularly when the past enemy is now termed a partner, and past presumably existential interests or nonnegotiable issues are now subject to compromise. To deal with these, custodians need to exhibit optimism as well as determination, a sense of stability, and confidence regarding security.[10] In addition to elucidating the path to be taken, custodians should make the rationale behind the interest in resolution clear.[11] One may base this on, or appeal to, shared values and the consistency or continued loyalty to these shared values and goals, as well as the relevance of the process to these values and goals.[12] Fears may be addressed, highlighting precautions taken or the positive nature of the situation that will emerge from the agreement. Similarly, there could be assurances that spoilers' interests will also be addressed, preserved, or somehow accommodated.

The handling of both fears and interests may be related to the cost/benefit calculation mentioned above, bearing in mind the theory that people are more concerned about loss than potential gain and likely to take greater risk to avoid loss. Coping, therefore, would require an appropriate definition of what might be lost if the process were spoiled. The possibility of a worse security situation or harsher enemy or leadership would be losses by comparison with the status quo—that is, if the process were halted. Losses might be framed in terms of shared values, goals, interests, status, influence, and so on, or even more concrete assets, rather than focusing on what could be gained. For many of these coping measures to work, however, attention must also be paid to the image of the adversary as credible, changed, and no longer the enemy but rather a partner. At the least, the adversary may be presented as varied and nonmonolithic, with emphasis not only on positive changes but also on signs of compliance and flexibility as distinct from bringing attention to violations or failures of some among the adversary to comply or cooperate.

Finally there is the potential role of a third party in coping with spoilers. Custodians may try to engage third parties—that is, parties not directly involved in the conflict, or, more commonly, a third party involved as mediator or facilitator.[13] They may be an international organization (most often, the UN), a state or group of states (e.g., the Quartet), or nongovernmental organization or group of interested parties such as the Church of Saint Egidio. Third parties may employ many of the coping tactics adopted by custodians, from organizing dialogue and track-two encounters to offering incentives or inducements, such as the promise of benefits (material, political) or support for some or all of the spoilers' demands. This may even extend to providing concessions or guarantees necessary to accommodate spoiler demands—for example, the provision of military protection to reduce fears born of mistrust.

Stephen Stedman has suggested "socialization" in the form of holding spoilers to certain norms or providing a system of rewards and punishments in return for allowing spoilers into the process (thereby according them legitimacy) or meeting their demands (provided they are not total spoilers).[14] A third option is coercion, specifically the threat or actual use of punishment to deter the spoiler. One form would be to simply exclude or eject spoilers, specifically the players most likely to veto, from the process. The advantage of the third party is that it can determine who will participate in the process. It may deal piecemeal, including groups separately and sequentially, although this could limit flexibility as the process moves to later groups. Even in this case, the separate, piecemeal approach could facilitate third-party use of the departing train tactic: "If you cooperate you can be part of the process; if not, you will be left behind as we move forward with others."[15] A variation of this may be what Stedman calls "withdrawal"—the threat by the third party to withdraw from the process, although this would have limited utility if the spoiler were a total spoiler or had no particular interest in positive relations with or involvement of the third party. Still other tactics might be the engagement of additional third parties, particularly—if possible—from among outside supporters and allies of the spoilers (e.g., diaspora, as well as states or organizations) or, conversely, blocking the support (political, material) provided to spoilers from outside sources.

The Example of Northern Ireland

The case of the Good Friday Agreement in Northern Ireland, and, in particular, the campaign around the referendum on the agreement provides an example of almost all the various coping measures regarding spoilers (including potential spoilers and skeptics) in a peace process. Many factors led to the successful conclusion and approval of the agreement, not least of which were various international developments and, domestically, the willingness to involve all the protagonists, on the basis of promised decommissioning of armed groups. Indeed there is a good deal of literature on the conflict in Northern Ireland, coping with violence there, and the many efforts at resolution over the years. Once the matter of violence was addressed, coping measures were required, nonetheless, to prevent, neutralize, or minimize other forms of spoiling and obtain a "yes" vote in the referendum on the Good Friday Agreement.

Four major coping measures were taken with regard to the negotiations themselves: (1) the direct participation of the patrons (and past spoilers) of the main protagonists, namely, Great Britain and the Republic of Ireland; (2) the involvement of a third-party mediator (from the United States, which through its powerful Irish diaspora had played various roles in the conflict in the past, including the engagement of President Clinton); (3) the inclusion of past veto players accompanied by monitoring and the threat of penalties and exclusion for the use of violence; and (4) the popular election of a forum consisting of political parties (the ten receiving the most votes) to conduct the negotiations. This last coping measure (election of a forum) was designed both to create legitimacy and to involve grassroots peace/human-rights activists, represented by two cross-community groups, including the women's coalition NGO that successfully ran as a party in the election. The promise of a final voice for the public, namely, a referendum on whatever agreements were reached, was, perhaps, the ultimate coping measure.

There were spoiling tactics by both major leaders, David Trimble of the Ulster Unionists[16] and Gerry Adams of Sinn Fein, during the talks themselves. These, however, were of the limited type rather than the total. These leaders were not "devious actors," but each sought not only to have his demands and grievances addressed but also to placate constituents and spoilers from his own side. Thus, both engaged in what many saw as stalling measures, exhibiting great cautiousness and suspicions. Trimble refrained from use of the word "peace," acknowledging only that "talks" were taking place.[17] He demanded a very tightly defined agenda and tried to limit concessions. Refusing to meet directly with Sinn Fein, he continued to portray the Republicans negatively, as untrustworthy and unchanged.[18] Adams did use the word "peace," referring to changes on the other side, but he also stressed Irish patriotism (as well as justice and freedom) in keeping with his constituents' values and demands. He is also said to have maintained links with the IRA, using delaying tactics on the decommissioning issue in order to gain better conditions.[19] There was an attempt, however, to provide information to militants within each party in order to give them a sense of ownership of the process, to the degree possible.[20] Ultimately, the third-party mediator, Senator George Mitchell, employed "departing train" tactics to end the foot dragging and arguing over details, as distinct from principles (tolerating, perhaps even preferring some vagaries).[21]

Once the agreement was signed, after long, generally secret negotiations, the task of the leaders (now "custodians") was to neutralize spoilers on both sides. This could be done by reference to the content of the agreement itself, with its power-sharing clauses, group autonomy, regulatory approach to sovereignty, monitoring and periodic reviews, and other measures. While these were all measures designed to respond to the grievances as well as fears of the protagonists, public-relations firms maintained that concentration on the content would invite defense, rebuttals, and confusion.[22] Generally this advice was accepted as the custodians geared their efforts to winning over not only many in their own parties but also, mainly, spoilers among other parties or groups within their respective populations, Catholic or Protestant. Potential spoilers, primarily doubters vulnerable to the arguments of the total spoilers, and therefore capable of tipping the scales to a "no" in the referendum, became the main targets for the custodians.[23]

The tactics employed—many of which were prepared even as the talks were taking place—included the public appearances of leading figures from each side, as well as involvement of popular entertainers and sportsmen, among their own as well as the adversary's population. The more moderate John Hume, leader of the Social Democratic and Labour Party (SDLP), had to respond to skeptics within his own party regarding not just Protestant intentions but also cooperation with their militant rival Sinn Fein. Similarly, Sinn Fein leader Gerry Adams had to pacify militants within his own party.[24] Ulster Unionist Party leader David Trimble had the perhaps more difficult task. He had to contend with the efforts of the rival, total spoilers from the Protestant public: the Democratic Unionist Party (DUP) under Ian Paisley and the more marginal United Kingdom Unionist Party (UKUP). Trimble began cautiously, designating different representatives to deal with different groups such as past militias, police, or charity groups. In time he took direct action—for example, going into prisons himself to seek continued support.[25]

In fact, both Protestant and Catholic leaders sought to engage former prisoners, and both sides sought to involve families of victims, not only to counter opposition but also to engage them in the process as an alternative to spoiling.[26] However, the release and celebrated welcome of former IRA prisoners—a measure designed to placate Catholic spoilers, particularly from within the ranks of Sinn Fein—almost backfired. The triumphant nature of the event did little to allay the fears of the Unionist skeptics, and the event was exploited negatively by spoilers.[27] This was an example of "unintentional spoiling," the classic problem of trying to calm one's own spoilers without alienating the other side and possibly ruining the process. The appearance of the universally popular performers U2 and the Northern Ireland rock band Ash in favor of the agreement, helped reduce the damage from this near mishap. The Hume-Trimble handshake at the concert added to its efficacy.[28]

The media were also, reportedly, helpful. For example, a joint editorial in favor of the agreement, published by the Unionist *Ulster Newsletter* (considered a right-of-center, anticompromise paper) and the nationalist *Irish News*, was said locally to have played a critical role in defusing the threat of Unionist spoilers.[29] Similarly, grassroots groups, cross-community activists, workers, teachers, students, and particularly women held joint meetings, debates, and rallies, many of which included appearances by or special efforts among past victims and former prisoners. Indeed the "YES" Campaign was organized by leaders of established cross-community NGOs long active for peace and human rights, specifically the campaign's director, Quentin Oliver, who was former director of the Northern Ireland Council for Voluntary Action. Theoretically they operated independently of the political parties, but they in fact coordinated or even organized many of the political leaders' and groups' activities mentioned above.

The "YES" Campaign approach to potential spoilers generally was to deflect opposition by giving people the sense that they had a voice, that they were part of the process, not only through meetings—including track-two exchanges as well as grassroots activities—but also by conducting polls in which their voices could be heard.[30] Third parties also contributed to the effort in public statements, sometimes directly addressing spoilers. For example, there was a joint appearance by Tony Blair and Bill Clinton on BBC television, in addition to photos of Clinton with the Northern Irish leaders (and local families). The British support, which included former Prime Minister John Major as well, was of particular use in countering the "no" claims. Specifically such measures were used to counter claims by the total spoiler UKUP to the effect that the British identity of Northern Ireland would be lost forever if the agreement, characterized as a prelude to a "United Ireland," were accepted.[31]

Aside from activities and "helpers," the framing and "selling" of the agreement was clearly designed to neutralize, not actually engage spoilers. The words of rock star Bono of U2 echoed one of the main messages of the rhetoric employed: "We're here to try to convince some of the people who have real concerns, genuine concerns, about the peace agreement still to vote yes," he said, "because to vote no is to play into the hands of the extremists who've had their day. Their day is over as far as we're concerned. We're on to the next century here."[32]

Leaving the past behind (i.e., the violence and suffering of the "Troubles") and benefiting from a different future was, indeed, a major theme even of the same leaders who had exhibited skepticism and mistrust during the negotiations.[33] Now the changed nature of circumstances and, especially, of the other side was emphasized by the Catholics (Nationalists/Republicans) but also, to a lesser extent, by the Protestants (Unionists/Loyalists). The latter had to counter Paisley's efforts to delegitimize Sinn Fein by claims that it remained unchanged. Trimble was relatively restrained and cautious regarding expectations, but he sought to dispel Unionists' sense of being under siege. Thus, he, like Adams, maintained that the other side was not monolithic, even as both asserted, nonetheless, that his own side was remaining loyal to its long-standing principles. This was in response to accusations of treason from Paisley's DUP and IRA militants, respectively.

Trimble's defensiveness in particular was apparent in his party's campaign slogan: "We are doing the right thing."[34] Both reassured their doubters that nothing would be lost, that they were giving up nothing, but that security would be obtained (and maintained) through peace. Appealing to patriotism, both leaders claimed that the needs of all in Northern Ireland would be met. This was not only the claim that there was something in the agreement for everyone; it was also an effort to create public ownership by references to the "people" making it happen, making history.[35]

The "YES" Campaign echoed many of these messages around several themes: the unique opportunity afforded by the agreement, meaning both that there was no alternative—except the unacceptable loss of an end to the fighting (achieved by the cease-fire) and a return to the "Troubles"—but also that change was coming and one should not be left behind (departing train). The agreement was presented as a "last chance" for a peace dividend, constituting a fresh start worth trying "for the sake of our children."[36] The campaign employed the families of victims in the call for saving a new generation from suffering, playing on fears and the costs of failure, clearly suggesting that a "no" vote offered no future, no hope. This was shown graphically by a central logo of the "YES" Campaign (fig. 7.1).

The third party "helpers," such as former Prime Minister John Major, along with Blair and Clinton, also emphasized the "no alternative" and "unique opportunity" ("departing train") themes, along with the promise of a positive peace dividend.[37] Both the British and Clinton suggested an incentive (or cost/benefit) tactic in the form of hints at economic benefits to accrue if the accords were implemented.[38]

The final vote in the May 1998 referendum (71.12% "yes" with exit polls showing 51 to 57% of Unionists voting "yes" and 96-99% of Nationalists[39]) marked a clear victory, indicating successful neutralization of the spoilers. The massive support from the Catholics was most likely a sign of successful dealing with skeptics and limited spoilers, but the achievement of a majority—however slight—from the Protestants was evidence of the more impressive success in overcoming the DUP-led total spoilers. Just which tactic or tactics were responsible for these successes is difficult to determine. The polls showed a direct relationship between actions, specifically the youth-targeted concert (and the Hume-Adams handshake there), on the one hand, and changes in Unionist opinion, on the other hand.[40] However, the massive and varied "YES" Campaign, conducted by civil society and largely coordinated with the custodians from both sides,

Figure 7.1. Publicity for the "YES" Campaign. By Quintin Oliver, reprinted with permission.

was indispensable. Indeed, it is impossible to know if the vote could have been achieved without this campaign—its framing of the issues and the "helpers" it engaged, including the media, NGOs, former prisoners, and, actually, people from all levels, background, and walks of life. Through both the framing and the actions undertaken, the leaders themselves—the custodians—played a central role, ultimately demonstrating consistent, firm, and united support for the agreement (as did the critical third parties, particularly Britain). Thus, determined leadership was also an important element in marginalizing, deflecting, or reducing the ranks of the spoilers.

Other Examples

Many of these or similar coping measures have been employed in other conflicts as well. Going back to the Cold War period, Kissinger dealt with potential spoilers by dealing secretly in relations with China, centralizing the conduct of the negotiations, even issuing disinformation. He revealed the whole process only once it was successfully completed. Kissinger's policy of détente was a more gradual and public process, plagued by spoiling efforts by opponents in Washington. He focused on US interests in détente and the greater concessions purportedly being made by the Soviets (e.g., in arms talks)—something that actually hurt the Soviets' efforts to deal with their own spoilers. Prime Minister Margaret Thatcher dealt with opposition within her own party by depicting a changed enemy (or at least a nonmonolithic adversary) in her declaration "Gorbachev is a man I can do business with."[41]

In Rhodesia and later in Guatemala, more than one group of fighters was included in the negotiation to prevent their spoiling the process. In South Africa, Nelson Mandela sought to placate spoilers among the white population in a gesture signaling a generosity of spirit by attending the Rugby World Cup final and shaking hands with the (mainly Afrikaner) players.[42] And in connection with the referendum on UN Secretary General Kofi Anan's plan for Cyprus, a number of confidence-building measures were introduced by both sides, including lifting of travel restrictions, along with joint appearances and the avoidance of offensive symbols, flags, and so forth in public places.[43]

In talks with Colombian rebel groups, the government employed several coping measures particularly with regard to its own military's opposition to the talks. The government brought some elements of the military into the early, design stage of the process so as to weaken their incentive to spoil. It consulted with them during the talks and offered assurances that the army would not be curtailed. The government also assigned a "peace counselor" to mend fences with the more recalcitrant military (though the person selected apparently was not sufficiently committed to the task). To rebel groups (as well as military, who might be negatively affected) they suggested the incentive (or compensation) of political benefits through standing for election, in some cases promising official positions. At the same time, the departing train tactic was used—cooperate or be left behind in the structural transformation of the country that was to ensue. For the spoilers among the public, public hearings (*audiencias publicas*) were held in which citizens could submit proposals for peace building (which did cause delays and added complications).[44]

In a similar effort to engage or at least appease the public, in both Liberia and Guatemala powerful women's grassroots groups were consulted (in different ways) outside the negotiations as they took place.[45] But, in another example, coping took on a negative, even coercive nature, in regard to spoilers from the Bosnian Croatian party HDZ-BiHD during the effort to end the war. Many were ousted from public office, the group's financial resources were blocked or confiscated, and postwar economic assistance was conditioned on political cooperation.⁴⁶

Third parties also dealt with spoilers, for example, in the negotiations between government and RENAMO rebels in Mozambique. The UN provided an incentive to induce reluctant rebels from the organization to accept the agreement: a trust fund providing $300,000 per month to the organization.⁴⁷ In the case of the Cyprus referendum, EU membership was theoretically an incentive to the Greek Cypriots to accept Kofi Anan's plan or at least to hold the referendum (although support for the proposal was not a condition for membership). For the Kurds in Iraq, it was sufficient incentive to cooperate in exchange for limited independence even though they sought full independence.⁴⁸ In Cambodia, the UN opened a radio station (December 1992) with broadcasts designed to neutralize Khmer Rouge propaganda.⁴⁹ It also worked to reduce backing or assistance to the Khmer Rouge from patrons China and Thailand.

In another form of coping, the intervening outside powers simply excluded the Bosnian Serbs, viewed as total spoilers, from the Dayton Agreement talks.⁵⁰ The UN tried to discourage or distance Khmer Rouge backers such as China. The failure of the international community to distinguish between limited and total spoilers in Rwanda led, it has been argued, to the success of the total spoilers. Coping measures could have been introduced by the third party, for example, as protection of the moderates by the introduction of a larger, more proactive peacekeeping force, clear and credible threats against the spoilers, and the "defanging" of extremists.⁵¹

Diasporas, a third party of a different type, have sought in many cases to break down spoiler resistance by holding dialogue and track-two meetings abroad.⁵² The African Diaspora Policy Center in Holland was particularly active in this respect, bringing together dissenters (spoilers and potential spoilers), as well as adversaries, for training and dialogue.⁵³ Indeed, training, while legitimate and useful, is often a pretext or incentive for bringing opponents together in many NGO as well as diaspora efforts. More direct action reportedly was undertaken by Tamils in diaspora. Like many diaspora, Tamils abroad were generally considered to be more militant than those in the home country. Nonetheless, experiencing discrimination following 9/11, a Tamil group from North America is said to have traveled to Sri Lanka and successfully persuaded spoilers to support the cease-fire of December 2001. Reportedly they used the stick (rather than carrot) of reduced contributions.⁵⁴

Israeli Examples: Menachem Begin and the Peace Talks with Egypt

From the time of his election in May 1977, Prime Minister Menachem Begin sought a peace agreement with Egypt, initiating secret contacts that led ultimately to Egyptian President Anwar Sadat's historic visit to Jerusalem in November 1977. Begin's policy was both a reaction to the intolerable loss of Israeli lives in the Yom Kippur War and an effort to deflect pressure from the new American president, Jimmy Carter, for a reconvening of the 1973 Geneva Conference to reach a comprehensive peace. Such a conference, as Carter made clear, would involve Palestinian rights and the future of the West Bank and Gaza, which in Begin's eyes were both part of the land of Israel (*Eretz Israel*).

Sadat's visit proved to be a significant, possibly critical measure for coping with potential spoilers to the peace process with Egypt. In keeping with Robert Putnam's two-level model of directly addressing domestic opinion on the other (Israeli) side, Sadat provided living proof of the "changed nature of the adversary" (Egypt). He also offered the prospect of a new—more secure—future in his repeated promise of "no more war," along with a view of what could be lost: acceptance of Israel as a neighbor in the region, if the opportunity for agreement were missed.[55] These comments and the visit clearly impacted public opinion, as depicted through positive changes in both the public belief that peace was possible and a willingness to withdraw from Sinai.[56] But serious spoilers remained within the public and, especially, within the leading political echelons.

Prior to the 1973 war, there had been left-wing (Labor Party) opponents to withdrawing from the Sinai peninsula, primarily for what were perceived as security considerations. After the war, Labor did agree to partial withdrawals, first in a postwar disengagement of forces and then in the Interim Agreement of 1975, albeit not without resistance and right-wing spoiler efforts. Some in Labor remained opponents to withdrawal, but during Begin's negotiations with Egypt spoiling action came almost exclusively from the settler movement, their ideological and/or religious supporters, and the right wing of the political spectrum. These included Begin's coalition partners, especially the National Religious Party (representing most of the settlers), Begin's own party, and even some in his own coterie. Thus, Begin had to cope not only with spoilers from among his natural constituencies or supporters, but also with opinions that in many ways mirrored his own reservations and ideological opposition to giving up territory or evacuating settlements, along with mistrust of the Arabs (and to some extent the Americans). The key to the essential difference between Begin and these spoilers was that Begin did not consider the Sinai to be part of *Eretz Israel*. Therefore, this specific territory was secondary, even expendable, in order to maintain their common goal of keeping the West Bank and Gaza.[57]

Until the signing of the Camp David Framework Agreement in September 1978, Begin relied primarily on measures of persuasion. As early as the government meeting immediately following Sadat's visit, Begin calmed those skeptical colleagues worried that he might have been deceived by Sadat's rhetoric. He explained that he thought Sadat was sincere, but he went on to quote a traditional saying: "One should respect people but not trust them too much."[58] This did not placate all. Following Sadat's visit, Begin's close friend and Minister of Information Shmuel Katz resigned and created the Circle of Herut Loyalists (to Herut principles).[59] This group linked efforts with the already-existing Movement for Greater Israel and the settler group, *Gush Emunim*, along with individuals from the right and from Labor.[60] Criticizing Begin's autonomy plan (made public December 1977), right-wing opponents called it "a new White Paper," and a betrayal of the legacy of Jabotinsky. From within the government, Minister of Agriculture Sharon accused the government of "weakness" regarding the settlements. Begin's response was that he was in fact carrying out the approach of his mentor, Zeev Jabotinsky, "to the letter."[61] In response to the spoilers' campaign of demonstrations and propaganda over the next months, he met with *Gush Emunim* leaders and groups of settlers himself or sent emissaries from the government or the party.

Going beyond mere persuasion, Begin also took action on the ground by acquiescing to *Gush Emunim* pressure, supported by Sharon, and allowing the expansion of settlements in northern Sinai, as well as in the West Bank. This was despite a general slowdown in settlement action that he had initiated for the negotiation period.[62] In addition, it may be that Begin's increasingly hard positions in the post-visit talks with the Egyptians were also motivated if not actually designed to counter the spoilers' measures. In any case, third-party (US) criticism of Begin's hard line in this period presumably helped him counter the spoiler accusations.[63] It was this hard-line position that had obstructed the negotiations to the point of American intervention calling for a summit at Camp David. But for the benefit of the spoilers, prior to his departure for Camp David talks in September 1978, Begin promised both the government and settler leaders that under no circumstances would his delegation to Camp David agree to the removal of any settlements from Sinai.[64] He reportedly told settlers from the Sinai settlement *Yamit* that if such a demand were made, the delegation would "pack our bags and go back home."[65]

At this time there were other efforts to counter the spoilers from those who saw themselves as custodians of the process, both within and outside the government. Likud Minister of Defense Ezer Weizman expressed at least one threat to resign if settlement expansions were not halted. He also pressed Begin to take a more flexible position than the one that had made the convening of the Camp David summit necessary.[66] Outside the government, a movement was formed in civil society (later named Peace Now), urging greater Israeli flexibility in the negotiations. The movement—the first and only mass peace movement in Israel—was formed some months earlier by reserve officers and soldiers in reaction to the hard line taken in the talks with Egypt, which, in their opinion, threatened the opportunity for a peace agreement "now" with Egypt.[67] This was similar to the later use of former fighters in support of peace in Northern Ireland, whereby sacrifice and loyalty were meant to demonstrate the legitimacy of support for peace. Unlike the later Irish example, Peace Now did not coordinate with the "custodians" in the government, although they did have informal contact with parties in the parliamentary opposition. Their intention was to counterbalance the pressure of the spoilers; thus, their major slogan was "Peace is greater than Greater Israel." On the eve of Begin's trip to Camp David, Peace Now held a massive demonstration in Tel Aviv, one of many actions they were to undertake over the next months.[68] While Begin would most likely not have suggested Peace Now as "helpers," criticism from civil society, as well as from Labor and the United States, regarding inflexibility was useful to some degree in dealing with the critics from the right. Later Begin was to refer to the peace demonstrators almost as an excuse, arguing that he had felt he could not return empty handed after such a show of support for peace.[69] This was the hoped-for effect sought by the movement and the custodians, for their target was not the public—which in fact overwhelmingly supported the peace process—but rather the decision-makers who might be affected by the spoilers.

At Camp David itself, Carter insisted on total exclusion of the media, which, according to one of the participants constituted a major measure for coping with spoilers.[70] However, following the meeting, spoiler action became much greater and more strident in the wake of the Camp David

Framework Agreement. Begin was greeted at the airport on his return with signs reading "traitor" and people holding black umbrellas, shouting "Munich." Between Camp David and the signing of the final peace agreement, Begin not only complained of the actions of the settler spoilers but also occasionally refused to meet with them, sending instead Housing and Construction Minister Gideon Patt.

Begin's immediate effort, however, was to counter the spoilers inside—that is, to gain government and Knesset approval of the Camp David Agreement, although he was not bound by law to do so. Knowing that he would have a Knesset majority (counting on opposition support), he presumably went to the Knesset to gain the legitimacy for the process that would now be needed to placate spoilers both inside and outside the formal political arena. In addition to legitimacy, the Knesset vote could create a sense of ownership and even shared responsibility for the agreement, which could also be useful. Begin's decision to allow coalition MKs a free vote, without party discipline even in his own party, was part of this objective (some might say "ploy") of sharing responsibility for the decisions. The vote was to be free, but Begin avoided an internal party discussion. While he did hold a meeting with the Likud Knesset action, he limited his responses only to written questions. Potential influence of spoilers in that discussion was further limited by the fact that the meeting, along with one with the Foreign and Security Affairs Committee, was held only the day after Begin presented the agreement to the Knesset (September 25) and just one day before the Knesset vote (September 27).

Another measure Begin tried to use to deal with the major objections to the agreement, regarding the issue of the Sinai settlements, was a separate vote on the Sinai settlements evacuation clause as distinct from a vote on the rest of the agreement. The separate vote had been a condition proposed by Aharon Barak at Camp David to facilitate agreement on the settlement issue. It was also a tactic Begin had previously used, for example, in the 1970 government decision on Washington's Roger's Initiative for a cease-fire in the War of Attrition. At that time, as a member of the unity government, Begin sought a vote on a cease-fire separate from the Roger's Initiative's clauses regarding UNSC resolution 242, which he opposed. Once he announced a similar measure ("ploy") for the Camp David Agreement, critics and especially the media responded with accusations that Begin was trying to dissociate himself from or shirk responsibility for the evacuation concession, or that he hoped it would be defeated while the rest of the accord approved.[71] As a result of such criticism, he in fact abandoned separation of the vote after Camp David.

The rhetoric and arguments Begin employed to "sell" the accord—to the cabinet on September 24 and to the Knesset (the Likud faction, the Foreign and Security Affairs Committee, and the Knesset plenary) the following days—took a similar form. To his own party, Begin modestly argued that the agreement was the best they could get, adding defensively that at Camp David all parties had moved from their original positions, but, he added, he had not deviated from his principles.[72] To the cabinet, he somewhat exaggerated Sadat's concessions, but he also told both the party and the Knesset of Sadat's absolute immovability regarding the settlements.

The settlements were the main thrust of Begin's pitch: their sacrifice in order to obtain peace. He related to this in terms, repeatedly, of "pain" likened to "birth pangs," adding the comment that "everything great is born through suffering."[73] Defensive—even apologetic—about his ultimately futile efforts regarding the Sinai settlements, and identifying with his "settler friends," Begin presented an either/or situation, which actually amounted to no alternative. Begin put it as a matter of settlements or peace, a choice between a historic opportunity for peace—"a great turning point," as he put it, after five wars and the loss of "12,000 or our best sons," constituting a "supreme national interest"—*or* settlements. The "settlements or peace" juxtaposition was in fact presented several times, with the comment that there really was no choice; peace was "the only way" according to the "laws of morality."

To the cabinet, Begin had even implied the "departing train" idea by saying that Sadat might backtrack if there were no approval of Camp David. To the Knesset he spoke of the pressure of time and need for a clear-cut decision, using loftier terms such as "historic event" and "the promise of life not only for our generation, but also for our children and our children's children," in what would be a decision of "moral significance" and "conscience" for each member of Knesset. These emotional appeals were interspersed with biblical quotations but also presented as a "practical" step, with the promise of concrete results such as a permanent border with Egypt, the use of the Suez Canal, or the broader possibility of peace with other Arab states. Further, he also related practically to the settlers, assuring them the assistance of Sharon (the second of two times he linked Sharon to the decision) regarding resettlement, and promising assistance for every family.

Another technique Begin used in his speeches to the Knesset was to spread responsibility for the sacrifices he had agreed to at Camp David.

He enumerated all the people who had participated in the Israeli delegation, providing their expertise—that is, their responsibility—for specific matters. Of these, the security issue was given particular attention, including the concession regarding the military air bases in Sinai. Explaining this to the Foreign Affairs and Security Committee, Begin invoked a past comment by Sharon that the bases were not needed, though he added that the Americans now promised to compensate with new bases not far away, in the Negev.

Allaying more than purely security concerns regarding the autonomy plan, he explained in all his presentations that the IDF would remain in the West Bank no matter what arrangements were made during the autonomy period. He employed his own somewhat stretched interpretation of the Camp David language regarding "redeployment" rather than "withdrawal." According to one account, Begin elaborated on this point in response to misgivings raised in IDF circles about the autonomy agreement.[74] Responding further to accusations that a precedent had been set and that autonomy would become the basis for a Palestinian state, Begin firmly asserted that Israel would not give up its claim to sovereignty over Judea and Samaria, nor would it permit a Palestinian plebiscite, nor "under any conditions" the creation of a Palestinian state, nor talks with the PLO (which he quoted Carter as having likened to "Nazis").

In addition, in order to avoid the impression of having set a precedent at Camp David regarding settlements, Begin maintained that settlement building in the West Bank and Gaza Strip would continue. Although Begin had earlier agreed to a three-month freeze on new settlements for the period of post–Camp David negotiations for the final peace treaty, there had in fact been some ambiguity at Camp David (and subsequent controversy) over the length of this freeze. This may have been purposeful ambiguity on the part of Begin; Carter had understood the duration to be throughout the whole five-year period of autonomy negotiations.[75]

In addition to his own interpretation of the security clauses in the autonomy plan and the ambiguity over the duration of the settlement freeze, in his speech to the Knesset, Begin also referred to what amounted to other ploys he had employed in the formulations of the accords. Whether these measures were introduced by Begin at Camp David in order to cope with the concerns of the spoilers back home, or if, rather, he insisted on them because he actually shared these concerns, is difficult to determine. In any case, in his comments to the government and to the Knesset, Begin dealt with some of them in detail in what was clearly an effort to forestall spoilers.

For example, he explained to the Foreign and Security Affairs Committee that he had succeeded in keeping the preamble of UNSC Resolution 242 out of the text of the accords. Thus, the resolution's clause on the "inadmissibility of acquisition of territory by war" was not part of the accords but, instead, the whole resolution was only added as an annex. In his Knesset speech, Begin explained that he had American assurances that any reference to "Palestinians" or "'Palestinian people'" in the documents would be construed as "the Arabs of *Eretz Israel*"; similarly, he added, "in each paragraph where the expression 'West Bank' appears, it is being and will be understood . . . as Judea and Samaria." With regard to Jerusalem, separate (actually contradictory) letters had been given to Carter by both Begin and Sadat, but in his speech Begin spoke of only one letter, his, in which he reaffirmed Jerusalem as "one city, indivisible, the Capital of the State of Israel."[76]

Begin did not, however, invoke the Americans as a form of third-party pressure, although his housing minister, Patt, did so in talks with the settlers.[77] Since one of the spoilers' accusations had been that he had surrendered to the Americans, Begin took a different tack, praising Carter and crediting him with trying to help Israel withstand Sadat's demands on the settlements. He also pointed to the US solution to the airbase issue.[78] (He did not mention the Israeli request for financial aid from the United States for relocation of the settlers since this was still under negotiation with the United States.) Begin's only suggestion that third-party pressure or opinion had forced the Israelis to comply on the settlement issue was a remark that Israel would not be able to face the consequences, "not in the US, not in Europe, not before the Jews of other countries" if it had caused the failure of Camp David because of this issue.[79]

In the final Knesset vote on the accords, seven Likud MKs voted against as did three from other coalition parties; nine Likud MKs abstained as did four other coalition MKs; the final vote was eighty-four in favor, nineteen against, and seventeen abstentions. Thus, the spoilers were effective to the extent that the Camp David Accords would not have been approved without support from the opposition.

Spoiler action both in political circles and on the ground continued, indeed increased after the vote. One coping measure, that of building settlements, continued, although Begin had his own ideological reasons to demonstrate that the concession on settlements in Sinai would have no effect on policy toward the West Bank, then or in the future. Shortly after the

Knesset debate, the government announced a "thickening" of settlements in the West Bank—a concession Begin reportedly promised to the cabinet in order to gain support for a draft of the peace treaty under consideration.[80] A month later, in violation of even the three-month freeze, the government announced plans to build eighteen to twenty new settlements in the Jordan Rift Valley, possibly a response to demands of the IDF to maintain the Jordan River as Israel's border under the autonomy agreement.[81] A further effort to placate spoilers may have been the elevation of the status of *Gush Emunim's* settlement organization, *Amana*, to that of an official settlement movement similar to the status of the kibbutz and moshavim movements, eligible for Jewish Agency aid. This was a move expected after Likud's election in 1977, but given the timing, it was most likely intended as a coping measure, designed, according to then–NRP MK Yehuda Ben Meir, to demonstrate support in a practical manner.[82]

As sympathetic as Begin appeared, he did not, however, approve every settlement initiative of the settlers. He actually used coercion (ordering the blocking of access) on a number of occasions, in order to maintain government authority and control over settlement building, both before and after the Knesset vote. On one such instance, in January 1979, Begin explained this to *Gush Emunim* leaders by returning to the "pain" motif: "I want you to believe me that my heart pains me when I think of *Gush* members out on the highway near *Kaddum* in this cold and rain." Nonetheless he asserted: "I want you to urge them to give up their demonstration. Let them put their proposals forward. But they cannot dictate to the Government."[83]

The period until the signing of the Israel-Egyptian Peace Treaty (now separate from the autonomy agreement negotiated at Camp David) was one of difficult negotiations, in part due to Egyptian efforts to pin down the timing of autonomy and other matters. Much of the trouble, however, was attributed to Begin's increasing resistance to US and Egyptian suggestions, and this in turn was said to have been the result of spoiler action within the government. According to one source, Begin's hard line was a concession to recalcitrant coalition members, such as NRP Zvulun Hammer, who actually threatened to resign on one occasion.[84] The decision to strengthen the settlements reportedly was a direct response to this, and Begin actually wrote Carter that this had been necessary in order to placate "discontented political allies."[85] This was a convenient argument to present to the Americans, but conceding to hard-line demands regarding the drafts of the final peace treaty's clauses was frequent and became something of a pattern.

Thus Begin also acceded to colleagues' insistence on American guarantees regarding future oil supplies, financial assistance for the withdrawal from Sinai, completion of airbases in the Negev, and other matters.[86] Begin hoped in this way to satisfy at least the limited spoilers, but he also demanded full government deliberations on each of the Peace Treaty clauses so as to bolster the legitimacy of the final product in the face of remaining spoilers.[87]

Finally, it once again became necessary for Carter to take direct action. In March 1979 Carter came to the region primarily to press Begin to finalize the treaty. This was not a Begin initiative to bring in a third party to assist in countering spoilers; Begin himself continued to hold out on many issues. But once he finally did agree to the Treaty, Begin had Carter meet with the government and the Knesset Foreign and Security Affairs Committee, and address the Knesset, presumably to strengthen his, Begin's, position vis-à-vis his still recalcitrant colleagues. Carter directly addressed the skeptics and opponents, identifying with their concerns particularly on the background of Jewish history. He spoke of what would be a "tragic loss" of an opportunity and, alternatively, the "legitimate exaltation" if the treaty were signed. With numerous biblical and historical references, he spoke expansively and reassuringly of America's commitment to Israel.[88]

In his own speech to the Knesset, presenting the treaty for approval, Begin employed a very different tactic from the emotional one he had used for the Camp David Accords. Going through the treaty almost article by article, Begin presented exhaustive (and exhausting) legalistic detail, spelling out the background discussions, defending provisions, and explaining formulations that he had achieved with great effort (including some of the items he had explained after Camp David) to protect Israeli interests. It was virtually a war of attrition, and in the end, he got approval.

Whether a result of the coping efforts and reassurances detailed in the speech or the various measures taken over the preceding months to placate opponents, at least some of the political spoilers were converted. In the final Knesset vote (ninety-five for, eighteen against), five Likud MKs and three NRP MKs who had either abstained or opposed Camp David now switched to support.[89] Nonetheless, in Begin's own party, seven still opposed (including Sharon), two abstained and two did not vote. Once again the opposition Labor Party made the difference.

Spoiling action continued even after the treaty was signed, focusing primarily on the West Bank, but it became relatively clear quite soon that Begin did not intend to implement the autonomy agreement. Right-wing efforts to prevent the withdrawal from Sinai were intensified, including wildcat attempts to create new settlements in Sinai. Reluctant to use force, Begin met with Sinai settlers, explaining that there was no alternative to peace. Nonetheless he promised to find solutions for them; he set up a committee to deal with them and ultimately offered generous compensation packages in what might be viewed as an effort to buy the spoilers off.[90] Begin sought to deal gently with the settlers. For example, while he was in Washington for the signing of the peace treaty, settlers created an outpost encampment near the Sinai settlement of *Yamit*. Begin denied access to the outpost, rather than try forcibly to remove the settlers. Later he quietly moved the group into the Gaza Strip.[91] In the end, however, he was willing to use coercion,[92] though not violence, to remove the last settlers who had gone to *Yamit* to resist its evacuation.

Prime Minister Yitzhak Rabin and the Oslo Accords

Rabin had a more difficult task than Begin in coping with spoilers, mainly because Rabin's adversary—the PLO—could not or would not cope with violent, total spoilers on the Palestinian side. Terror attacks by Hamas and Islamic Jihad that began almost immediately after the signing of the Oslo Accords in September 1993. These events nearly derailed the process on a number of occasions and clearly complicated the efforts of the "custodians" to placate or neutralize spoilers on the Israeli side. Rabin did not have Begin's advantage of being able to count on the opposition to add support in case of need. In fact his own coalition was shaky, with just sixty-two MKs at the beginning of the process, six of whom from the less dependable Shas (forty-four Labor, twelve Meretz, six Shas, plus the support of two Arab Democratic Party MKs and three from Hadash).[93] Weakness of the coalition constituted a serious problem of legitimacy for government decisions.

In addition, spoiler activity was far stronger than that facing Begin inasmuch as Rabin, with the Oslo Accords, was dealing directly with the core of the conflict: the dispute with the Palestinians over the same piece of land. Although the 1988 PLO decisions limited their demand to the West Bank, including East Jerusalem, for total Israeli spoilers the issue remained relinquishing any part of *Eretz Israel*. Moreover, in Rabin's struggle, the ranks of potential or limited spoilers were far greater than in Begin's effort, given the high degree of mistrust of the Palestinians among the general population. Although the First Intifada had contributed significantly to a general willingness to compromise, maintaining the status quo in the West Bank had long been a preference for most Israelis.[94] Therefore, while the Oslo Accords were greeted positively by some 61 percent of the population, nevertheless, the potential for spoiler success was great.[95]

Rabin's awareness of this was evident from the beginning, both in his rhetoric and in the design of the peace process itself. Like Begin, he shared some of the spoilers' concerns regarding trust. Reiterating a statement made by all of Israel's prime ministers before him, Rabin had once said "no Arab leader will ever make genuine peace with us."[96] However, unlike most of his predecessors, he believed that this could change. He told President Gerald Ford in 1974, "There is an accumulation of suspicion that must be cleared on the way to peace.... In order to change attitudes in the area it would take a very long time."[97] For this reason, he favored partial or interim agreements in order to test the other side but also to cope with—and change—attitudes on both sides. Thus, Oslo was only an interim agreement of gradual stages designed to test the other side but also to build up trust among the public as well, so that a final peace agreement could be signed after five years.[98]

Another measure built into the accords that may have been *at least partially* connected to concern over spoilers was Rabin's refusal to deal with the settlements until the final status talks. Presumably he preferred to defer confrontation with the settlers until it would be absolutely necessary. The same might be said about the explicit exclusion of Jerusalem from the interim arrangements and from the jurisdiction of the autonomy organs to be created. However, as distinct from the settlement enterprise, which Rabin did not entirely support, sovereignty over all of Jerusalem was an interest he shared with the spoilers and the majority of the public. Thus, like Begin, he could use his insistence on these measures also as tools to placate spoilers. The same might be said regarding such Oslo provisions as continued Israeli responsibility for the security of the settlers (via bypass roads and other devices) or limitations on the arms (light weapons) allowed the Palestinian police, and other measures until the final status accords were negotiated.

Rabin himself undertook very few if any direct measures to placate the major spoilers: the settler organizations and their supporters.[99] In fact he had very little patience with them and often responded strongly and negatively, particularly when they began a campaign for soldiers to refuse any order to evacuate settlements that might be given. Thus, rather than use persuasion or try to placate them, he may have provoked them further. Eventually Rabin had hundreds of illegal settlers arrested. He also announced that any soldier disobeying orders would be arrested. In addition, following near-violent spoiler actions such as a procession carrying a coffin labeled "Zionism killed by Yitchak Rabin" or a demonstration with signs depicting Rabin in SS uniform, the attorney general announced his intention to bring indictments against inciters. After the settler Baruch Goldstein's massacre of Muslims at prayer in Hebron, two parties, Kach and Kahane Chai, were outlawed by the Knesset. Rabin stopped short, however, of removing the settlers from the heart of Hebron.

Nevertheless, and in violation of campaign promises, Rabin allowed the continuation of building in the settlements; some thirty-five thousand settlers were added during the Labor government July 1992 to May 1996. And while he himself made disparaging comments about the settlers and refrained from meeting with them, his deputy defense minister, former IDF chief of staff Motta Gur, was designated (at Gur's initiative) to hold regular discussions with settler leaders. President Ezer Weizman also visited settlements and met with their rabbis, generally after Palestinian terror attacks. Weizman's visits, however, were after a *"din rodef"*[100] edict was issued by settler (and American) rabbis against Rabin. Other custodians, for example, Rabin's military secretary, Danny Yatom, also maintained contact with the settlers, while both then Foreign Minister Peres and his deputy Yossi Beilin made public appearances issuing assurances that settler interests would not be abandoned (saying, for example, that most settlements would not be dismantled).[101]

Others who saw themselves as custodians were also active, usually on their own initiative, in varied efforts to counter the spoilers' campaign and to preserve the process in light of continued terrorism. People-to-people activities and dialogue groups were actually part of the process outlined in the Oslo Accords, though most often they were organized by civil society groups and even private individuals.[102] These were generally intended to persuade skeptics, by means of encounters with Palestinians, and to allay fears by demonstrating the diversity of the adversary or its changed and now-sincere character. One of the more ambitious of these efforts was Project Charley, which brought settlers and Palestinians together in dialogue.[103] It was based on an expectation that Oslo would lead to peace, and its purpose was to try to find a way for these two sides to deal with each other in the future—in the belief that if successful, spoiling efforts could be neutralized or stopped. While a private initiative, the meetings were known to Rabin through reports conveyed via Danny Yatom. Another group, reportedly with more direct links to the government (and the PLO), was an Israeli-Palestinian-American track-two effort at working together to find ways of dissuading spoilers on each side.

Other dialogues and public events were organized by extraparliamentary movements, including a women's peace group, the Jerusalem Link, organized primarily for this purpose, and the Israeli peace movement, Peace Now. Both engaged in bringing Palestinian speakers to Israeli audiences and even meetings in Israeli homes.[104] Peace Now also organized demonstrations in support of the peace process, usually employing slogans such as "There Is a Mandate for Peace" to counter those of the settlers seeking to delegitimize the process. While these and other civil society groups had contact with individuals in the coalition parties, Labor and Meretz, their activities were not coordinated with the government. In fact, one of the later criticisms of the Rabin government was that it did not organize activity on the street to counter that of the spoilers—until it was too late.[105] Rabin sought to avoid a leftist Peace Now tint lest it render the process still more difficult to sell. Thus, even when he did agree to a demonstration of support, the massive but fateful November 4, 1995, demonstration in Tel Aviv, he insisted that it have no party or organizational label, and he would not permit a speaker from Peace Now (even though the movement was deeply involved in organizing the event).

In addition to these "unsought" Israeli civil society helpers, there were also third-party civil helpers, in the American Jewish Diaspora. For example, the Israel Policy Forum, Americans for Peace Now, and Project Nishma each organized public events, media ads, and dialogues, often including Palestinians as well as Israelis. Their actions and statements were designed mainly to counter spoilers from among the Diaspora itself (who were often assisted by spoilers sent from Israel[106]) such as the Zionist Organization of America (ZOA), as well as spoilers or potential spoilers within the main pro-Israeli organizations, including AIPAC.[107] In a secret meeting following his election in 1992, Rabin, believing AIPAC to be biased toward the Likud, had already chastised AIPAC leaders for their hard line.[108] Indeed on occasion Diaspora spoiler action threatened to harm the peace process—for example, when the ZOA and others lobbied to limit US financial assistance to the PLO or promoted a resolution in the US Congress to move the US embassy from Tel Aviv to Jerusalem. The Orthodox Rabbinical Alliance of America was also active against the Oslo Accords on religious grounds, with its president, Rabbi Abraham Hecht, ultimately issuing a *din rodef* against Rabin, stating on US television that it would be a mitzvah (Jewish commandment) to kill Rabin.[109]

To counter these statements and actions, Israeli leaders met with US rabbis and others in the Diaspora. An American Desk was set up in the Labor Party (under the direction of Itzhak Herzog), and emissaries such as Peres and Beilin, along with Israeli diplomats, Labor Party MKs and young activists, were sent to speak to Jewish leaders and communities.[110] Rabin called the extremist US rabbis "ayatollas" and strongly criticized Jewish groups "that pressure Congress against the policies of the democratically elected government of Israel." He also intervened directly.[111] For example, he addressed AIPAC by teleconference and, on one occasion, he spoke by teleconference with American Jewish leaders in some seventy US cities. Twice he traveled to North America to address the annual meeting of the General Assembly of Jewish Federations, although generally he avoided personal appearances, leaving much of the effort to Peres and others.[112]

Another "third party," the US government, was rarely called on to assist in the "selling" of the process to Israelis. Aside from the signing of the Oslo Accords on the White House lawn, which provided backing for the process, the American role came mainly only in the later negotiations for the Oslo II Interim Agreement. The Americans were given a role in new monitoring and security arrangements, but this presumably was intended to improve those functions. Such participation was only indirectly useful for coping with spoilers inasmuch as it strengthened efforts against terrorism.

Rabin's major means of coping was to exhibit authority and increasingly firm determination throughout the process—for example, by his pronouncement "We must fight terrorism as if there's no peace process, and work to achieve peace as if there's no terror," (rephrasing, for the sake of legitimization, David Ben Gurion regarding the British White Paper of 1939).[113] Rhetoric, or framing, was an important part of the effort to sell the peace process to the skeptics and potential or limited spoilers, and to limit the impact of the total spoilers. The government was later criticized for failing to prepare a media campaign, and Rabin himself complained that the media were according disproportionate attention to "extremists" opposed to Oslo.[114] But in fact, possibly even instinctively, Rabin himself, and also Peres, relied primarily on rhetoric, believing, as Rabin said, that the government "must do everything to prove that the line it believes to be right is the correct one, and must try to influence public opinion [to that effect]."[115]

From the day he came to office, Rabin undertook such persuasion. In his first speech to the Knesset (before Oslo) and almost every subsequent speech and interview, he referred to the changed environment in which Israel found itself, directly challenging Israelis' deeply ingrained sense of victimhood and isolation: "No longer are we necessarily 'a people that dwells alone,' and no longer is it true that 'the whole world is against us.' We must overcome the sense of isolation that has held us in its thrall for almost half a century."[116] In this effort to change deep-seated attitudes, he also employed the departing train motif (albeit in a more general way than specifically referring to the process about to begin): "We must join the international movement toward peace, reconciliation and cooperation that is spreading over the entire globe these days—lest we be the last to remain, all alone, in the station."

The image of the adversary also had to be changed, and Rabin tackled this by enumerating the commitments he had wrested from the PLO regarding both ideology and methods: recognition of Israel's right to exist in peace and security, elimination from the PLO Charter all references incompatible with Israel's right to exist and with the peace process, and renunciation of the use of terror and a pledge to resolve differences through negotiation.[117] To the same end, he also claimed explicitly that the PLO had changed, and in time, he took pains to distinguish between Arafat (the PLO) and those continuing to commit terrorism, Hamas and the Islamic Jihad.[118]

Although the Oslo breakthrough raised expectations, Rabin himself was cautious, repeatedly emphasizing that this was "a chance" for a different future, though one fraught with some risk or danger.[119] For the latter, he also had answers. Implicitly deriving his legitimacy from his security credentials, at no time did Rabin let the public forget that he was first a military man, and therefore personally keenly aware of Israelis' losses and sacrifices in the past. Beyond legitimacy, these references indicated that realism and empathy are difficult for spoilers to challenge. However, references to his security credentials also conveyed a capacity for understanding and dealing with future dangers, while he explicitly referred to the continued reliance on Israel's strength, the IDF.[120] The emphasis on security and reliance on the IDF, as distinct from relying on the trust of the adversary was a theme used in the Diaspora as well.[121]

Generally it was left to Peres to present a vision of the future (a "New Middle East").[122] Still, in presenting the Oslo II Agreement to the Knesset,

Rabin used some of the same rhetoric as Begin had regarding the peace treaty with Egypt, for example: "a new stage for the Jewish people," a "new path" as well as an end to bloodshed and terrorism.[123] He also invoked ideological continuity, speaking of the Jews' "rightful ownership of the land," though he added that there was also another people on this land. He also mentioned Labor's traditional position in favor of a Jewish majority in the state of Israel as distinct from the danger of a binational state.

An explicit reference to the alternative, a binational state, should the peace process fail, came very late in Rabin's approach, possibly because he felt it necessary to appeal to the very basic aspirations of Zionism. Thus, in order to counter the increased violence of the spoilers, their charges of "treason" and "Jew killer," alongside the continued terrorism by Palestinian Islamists, Rabin spoke of fear of losing a Jewish majority in the country.[124] At the same time, in his speech presenting the main points of Oslo II, Rabin outlined his positions for the final status negotiations, repeating assurances he had been expressing all along: there would be no return to the June 4, 1967 lines, no Palestinian state (he spoke of "an entity less than a state"); Israel's eastern border would be in the Jordan Rift Valley; Jerusalem would remain united under Israeli sovereignty; settlement blocs would be maintained; and, during the Interim period, no settlements would be evacuated or natural growth limited.[125] As had been the case for Begin, these assurances reflected most of Rabin's own interests and concerns. However, enumerating them in support of the new agreement was also designed to placate the spoilers. Indeed, Rabin's references to full Israeli control over the security arrangements, specifically the scope of the redeployments, was most likely aimed at potential spoilers from military or ex-military colleagues—for example, former chief of staff Ehud Barak, who voted against Oslo II in the cabinet.

Unlike Begin (who had been able to count on support from the opposition), Rabin had some difficulty gaining a majority in the Knesset for Oslo II. He had faced serious problems keeping his coalition together. As noted above, *Shas* had taken its faction of six out of the government at the beginning of the peace process (though two former Likud MKs forming *Yi'ud* joined), leaving Rabin with a fifty-eight-person coalition, supported by five additional MKs from outside the coalition. The final vote for Oslo II was sixty-one to fifty-nine, with two Labor MKs voting against.[126] Given the slim majority, obtained only with the help of the mainly Arab MKs, the vote did little to secure legitimacy for the process in the eyes of the spoilers.

Even limited spoilers apparently were unconvinced; Israeli Jewish support for Oslo had declined from 61 percent at the time of the signing in 1993 to just 31.1 percent by March 1995.[127] One month after the Knesset vote, Rabin was assassinated by a right-wing religious student of law from Bar Ilan University.

Quite clearly the coping measures employed by Rabin and the various custodians failed to overcome the spoilers. There were many reasons for the failure of Oslo, but if we examine it from the point of view of the coping measures employed or those that might have been employed, the conclusions are also numerous. From this point of view, steadfastness despite Palestinian terror, efforts to distinguish between a changed PLO (including Arafat) and the terrorists, and reassurance to the Israeli public that the government was and would be in control of security did not succeed in fully waylaying fears or reducing the intensity of the spoilers' actions.[128] In July 1995 some 48 percent of Israelis reported feeling less secure as a result of the peace process.[129] The choice of a gradual approach—during which time opponents on both sides could gather forces and act—may have been the wrong choice, as distinct from a swift move to full agreement, as suggested in theory.[130]

It has been argued that the government did not sufficiently prepare for dealing with spoilers, for example, with regard to a media campaign. Nor did it make an effort to educate the public.[131] And Rabin's efforts to marginalize them by his disdainful comments and criminalization of the extremists may have had the opposite effect of that desired, escalating spoilers' charges to that of tyranny as well as treason.[132] The bottom line is that the total spoilers were motivated by religious and extreme nationalist ideology, and the agenda was the core issue of "giving up" any part of (God-given) *Eretz Israel*. Thus, it is unlikely that they could have been dissuaded. However, the fact that they were not totally marginalized was more the result of the Islamists' terrorism (and Arafat's failure to curb it), along with problems within the accords themselves and their implementation, rather than the result of spoiler actions. Indeed, it is conceivable that if Rabin—given his security credentials—had lived to continue the process, with Arafat's eventual though tragically belated crackdown on the Islamists, it may well have been possible to bring skeptics and limited spoilers back into the fold. Whether this would have made a difference for the possibility of reaching a final peace agreement is a matter of speculation. Presumably, *successful* negotiations for a final peace agreement would have constituted the most promising coping measure.

Notes

1. For example, Marie-Joelle Zahar, "Understanding the Violence of Insiders," in *Challenges to Peacebuilding*, ed. Edward Newman and Oliver Richmond (New York: United Nations University, 2006), 40–58; Michael Doyle and Nicholas Sambanis, *Making War and Building Peace* (Princeton, NJ: Princeton University Press, 2006), 58–59; Miriam Ellman, "Preventing and Managing the Spoilers of Peace," in *Negotiations in Times of Conflict*, ed. Gilead Sher and Anat Kurz (Tel Aviv: INSS, 2016).

2. Discussed in Edward Newman and Oliver Richmond, eds., *Challenges to Peacebuilding* (New York: United Nations University, 2006), 59–77.

3. Stephen Stedman, "Spoiler Problems in Peace Processes," in *International Conflict Resolution After the Cold War*, ed. Paul Stern and Daniel Druckman (Washington, DC: National Academy Press, 2000), 185; Louis Kriesberg and Bruce Dayton, *Constructive Conflicts* (New York: Rowman and Littlefield, 2012), 815–88.

4. Gabriel Blum, *Islands of Agreement* (Cambridge, MA: Harvard University Press, 2007), 7–52.

5. David Cunningham, "Veto Players and Civil War Duration." *American Journal of Political Science* 50 (2006): 875–892; Christopher Mitchell, *Gestures of Conciliation* (London: Macmillan, 2000), 242.

6. Karen Aggestam, "Internal and External Dynamics of Spoiling," in Newman and Richmond, *Challenges*, 25.

7. Peter Wallensteen, *Understanding Conflict Resolution* (New York: Sage, 2007), 46; Mitchell, *Gestures*, 242–3.

8. Thania Paffenholz, "Civil Society and Peace Negotiations: Beyond the Inclusion-Exclusion Dichotomy, *Negotiation Journal* (January 2014): 73–74.

9. Ifat Maoz, "The Women and Peace Hypothesis? The Effect of Opponent-Negotiators' Gender on Evaluation of Compromise Solutions in the Israeli-Palestinian Conflict," *International Negotiation* 14 (2009): 521–538.

10. Nimrod Rosler, "Not as Simple as That: The Challenges Leaders Faced in Pursuing a Peace Process towards Reconciliation in Northern Ireland," unpublished paper.

11. Kristine Hoglund, *Peace Negotiations in the Shadow of Violence* (Leiden, Netherlands: Nijhoff, 2007), 177, 182, 183.

12. Hoglund, *Peace Negotiations*, 182. Zahar speaks of value-based loyalty to the process, as distinct from process based (being part of the process, having a voice and having invested in it by participating), and instrumental loyalty—gaining something from the process. Newman and Richmond, *Challenges*, 43.

13. There is a vast literature on mediating; the measures discussed here are those specifically related to coping with spoilers.

14. Stephen Stedman, "Spoiler Problems in Peace Processes," *International Security* 22 (1997): 12.

15. David Cunningham, "Who Should Be at the Table: Veto Players and Peace Processes in Civil War," *Penn State Journal of Law and International Affairs* 2, no. 1 (2013): 43.

16. The two other Unionist parties had already withdrawn from the talks and remained total spoilers.

17. Rosler, "Not as Simple."

18. Roger Mac Ginty, "Northern Ireland: A Peace Process Thwarted by Accidental Spoiling," in Newman and Richmond, *Challenges*, 165.

19. Mac Ginty, "Northern Ireland."

20. Cathy Gormley-Heenam, *Political Leadership and the Northern Ireland Peace Process* (New York: Palgrave, 2007), 76; John Darby and Roger Mac Ginty, *The Management of Peace Processes* (New York: Palgrave, 2000), 88.

21. George Mitchell, *Making Peace* (New York: Knopf, 1999), 57.

22. Richard Couto, "The Third Sector and Civil Society: The Case of the 'Yes' Campaign in Northern Ireland," *Voluntas: International Journal of Voluntary and Nonprofit Organizations* 12, no. 3 (2001): 227.

23. The objective was to get more than a majority.

24. Approximately 7 percent of Sinn Fein members were said to be opposed to the agreement. Ian Sommerville and Shane Kirby, "Public Relations and the Northern Ireland Peace Process: Dissemination, Reconciliation and the Good Friday Agreement Referendum Campaign," *Public Relations Inquiry* 1, no. 3 (2012): 246. (This article has quite detailed analyses of the tactics used by each of the parties.)

25. Gormley-Heenam, *Political Leadership*, 76–77; Darby and Mac Ginty, *Management*, 88.

26. Darby and Mac Ginty, *Management*, 88.

27. Landon Hancock, "There Is No Alternative: Prospect Theory and the 'Yes' Campaign and Selling the Good Friday Agreement," *Irish Political Studies* 26, no. 1 (2011): 97; Couto, "Third Sector," 34. See also Landon Hancock, Joshua Weiss, and Glen Duerr, "Prospect Theory and the Framing of the Good Friday Agreement," *Conflict Resolution Quarterly* 28, no. 29 (2010): 183–203.

28. Sommerville and Kirby, "Public Relations," 248. They calculate that the concert, with the handshake, contributed significantly to the swing of 15 percent in support of the agreement from within unionist voters in the final week of the campaign; 248, 252.

29. Gadi Wolfsfeld, "The News Media and Peace Processes: The Middle East and Northern Ireland," Paperwork No. 37, United States Institute of Peace, Washington, DC, January 2001, 1–54.

30. Landon Hancock, "The Northern Irish Peace Process: From Top to Bottom," *International Studies Review* 10 (2005): 226–228.

31. Sommerville and Kirby, "Public Relations," 249–250. There was also a visit by Tony Blair to the constituency of UKUP leader Robert McCartney's constituency. Hancock, "No Alternative," 104.

32. *Washington Post*, May 20, 1998, accessed June 1998, http://www.atu2.com/news/in-name-of-peace-u2-rocks-in-belfast.html.

33. Trimble, for example, asserted that "voting No would guarantee a return to violence." Cited in Hancock ,"No Alternative," 111.

34. Sommerville and Kirby, "Public Relations," 245. Trimble maintained that the agreement would keep Northern Ireland in Britain. The DUP and UKUP both used the slogan "It's right to say 'NO.'" Sommerville and Kirby, "Public Relations," 249.

35. Sommerville and Kirby, "Public Relations," 243.

36. Hancock, "No Alternative," 99; Hancock, Weiss, and Durerr, "Prospect Theory," 188–200.

37. Hancock, "No Alternative," 111.

38. Hancock, Weiss, and Durerr, "Prospect Theory,"196.

39. Couto, "Third Sector," 231.

40. Sommerville and Kirby, "Public Relations," 251.
41. Mitchell, *Gestures*, 248.
42. Darby and Mc Ginty, *Management*, 235.
43. Robert Rotberg. "Conflict Resolution in Cyprus: The Absence of Committed Leadership," *Canadian Foreign Policy Journal* 19, no. 1 (2013): 60–74.
44. Newman and Richmond, *Challenges*, 226–229.
45. In Liberia the women virtually forced their way into a discussion with the negotiators; in Guatemala they formed an officially accepted accompanying forum aside the talks.
46. Vesna Bojicic-Dzelilovic, "Peace on Whose Terms? War Veterans' Association in Bosnia and Herzegovina," in Newman and Richmond, *Challenges*, 216.
47. Kelly Greenhill and Soloman Majerk, "The Perils of Profiling Civil War Spoilers and the Collapse of Intrastate Peace Accords," *International Security* 31, no. 3 (2006–2007): 25–27.
48. Greenhill, *Perils*, 27.
49. Stedman, "Spoiler Problems," 31. Such use of media is a tactic often employed by NGOs, most notably Search for Common Ground. Galia Golan and Adir Gal, "Globalization and the Transformation of Conflict," in *Conflict Transformation and Peacebuilding*, ed. Bruce Dayton and Louis Kriesberg (London: Routledge, 2009), 124–125; Loretta Hieber, "Media as Intervention," *Track Two* 7, no. 4 (1998), http:/ccrweb.ccr.uct.ac.za/archive/two/7_4/16_intervention.htlm.
50. Stephen Stedman, Donald Rothchild and Elizabeth Cousens, *Ending Civil Wars* (Boulder, CO: Lynne Reinner, 2001), 207. Karadžić was theoretically represented by then Yugoslav Serb leader Milosovic.
51. Stedman, "Spoiler Problems," 25.
52. Golan and Gal, "Globalization," 128.
53. http:/www.diapora-centre.org, accessed January 10, 2012, site closed 2013.
54. C. C. Fair, "Diaspora Involvement in Insurgencies: Insights from the Khalistan and Tamil Eelam Movements," *Nationalism and Ethnic Politics* 11 (2005): 125–156.
55. "Documents Related to the Peace Process between Israel and Her Neighbors," accessed June 2015, http:/www.knesset.gov.il.
56. Asher Arian, *Security Threatened* (Cambridge: Cambridge University Press, 1995), 102.
57. In the postwar government meetings of June 18–19, 1967, Begin did not object to returning Sinai to Egypt, minus Gaza. Israel State Archives (ISA), Documents 1–6: a-8164/7; a-8164/8; a-8164/9, and a-7634/5, Government Publications, Periodic History, Stenographic Minutes of Meetings of the Government, June 18 and 19, 1967, April-June 1967 including Six Day War. In 1977, there were some outside as well as inside the Likud—for example, Moshe Arens, at the time ambassador to Washington—who opposed withdrawal primarily on security grounds. Others, such as Labor leaders like Shimon Peres, objected to evacuating settlements, but they did not join the spoilers.
58. ISA, a-4270/1, "Meeting of the Government; 24 November 1977."
59. Herut members of the Likud accounted for approximately one-fourth of the members of the Knesset.
60. Yaacov Bar-Siman-Tov, "Peace Policy as Domestic and Foreign Policy," in *Peacemaking in a Divided Society* (London: Frank Cass, 2001), 41.
61. Colin Shindler, *Israel, Likud and the Zionist Dream* (London: I.B. Tauris, 1995), 94.
62. "Settlement Fever and the Peace with Egypt, 1977–1982," accessed May 2013, http:/www.ariel-sharon-life-story.com.

63. Shindler, *Israel, Likud*, 93. As early as December 1978 the government established a new settlement and approved the establishment of two additional ones; in January 1978 it announced large-scale plans for more. In February Gush Emunim claimed the promise to establish Shilo was not fulfilled, due to Begin's acquiescence to US pressure for a settlement freeze, but Begin did not try to evacuate the Shilo settlers and allowed other settlements, and, possibly in return, protests from Gush Emunim subsided until the Camp David talks. David Weisburd, *Jewish Settler Violence* (University Park, PA: Pennsylvania State University Press, 1989), 39–40.

64. Yaacov Bar-Siman-Tov, *Israel and the Peace Process* (Albany: State University of New York, 1994), 110.

65. Bar-Siman-Tov, *Peace Process*, 137.

66. Shindler, *Israel, Likud*, 94.

67. Benny Morris, *Righteous Victims* (New York: Alfred Knopf, 1999), 461–463; Bar-Siman-Tov, *Peace Process*, 93–95, 100, 110–112.

68. The demonstrators were numbered at an estimated one hundred thousand, the largest such gathering up to that time.

69. Mordecai Bar On, *Peace Now: A Portrait of a Movement*, in Hebrew (Tel Aviv: Kibbutz Meuchad, 1985), 31–32; although Weizman said that no government decision was actually affected by this. Ezer Weizman, *The Battle for Peace* (New York: Bantam, 1981), 306.

70. Elyakim Rubinstein, *Paths of Peace*, in Hebrew (Tel Aviv: Ministry of Defense Press, 1992), 99–100.

71. Bar-Siman-Tov, *Peace Process*, 138.

72. Bar-Siman-Tov, citing Uzi Benziman, *Prime Minister Under Siege*, in Hebrew (Jerusalem: Adam, 1981), 206 (on the cabinet); and *Ma'ariv, Yediot Ahronot, Jerusalem Post*, September 27, 1978 (on the Foreign and Security Affairs Committee).

73. Quotations are from Begin's September 25 and 27, 1978, speeches to the Knesset plenary. Ministry of Foreign Affairs (MFA), "Statement to the Knesset by Prime Minister Begin on the Camp David Agreements," http:/www.mfa.gov.il, accessed June 2015, in the full text of the Knesset debate, Netanel Lorch, *Major Knesset Debates* (Jerusalem: Jerusalem Center for Public Affairs, 1981), 2232–2274.

74. Morris, *Righteous Victims*, 477. The reference to Sharon regarding the air bases was also, reportedly, in answer to IDF concerns.

75. Jimmy Carter, *Keeping the Faith, Memoires of a President* (New York: Bantam, 1982), 397.

76. William Quandt, *Camp David* (Washington, DC: Brookings Institution, 1986), Appendix G, 386. Sadat's side letter to Carter said, "Arab Jerusalem is an integral part of the West Bank." Quandt, *Camp David*, 385.

77. Bar-Siman-Tov, *Peace Process*, 152.

78. Bar-Siman-Tov, "Peace Policy," 39.

79. Lorch, *Knesset Debates*, 2271.

80. Morris, *Righteous Victims*, 479; Quandt, *Camp David*, 277.

81. Morris, *Righteous Victims*, 480. For some time the government had been placing settlers in IDF bases, later changing their status to civilian settlements.

82. Interview with Ben Meir in Marcia Drezon-Tepler, *Interest Group and Political Change in Israel* (Albany, NY: State University of New York, 1990), 212.

83. Weisburd, *Settler Violence*, 42–43, citing *Jerusalem Post*, January 5, 1979. Used "pain" motif again in talks with Herut Central Committee. Morris, *Righteous Victims*, 481.

84. Moshe Dayan, *Breakthrough* (London: Weidenfeld and Nicholson, 1981), 225.
85. Carter, *Keeping the Faith*, 408.
86. Bar-Siman-Tov, *Peace Process*, 159; Quandt, *Camp Daivd*, 289; Morris, *Righteous Victims*, 480.
87. Bar-Siman-Tov, *Peace Process*, 161.
88. Address of US President Jimmy Carter to the Knesset, March 12, 1979, accessed June 2015, http:/www.mfa.gov.il.
89. Bar-Siman-Tov, "Peace Policy," 43.
90. Morris, *Righteous Victims*, 491.
91. Weisburd, *Settler Violence*, 43.
92. Using water cannons and foam sprayers.
93. Shas left the government September 14, 1993, but a small Likud breakaway faction, Yi'ud, joined the government on January 9, 1995. After Shas left and Yi'ud entered, the number of MKs who supported the government fell to fifty-eight coalition members plus the five MKs from the mainly Arab parties outside the coalition.
94. Asher Arian, *Israel and the Peace Process: Security and Political Attitudes in 1993*, Jaffee Center for Center for Strategic Studies, Tel Aviv University, 1993, 10; Jacob Shamir and Michal Shamir, *The Dynamics of Public Opinion on Peace and the Territories*, Final Research Report, September 1993, cited in Galia Golan, "Israel and Palestinian Statehood," in *Global Convulsions: Race, Ethnicity, and Nationalism at the End of the Twentieth Century*, ed. Winston Horne (New York: New York University Press,1997), 176; Hanna Levinsohn and Elihu Katz, "The Intifada is Not a War: Jewish Public Opinion on the Israel-Arab Conflict" in *Framing the Intifada: People and Media*, ed. Akiva Cohen and Gadi Wolfsfeld (Norwood, NJ: Ablex, 1993), 53–61.
95. Dan Leon, "Israeli Public Opinion and the Peace Process," *Palestine-Israel Journal* 2, no. 1 (1995): 57.
96. Yitzhak Rabin, *The Rabin Memoirs* (Berkeley: University of California Press,1996), 263.
97. FRUS, XXVI *Arab-Israeli Dispute, Doc*.183, Memorandum of Conversation, June 11, 1975.
98. This was basically Begin's autonomy plan, but with the PLO, not Jordan, representing the Palestinians.
99. Leading spoilers were the settler umbrella organization The Council of Judea and Samaria (YESA) with strong ties to the National Religious Party, and the most active, extreme settler group, Zo Artzenu, established in 1993.
100. Literally "law of the pursuer," roughly equivalent to "going after a traitor."
101. Reuven Hazan, "The Labor Party and the Peace Process," Davis Institute Occasional Papers, 1998.
102. Many of these were in fact initiated by Palestinians.
103. Yossi Alpher, *And the Wolf Shall Dwell with the Wolf: Settlers and Palestinians*, in Hebrew (Tel Aviv: Kibbutz Hameuchad, 2002).
104. Jerusalem Link, a joint Israeli and Palestinian organization consisting of Bat Shalom in West Jerusalem and the Jerusalem Center for Women in East Jerusalem.
105. Ehud Sprinzak "The Shaping of the Right and Its Current Attitudes," in Alan Dowty, Ilan Peleg, Abraham Diskin, Ehud Sprinzak, Hillel Frisch, Hans-Joachim Lauth, *The Role of Domestic Politics in Israeli Peacemaking* (Jerusalem: Leonard Davis Institute, 1997), 39.
106. For example, both Itzhak Shamir and Arik Sharon spoke against the Oslo Accords at the Conference of Presidents of Major Jewish Organizations, November 1993.

107. For the split within AIPAC, see Ofira Selitkar, *Divided We Stand* (Westport, CT: Praeger, 2002), 119–149, which has a very thorough account of the Jewish Diaspora activities in this period. See also Yossi Shain, "Jewish Kinship at a Crossroads," *Political Science Quarterly* 117, no. 2 (2002), 301, on US Diaspora funding of campaign against Rabin.

108. Selitkar, *Divided*, 133.

109. October 9, 1995 interview in *New York Magazine* and Yoram Peri, *The Assassination of Yitzhak Rabin* (Stanford, CA: Stanford University Press, 2000),110.

110. David Singer and Ruth Seldin, eds., *American Jewish Yearbook—1994* (Philadelphia: American Jewish Committee, Jewish Publication Society, 1994); Selitkar, *Divided*, 132.

111. Selitkar, *Divided*, 143.

112. Singer and Seldin, *American Jewish Yearbook—1994*.

113. Quoted in Clyde Haberman, "Peace and Terror in Israel," *New York Times*, April 1, 1993, although Rabin said this more than once.

114. Hazan, "Labor Party," 218; Oded Haklai, "Linking Ideas and Opportunities in Contentious Politics: The Israeli Nonparliamentary Opposition to the Peace Process," *Canadian Journal of Political Science* 36, no. 4 (2003): 791–812; Chanan Nevo, "The Role of the Media in Shaping Israeli Public Opinion," in Sofer, *Peacemaking*, 219 (quoting Beilin).

115. Interview with *Davar*, September 16, 1974, http:/www.mfa.gov.il.

116. MFA, Address to the Knesset by Prime Minister Rabin Presenting His Government, July 13, 1992; Address by Prime Minister Yitzhak Rabin at the Levi Eshkol Creativity Awards Ceremony, Tel Aviv, October 6, 1994, Rabin Center Archives; Speech to National War College: Perry, in Rabin, *Memoirs*, Appendix D, 397–398. For an analysis of the rhetoric used, see Nimrod Rosler, "Political Context, Social Challenges, and Leadership: Rhetorical Expressions of Psycho-Social Roles of Leaders in Intractable Conflict and Its Resolution Process—the Israeli-Palestinian Case," PhD thesis, Hebrew University of Jerusalem, 2012. Rabin's media advisor, Eitan Haber, reportedly said that he added biblical phrases to Rabin's peace process speeches. Nevo, "Role of Media," 218.

117. "Excerpts of PM Rabin Knesset Speech," September 21, 1993, http:/www.mfa.gov.il.

118. Prime Minister Yitzhak Rabin: Ratification of the Israel-Palestinian Interim Agreement, October 5, 1995, http:/www.mfa.gov.il.

119. Rabin to Knesset, September 21, 1993; Address by Prime Minister Yitzhak Rabin at the Levi Eshkol Creativity Awards Ceremony, Tel Aviv, October 6, 1994 Rabin Center Archives.

120. Perry, "Afterword," in Rabin, *Memoirs*, 406–407 (slightly more complete than the MFA excerpted version of the speech). Speech December 1993, no exact date or occasion listed, Perry, Appendix G, in Rabin, *Memoirs*, 413.

121. Lawrence Grossman, "Jewish Communal Affairs," *American Jewish Yearbook—1995*, 154, 158.

122. Rabin's biographer Yoram Perry maintains that Peres "was able to lift the public on the wings of his vision," in contrast to Rabin's more hesitant, plodding, and cautious approach. Savir characterized the two leaders as "visionary" and "pragmatist" respectively. Rabin, *Memoirs*, 374; Uri Savir, *The Process* (New York: Vintage Books, 1998), 78.

123. Rabin, Ratification, October 5, 1995, http:/www.mfa.gov.il. Also similarly to Begin, Rabin accorded responsibility to others: "dozens perhaps hundreds of civil servants" who helped design Oslo II, naming also Peres, perhaps as a gesture of sharing the credit as well as responsibility, since demonstrating government unity despite their rivalry was also a coping measure.

124. http:/www.michaelkarpin.com or http:/www.learntoquestion.com; https://www.youtube.com/watch?v=8Wlgag6XTuE.
125. Rabin, "Ratification," October 5, 1995, http:/www.mfa.gov.il.
126. The two (Kahalani and Zissman) later left Labor and formed a new party, mainly because of opposition to Rabin's negotiations with Syria.
127. Leon, "Israeli Public Opinion," 57 (poll of Jewish Israelis); Peace Index, 1995 http://www.peaceindex.org/files/peaceindex1995_10_6.pdf. (There was no index on Oslo for 1993.) See also, Shamir, Jacob and Michal Shamir, 2000. *The Anatomy of Public Opinion*, Ann Arbor: University of Michigan Press. 192–193.
128. It is argued that Rabin did not aggressively attack the insecurity themes of the right wing. Sprinzak, "Shaping of the Right," 39.
129. Peace Index, July 1995.
130. Mitchell, *Gestures*, 242.
131. Sprinzak, "Shaping of the Right," 39; Hancock, "Prospect Theory," 427–452; Robert Rothstein, "A Fragile Peace: Could a Race to the Bottom Have Been Avoided?" in *The Israeli-Palestinian Peace Process*, ed. Robert Rothstein, Moshe Maoz, and Khalil Shikaki (Brighton: Sussex University Press, 2002), 10.
132. For example, Moshe Feiglin, *Zo Artzenu* cofounder, indicted for sedition in 1997 and later deputy speaker of the Knesset from the Likud, accused Rabin of "tyrannical democracy." "The Ideological Failure and the Tactical Foul-up," *Nekuda*, 179, 1994, 44–46, cited in Haklai, "Linking Ideas," 801. See also Haklai, "Linking Ideas," 805, on exacerbating the protestors.

GALIA GOLAN is Professor Emerita of Political Science at the Hebrew University of Jerusalem. The most recent of her many publications is *Israeli Peacemaking since 1967: Factors behind the Breakthroughs and Failures*. Golan is the recipient of the 2016 Distinguished Scholar Award of the International Studies Association (ISA) for her work in peace research.

INDEX

1967 War (Six Day War), 5, 87

Abbas, Mahmud, 12–13, 23–24, 26, 42–44, 48, 55
Abed Rabbo, Yasser, 13
Adams, Gerry, 161–164
ADPC (African Diaspora Policy Center), 167
African national congress, 16
al-Assad, Hafez, 36, 42
Alfei Menashe, 66
Algeria, 20–21, 28, 130
American guarantees, 176
American Jewish committee, 95, 112
American Jews, 94–96, 98, 107, 109, 110, 113, 115
Americans for Peace Now, 105, 109, 180
Americans for Safe Israel, 96
Amicay, 75
Amona, 69–71, 73–75, 88–90
Angola, 22
APIAC, 94, 99, 101–103, 108–110, 112, 114, 180, 181
Arab democratic party, 177
Arafat, Yasser, 14, 18, 97, 100–101, 104–105, 110–113, 124–126, 182, 184
A-Shara, Farouk, 36
autonomy plan, 169, 173, 189

Bar Ilan University, 85, 184
Barack, Aharon, 87, 90, 171
Barak, Ehud, 6, 17–18, 36–41, 49–54, 107–113, 117, 183
Bargil case, 64, 66
Bedouin communities, 61
Begin, Menachem, 96, 168–179, 183, 187–189
Beilin, Yossi, 101, 103, 179, 181, 190
Ben Meir, Yehuda, 175, 188
Ben-Aharon, Yossi, 36
Ben-Ami, Shlomo, 17, 19
Beth El case, 59, 62
bi-national state, 42

Blair, Tony, 39, 163–164, 186
Bolling Airforce Base, 17
Bosnia and Herzegovina, 22, 187
Bruchin, 71

cabinet, 172
Cambodia, 22, 167
Camp David (2000), 6, 120
Camp David framework agreement, 169
Camp David, 6, 11, 14, 17, 18, 25, 29, 109, 110, 113, 114, 120, 123, 169, 170–176, 188
Carter, Jimmy, 168, 170, 173–176, 188–189
China, 130, 165, 167
Church of Saint Egidio, 159
civil society, 3, 156, 157, 164, 170, 179, 180
Clinton administration, 100, 105–108, 112
Clinton parameters, 17, 24, 85
Clinton, Bill, 13, 17–19, 24–25, 37–39, 41, 49, 63–54, 56, 85, 100, 105–108, 110, 112, 160, 163–164
Colombian rebel groups, 166
conference of presidents, 94, 99, 102, 110, 189
courts, 4, 60, 82
Cyprus, 166–167, 187

Dahlan, Mohammad, 14, 18
Dayton agreement, 167
De Gaulle, Charles, 20–21
declaration of principles, 95
Democratic Unionist Part (DUP), 162
diaspora, 3, 4, 36, 93, 94, 113, 160, 167, 180–182
disengagement from Gaza, 143

East Jerusalem, 5, 24, 91, 98, 106, 107, 112, 177, 189
Egypt, 2, 5, 6, 38, 61, 66, 135, 168, 170, 172, 183
Egyptian-Israeli peace treaty of 1979, 5, 175
El Salvador, 15
Elon Moreh, 62, 63, 65, 70, 74, 86, 87, 91
Erekat, Saeb, 18–19, 43, 49

193

Eretz Israel, 5, 96, 103, 168, 169, 174, 177, 184
EU (European Union), 84, 90, 167
Evian accords, 20

Fayad, Salam, 43
final status negotiations, 12, 183
forced evacuation, 5, 133–141, 144–148
Ford, Gerald, 178
Foreign Affairs and Security Committee, 173
Freeman Center for Strategic Studies, 97, 104
French occupation (of Algeria), 21

Gaza disengagement, 67
Gaza, 6, 24, 43, 67, 69, 87, 88, 133, 135, 136, 143, 168, 169, 173, 177, 187
General Assembly of Jewish Federations, 181
Geneva conference, 168
Geva Binyamin, 72
Golan Heights, 37, 107, 108
Goldstein, Baruch, 179
Good Friday Agreement, 15, 160
Gorbachev, Mikhail, 166
Grassroots groups/organizations, 51, 99, 157, 160, 162, 163, 166
Great Britain, 90, 160, 165, 186
Greek Cypriots, 167
Guatemala, 166–167, 187
Gur, Motta, 179
Gush Emunim, 169, 175, 188
Gush Katif, 136

HaBayit HaYehudi, 42, 48, 56
Hadash, 177
Hamas, 14, 43, 111, 113, 177, 182
Hammer, Zvulun, 175
Haresha, 71, 88
Hatnua, 42
HaYovel, 71
Hecht, Abraham, 96, 99, 180
Herut, 96, 169, 187
Holbrooke, Richard, 27–28
Horne, Alistair, 20, 18
Hume, John, 162, 165

ICC (International Criminal Court), 81, 92
ICJ (International Court of Justice), 65–66, 79, 81, 86–87

ideological settlers, 139–148
IDF, 67–69, 100, 104, 111, 112, 173, 175, 179, 182
illegal construction, 60, 68–76, 83, 92
illegal outposts, 59, 71–75, 81, 90
Indyk, Martin, 40, 54, 100, 105
interim agreement (1995), 6, 17, 86
interim agreement of 1975, 168
Intifada, 6, 93, 110, 114, 120, 122, 177
IRA, 161–163
Iraq, 167
Ireland, Republic of, 160
Islamic Jihad, 14, 111, 113, 177, 182
Israel Policy Forum, 105, 109, 180
Israel Political Affairs Committee, 94
Israeli government, 49, 56, 58, 59, 62, 63, 67–69, 71, 73–75, 77–79, 82, 86, 91, 102, 105, 108, 110
Israeli-Arab conflict, 5, 6
Israeli-Palestinian conflict, 59, 79, 83
Israeli-Syrian negotiation, 31, 36, 38–40, 42, 48, 49

Jewish agency, 175
Jordan Rift valley, 175, 183
Jordan, 5, 7, 24, 41, 66, 107, 175, 189
Joxe, Louis, 20–21
Judea and Samaria, 86, 92, 173, 174

Kach, 179
Kahane Chai, 179
Katz, Shmuel, 96, 169
Kerry talks (2013–2014 negotiations) 6, 23, 31, 42–46, 48–50, 52
Kerry, John, 6, 12, 23–24, 26–28, 31, 42–26, 48–50, 52, 54–55
Khmer Rouge, 167
Kissinger, Henry, 165
Knesset, 45, 47, 67, 88, 90, 101, 138, 139, 142, 146, 171–176, 179, 182–184, 187, 188, 190

Labor, 38, 93, 96, 98, 100–103, 105, 107, 110, 112–114, 168, 169, 170, 176, 177, 179, 180, 181, 183, 191
Lauder, Ron, 36, 38
Likud, 42, 94, 95, 98, 100, 102, 104, 107, 108, 112, 113, 115, 170–172, 174–176, 180, 183, 187–189, 191
Livni, Tzipi, 16, 42–43, 45–46, 48, 50, 54, 56

Ma'ale Adumim, 64
Madrid conference, 20, 36
Major, John, 163–164
Mandela, Nelson, 166
Meretz, 177, 180
Migron, 72, 73, 83
Milosevic, Slobodan, 22–23
Mitchell, George, 22–23, 27–28, 161, 186
Molcho, Yitzhak, 16, 43, 46
Moskowitz, Irving, 98, 106–107
Movement for Greater Israel, 96, 169

National Liberation Front, 12
National Party (South Africa), 15, 16, 166
nationalists/republicans, 163
Netanyahu, Benjamin, 6, 12–13, 16, 36, 39, 42–47, 49–52, 55, 68, 84–85, 88, 92, 94–95, 98, 105–108, 111–113, 149
New Migron, 72
NGO, 47, 64, 69, 90, 160, 162, 165, 167, 187
Northern Ireland Council for Voluntary Action, 162
Northern Ireland, 15, 16, 22–24, 160, 162–164, 170
NRP (National Religious Party), 37, 168, 175, 176, 189

Obama, Barack, 43, 44, 85, 89, 132
occupation, 5, 21, 45, 62, 63, 67, 83, 87, 93, 120
Ofra, 74, 90
Oliver, Quentin, 162, 165
orthodox Jews, 95, 96, 102
Oslo accords, 6, 20, 101, 138, 177–181
Oslo talks, 14, 20, 31, 93, 95, 120, 122
outpost evacuation, 68, 73, 75, 89

Paisley, Ian, 162–163
Palestinian Authority, 42, 86, 97, 100, 111
Palestinian Islamic Jihad, 14
Palestinian land, 58, 60– 63, 69, 72, 74, 75, 80
Palestinian landowners, 62, 76
Palestinian state, 17, 23, 68, 79, 80, 95, 97, 99, 124, 149, 173, 183
Peace Now, 64, 69, 71, 89, 90, 105, 109, 170, 180, 188
people-to-people activities, 179

Peres, Shimon, 6, 17, 42, 101, 104, 124–126, 179, 181, 182, 187, 190
Pillar, Paul, 18, 26–27
PLO, 6, 10, 13, 14, 86, 98, 100, 111, 128, 173, 177, 180, 182, 184
posttraumatic (syndrome), 136
pre-1948 mandated Palestine, 5
private Palestinian land, 58, 60, 61, 69, 72
project Charley, 179
project Nishma, 180
protestant, 16, 161–164
protests, 11, 119, 188
public hearings, 166
Putnam, Robert, 7, 13, 26, 168

quality of life (life quality), 139–142, 144–147, 151

Rabin, Yitzhak, 6, 36–37, 39, 41, 93, 96, 98–101, 103, 106–107, 111, 115–116, 122–123, 177–184, 189–191
Rabinvitch, Itamar, 36, 39, 54, 101, 103, 116
Rafah, 61
Rechelim, 71
regularization law, the, 81, 90, 92
RENAMO, 167
Richmond, Oliver, 3, 7, 28, 31, 33, 35, 49, 53, 56, 185, 187
rodef din, 179, 181
Ross, Dennis, 14, 37–38, 40–41, 53–54
Rujeib, 62, 63

Sadat, Anwar, 168–169, 172, 174, 188
Sagie, Uri, 37–38, 40–41, 49, 53–54, 56
Sansana, 71
Savir, Uri, 36, 190
Sebenius, James K., 15, 22, 27–28
settlement expansion, 170
settlements, 23, 44, 45, 47, 48, 50, 55, 58–91, 101, 133, 138–140, 151, 155, 169–175, 177–179, 183, 187, 188
settlers, 5, 21, 37, 50, 51, 58–60, 63, 67, 68, 70, 72–74, 77, 87, 91, 94–96, 110, 133–149, 168–170, 172, 174, 175, 177–180, 188
Shamgar, Meir, 64
Shamir, Yizhak, 23, 36, 189

Sharansky, Natan, 37
Sharm el-Sheikh memorandum, 13
Sharon, Ariel, 67, 108, 169, 172–173, 176, 186, 188, 189
Shas, 37, 42, 113, 177, 183, 189
Shepherdstown, 37, 39, 40, 41, 108
Shtayyeh, Muhammad, 43
Sinai peninsula, 5, 61, 78, 133, 135, 168
Sinn Fein, 161–163, 166
Social Democratic and Labor Party (SDLP), 162,
Stedman, Steven, 2, 7, 9–10, 26, 31, 95, 101, 110–111, 113, 115, 159, 185–187
Supreme Court (High Court of Justice), 60–67, 72–77, 79, 81, 82–85, 87, 88, 91, 113, 134
Syria, 6, 36–42, 48, 49, 107–109

Taba, 13, 17, 29, 120, 123
Tag Mechir (price tag), 45, 56
Tamils, 167
Thatcher, Margaret, 166
Trimble, David, 161–164, 186

Ulpanah, 72
Ulster Unionist Party, 16, 161–162

unionists/loyalists, 163
UNSC resolution 242
US Congress, 180

Wanis-St. John, Anthony, 21, 28
War of Attrition, 171
Weizman, Ezer, 170, 179, 188
West Bank, 5, 6, 24, 45, 58–61, 63, 64, 66–70, 72, 73, 75, 79, 80, 82–86, 91, 92, 96, 101, 108, 120, 122, 133, 135, 138, 139–143, 145–148, 168, 169, 173–178
women's rights, 157
Wye River memorandum, 6

Ya'alon, Moshe (Bogie), 46
Yamit, 170, 177
Yatom, Danny, 41, 179
Yesh Atid, 42
Yishai, Eli, 37
Yisrael B'aliyah, 37, 103
Yom Kippur war, 168

Zartman, Ira Willian, 16, 27–28
Zionism, 144, 179, 183
Zionist Organization of America, 97, 180

www.ingramcontent.com/pod-product-compliance
Lightning Source LLC
Chambersburg PA
CBHW021731220426
43662CB00008B/803